ALONE TOGETHER

ALONE TOGETHER

My Life with J. Paul Getty

TEDDY GETTY GASTON

WITH DIGBY DIEHL

An Imprint of HarperCollins*Publishers*

This is a work of nonfiction. The experiences detailed herein are all true and have been faithfully rendered as the author remembered them.

ALONE TOGETHER. Copyright © 2013 by Theodora Getty Gaston. All rights reserved. Printed in the United States of America. No part of this book may be used or reproduced in any manner whatsoever without written permission except in the case of brief quotations embodied in critical articles and reviews. For information address HarperCollins Publishers, 10 East 53rd Street, New York, NY 10022.

HarperCollins books may be purchased for educational, business, or sales promotional use. For information please e-mail the Special Markets Department at SPsales@harpercollins.com.

FIRST EDITION

Designed by Suet Yee Chong

Library of Congress Cataloging-in-Publication Data has been applied for.

ISBN 978-0-06-221971-8

13 14 15 16 17   OV/RRD   10 9 8 7 6 5 4 3 2 1

I dedicate this book to
my beloved daughter, Gigi, who came into my life in
my darkest hour and has been a lighthouse of hope;
my son, Timmy, whose spirit has never left me;
and my treasured friend and stepson,
the talented composer Gordon Getty

This above all: to thine own self be true,

And it must follow, as the night the day,

Thou canst not then be false to any man

—POLONIUS IN *HAMLET*, WILLIAM SHAKESPEARE

CONTENTS

PART II

A Prologue From J. Paul Getty

I have been quoted as saying, "Preoccupation with business has taken a heavy toll in my personal life" . Whether I ~~~ said that or not, it is true in my case. At least during the years covered by my dear Teddy in this book. A wife doesn't feel that she is truly a wife if she has to take a secondary role to her husband's business affairs. I suspect that if we all followed Francis Bacon, who said that wives were 'impediments to great enterprises' we would not advance the human race,though, for a short while,the virtue of business would dominate the heart of man.

I am not certain of what I may have missed on the wayside while working day and night,for I have not paused long enough to find out. Yet, when I read what Teddy has written about our life together - and about our son - I knew that she visited many peaks and walked through many valleys which I should not have missed had I not been so diligent and about my Father's business. Perhaps a strong sense of obligation to those working for me, a need to accomplish what I have started and an abiding faith that those around me understand that with which I am so totally involved has kept me from completly understanding the needs of a wife.

Certainly,Teddy is and was always someone   special

uncomparable, adorable and very much like a fairy princess
experiencing the enchanting and unbelievable while all those
about her are at her feet or carried along with her great
exuberance, an overflowing spirit of optimism despite all the
evidence to the contrary about her. I think this quality is
what attracted me then and attracts me in thought new. She was
never the single woman in the single role but the many parts
of the complete woman in, many roles. You may remember the words
of the German auther, Ina Seidel whe said, "A woman is a priestess,
a mether and an actress". That, too, was and is Teddy. She is
deeply religeous. I have seen her try to live her highest
sense of what her religeen teaches her. She is ene of the world's
most deveted methers, as I have experienced this side of her
during the brief but fulfilling years when we shared our beloved
sen Timmy. There can be ne deubt abeut her - being an actress
en stage and eff - for all the world is her stage She has
blessed it with her youth, maturity and devotien.

        In closing this brief cemmentary abeut what Teddy has
written, the memeries never beceme dulled with time when shared
with her. We relive an exciting era . During the marriage I
tried to pass en to a willing student whese thirsty ears and quick
intellect yearned fer infermation which had ceme my way. During
these same years, she gave me compassien, understanding, leve

and generously of her time and thought.

We can't relive our lives and we shall not pass down the same reads again, but if this were to happen to me, I would want to meet Teddy. I would want her acquired maturity to be there without less of that youthful spirit which saw no evil. And I would try to let her know that I would do it all over again in a better way next time.

Paul
PAUL.

—J. Paul Getty
Sutton Place
Surrey, England

January, 1976

ALONE TOGETHER

In May of 1935, I opened at the New Yorker, one of the smartest little dinner clubs in the city, located in a fine old house on East 51st Street. I can still remember walking out into the spotlight and singing some of that era's most beloved songs—"Night and Day," "Smoke Gets in Your Eyes," "Body and Soul," and "Alone Together." Although I had been on Broadway twice, I'd never had the chance to sing as part of a floor show and I loved it.

One night, just as the lights dimmed and I was to go on for the second show, there was a commotion downstairs. Minutes later a group swept up the spiral staircase and was ushered to a ringside table. By their laughter I recognized Betzi and Jeannie, my two dearest friends. Fred, Betzi's husband, had to be there as well, but who else was with them? It was too dark to see.

When I finished singing and the applause died down, I made my way over to their table. Three men stood up. In the half-light, I saw my brother Ware, Fred, and a man I had never seen before. "Teddy!" Betzi said excitedly, blowing me a kiss. "This is Paul, my friend from California."

I found myself looking into the bluest eyes of an immensely charming man—tall, slender, with sandy hair. "Hello, Teddy," he said. "What a beautiful voice you have! 'Alone Together' is one of my favorites."

"Thanks, mine too!" I replied.

At that very moment, the orchestra started playing. Paul had been holding out a chair for me, but before I could sit down, he grabbed my hand. "Let's dance," he said. In seconds I was in his arms, and we were dancing. He held me too close, but it was the beguine, music that made it seem right. I closed my eyes and let my body follow his. We moved as one to the beat of the drums. He was a fabulous dancer, but it ended too soon and then we were back at the table.

Sitting there in the semi-dark, sipping champagne, Paul smiled and said, "You're very beautiful, Teddy, and your voice is, too. I love the quality of it." I looked up and saw he was studying me. "You know," he went on, "you should study opera. You'd be a great Carmen, or Tosca."

At these words, I trembled. Although he had no way of knowing, it was my ambition to one day sing in concerts and the opera. I sat there amazed at this stranger who, after hearing me sing only once, was saying exactly what my teacher, Gene Berton, had been telling me. Intrigued by the sincerity in his warm, deep voice, I looked more closely at his hands. They were very masculine, but they were also artistic and expressive. Could he be a conductor? A composer? A critic?

"And what do *you* do, Paul?" I asked.

"He's in oil," Betzi cut in.

"*Oil?* What show is that?" I asked. Everyone started to laugh. "Of course!" I said. I felt like a fool.

PART I

CHAPTER 1

IN THE BEGINNING

When I was a little girl, my mother had a marvelous interior decorator, Anna Della Winslow, who not only had furnished my grandparents' magnificent duplex at 44 West 77th Street in New York City, opposite the Museum of Natural History, but she'd also redone their summer home, Thorncroft, in Vineyard Haven, Massachusetts. And then she helped my mother put her lovely things in our home in Belle Haven, Greenwich, Connecticut.

Annie, as we children called her, was born in Sweden, but was as American as apple pie. She loved doing for others, had great taste, adored the theater, and knew everyone who was anyone in or out of the theater and art worlds.

Annie kept an office in a boutique on the ground floor of the Great Northern Hotel on 57th Street, close to the famous Russian Tea Room, near Carnegie Hall. I'd always go along when Mother had an appointment with her. Inevitably, we'd have lunch at that famous tearoom, where

Annie would hold court. I could hardly eat, it was so exciting to meet so many great artists from the concert and opera world . . . and they all loved Annie.

In 1924, when I was eleven years old, Stravinsky stopped at our table, kissed Annie's hand, and wouldn't let go. Another time, the great contralto Marguerite d'Alvarez, all two hundred pounds of her, swept in and, after embracing Annie, Mother, and me, promptly sat down and ordered a luncheon large enough for two . . . completely forgetting those waiting for her at the next table. Once, the beautiful soprano Marguerite Namara came by for a moment, swathed in furs and Chanel, looking so romantic; every man in the restaurant was staring at her. *Dear God*, I thought, *I hope when I grow up, I can be as fascinating.* Of course, I hadn't realized that not only was she a great beauty, but she also had a voice that enthralled everyone.

I had a voice, too, even as a child, and loved to sing. But I was far from beautiful or glamorous. In fact, I felt ugly. I figured I had a lot of work ahead of me if I ever expected to sing on any stage and be like Namara. But this was my dream.

I was still young when my parents divorced, which meant that I never really knew my father, Walter Morris Lytton. After the divorce, he stayed in Chicago, where he was an architect, so I didn't see him often enough to know him. My mother met Frank J. Lynch, who'd been a friend of my father's, when I was five. I knew him first as Uncle Frank. He was handsome, with blue eyes and great charm. When he married Mother, he became my stepfather, but I called him Dad, and he adopted Ware and me. The two of us took his last name. We moved back east and settled in Greenwich, Connecticut. Henry, our oldest brother, remained Henry Lytton. He was always very serious and straitlaced. He didn't approve of

the divorce, but then again, Henry didn't approve of a lot of things. A lot of the time, that included me.

While waiting for the Belle Haven house to be finished, our family moved into a suite at the Greenwich Country Club. Saturday nights, when they held dinner dances, I would gulp down my supper and ask to be excused. Then I would stand near the orchestra and sing along with them, while Mother and Dad danced by. Sometimes couples would stop just to listen to me. That's when I knew in my heart I could, if I tried, have a career. That was so very important in my mind.

When we moved into the Belle Haven house, Ware went to Brunswick High, Henry was off to Yale, and I went to the Greenwich Academy. By this time, I had two younger sisters, Nancy and Barbara (Bobby). I was not quite a teenager when they were born. They were adorable . . . blond, blue-eyed, and bewitching. I loved them as babies, and still do. They were and still are my whole, not half, sisters.

I practiced singing every chance I could. Many nights Mother would play the piano after dinner, and Ware and I would stand beside her and sing. Sometimes my little sisters would tiptoe down the stairs and peek at us through the rails of the banister, until their nanny scooted them off to bed.

This should have been the perfect life for Mom and Dad. They had it all—good friends, a great social life, and five fairly well-behaved children. But something was wrong. I couldn't tell my mom, because it was about Dad. For years, my situation at home had been difficult. I figured his drinking made him do what he did to me, and like most abused children of that era, I remained silent. Singing wasn't just a career ambition for me. It was something to look forward to, a way out of a bad situation.

Often, I'd wake up to hear the crashing of furniture, doors slam-

ming, and Mother crying, "Frank . . . NO!" In seconds, I'd be out of bed and down those stairs to defend her! It was horrifying to see him looking quite out of his mind and Mother standing there, terrified. I never really knew what they were fighting about, but he was definitely very drunk and demanding the keys to the car, which she refused to give him. When he threatened her, I'd get between them, but I was small and he'd throw me aside. After that, he would plunge down the stairs and storm out the front door. Eventually, he'd come back, and finally fall asleep. In the morning, I'd go to school, unable to function, but I'd go.

The next night, Mom would forgive him. He'd tell her he wanted to have a talk with me, to say how sorry he was. As soon as I heard him coming up the stairs, I'd turn off my light and pretend to be asleep, but he'd still come in, very quietly. I'd hold my breath and freeze, hoping I wouldn't feel him if he touched me. He did.

"Babe," he'd whisper as his hands reached under the covers. "I'm sorry about last night . . . I don't want to hurt your mother—or you. I just wanted to come up and kiss you good night."

"Don't touch me, Dad, or I'll scream," I'd say, and suddenly he'd be gone.

Looking back, I can't remember just when it began, but when I was a very little girl, about five or six years old, he used to make me sit on his lap. When I was eleven, Mother started making me go with him in the car whenever he'd say he was "out of cigarettes" and had to drive into Greenwich to buy more. Mother thought this was his excuse to buy liquor instead, and she thought I'd prevent him.

One rainy night, alone in the car with him, driving through the dark, wet, empty streets of Belle Haven, he told me how grown up I was getting to be, and what a nice, strong body I had for such a young girl. As

he was speaking, he put his hand on my knee and slowly moved it up my leg. I tried to get away, but he gripped my thigh. "Be still!" he said as his fingers reached up between my legs. "I just want to feel you!"

"Stop, Dad!" I cried. "Are you drunk or something?"

"No, babe, I'm not!" he said, lowering his voice. "Be still . . . or I'll slam on the brakes and the car will skid and turn over." With that he laughed, enjoying how frightened I was.

"You wouldn't dare . . . you might kill us. I'll tell Mom."

"If you do, I'll tell her you asked me to touch you." His fingers found their mark . . . "There!"

"That's not true!" I screamed. I attempted to push him away, but his hand stayed put. Then I started to cry.

"Your mother will believe me, not you," he said, his breath hot on my face. "After all, you're very mature for your age, and girls who do things like this could be put away in an institution."

His threat stopped my tears. Terrified by his words, I pulled away from him. I grabbed the door handle on my side of the car, and held on tight. When we got home, I ran upstairs to my room, threw myself on my bed, and cried myself to sleep.

I never told my mother, not then, not ever. She would have been devastated. She loved Frank, they had those two adorable daughters, and I couldn't bear to hurt her. Besides, I was afraid that maybe, just like Dad said, she might not have believed me. From that night on, however, I avoided Dad, except when the whole family was together. I also started locking my bedroom door.

At the Greenwich Academy I studied singing, wrote poetry, and was on the field hockey, basketball, and riding teams. History, my favorite subject, made up for math, which I never conquered. I loved movies and

Saturday afternoon football games. Actually, I loved one of the players much more than the game itself. His name was Tim Crowley, he was a member of the Brunswick High football team. Once I left a junior dance at the Field Club to take a ride with Tim on his motorcycle, ending up in his arms on a couch in his mother's living room. My brothers burst through the door just in time to stop me from what I longed to do and brought me home. Henry told Mom, who promptly cried. Dad stormed up and down the hall and called me a whore. "We didn't do anything bad," I said, defending myself. "We just kissed!" Years later I figured out what really bothered him: he didn't want anyone else to touch me.

That night my parents decided to send me away to school in Europe. Less than two weeks later, Mom, Dad, and I were aboard the SS *Paris* en route to France. The memory of that trip has never left me. We had bad weather all the way across the Atlantic. Even worse than rough seas and high winds, however, was Dad's drinking. He and Mom returned to our suite very late after a party. I awoke to hear them arguing—again. When Mom cried out, I ran to help her, but Dad just threw me across the cabin. I hit my head on the edge of the bunk, and stayed there stunned and bleeding. There was a sudden knock on the door and two officers called out in French, "Is something wrong?"

"Merci . . . c'est rien," Mom replied. Moments later, she dissolved in tears as Dad staggered out, heading for the bar.

They took me to Marymount Convent, 72 Boulevard de la Saus-saye, Neuilly-sur-Seine, just outside of Paris, one block from the American Hospital. I stayed there for the next year and a half. On entering Marymount, one had to sign a paper promising not to speak English . . . ever. I learned French in a hurry—I had to, if I was going to eat. Even so, Marymount was a wonderful experience. I was the youngest student;

most of the other girls were of college age. I went with them to the Sorbonne for classes in literature and history. Even better, I studied singing with Maestro Maugiere of the Opera Comique, who taught me a duet, the barcarole *"Belle nuit, ô nuit d'amour,"* from Offenbach's opera *Les contes d'Hoffmann*.

I think that is when I really fell in love with opera. The seductive melodies, the stories, the passions enchanted me, transporting me into another world. When I finished my term at Marymount, Mother, Dad, my sisters, and my brother Ware came over on the SS *Majestic*, bringing a brand-new Packard touring car with them. After Mother hired a governess, a chauffeur, and a cook, we spent the next four months at the Villa Lalo in Saint-Jean-de-Luz, just south of Biarritz on the west coast of France. I was so happy to again be with my whole family that I never once thought about why I'd been sent to Marymount in the first place, nor did I think back on what Dad had done to me. I forgave him and forgot about it. It just seemed like a bad dream, something that happened long ago, and I pushed it out of my mind.

We came home on the SS *Berengaria*. It was another terrible crossing, with monstrous waves so high and frightening that no one was allowed on deck. We were a day late getting into New York. Still, it was great being back in America, and as a teenager I was allowed to choose my next school. I chose Harcum in Bryn Mawr, Pennsylvania, because it was widely acclaimed for its music department. Ware went off to Roxbury; Henry was still at Yale.

Along with my singing, French, Latin, math, English, and history classes, I played on the hockey, tennis, basketball, and riding teams. Not having enough to do, I also decided to take ballet with Mikhail Mordkin, Anna Pavlova's last partner. I made a lifelong friend in Jean Donnelly

from Scranton, who introduced me to the entire University of Pennsylvania football team. None of them were good dancers, so at proms I depended on Ware's friends from Roxbury as dancing partners.

I loved Harcum; I felt free and happy there—until the weekend when Dad drove down from Greenwich and took me into Philadelphia for a special outing. It was supposed to be a treat—he had reserved a suite for us at the Ritz. We dined, went to a movie, and called Mother to say good night. After thanking him for our time together, I went to my room, undressed, climbed into bed, and fell asleep.

I was awakened by the sound of the door opening. I heard him coming toward me. I was so frightened that I didn't dare move. I could tell by his breath he'd been drinking, but how could that be? He'd only had one cocktail at dinner. He pulled back the covers and crawled into my bed. I could feel his body; it was burning. We lay there, kind of in spoon fashion, for what seemed like hours. I was very scared, and when he touched my breasts, I started to tremble. "Dad, don't!" I pleaded.

This only made him angry. He yanked down my pajamas. His legs forced mine apart, and he moved on top of me. I tried to fight him off, but he was too strong. I cried out, but he covered my mouth. "Shush, babe, I'm not going to hurt you. I just want to put it between your legs."

"No, Dad, you can't do this to me. It's wrong!"

But he was doing it . . . He was having an orgasm, and it happened so fast—and then he lay still. He had not penetrated me, but it was sickening, and I died a thousand deaths.

"I hate you, I hate you!" I sobbed . . . and then I slapped him as hard as I could.

He looked at me, then slapped me back. The blow was quick and stinging. There was contempt in his voice when he said, "I haven't hurt

you, babe. It's what you deserve, because you're nothing but a dirty little Jew! Like your father!"

And with that, he got up and left.

For a moment, I lay there in the dark, stunned, not realizing what he meant, thinking he must be crazy. Afraid he might return and try again, I ran to the bathroom, washed myself, dressed, and packed my bag. I dashed out the door and took the first train back to Bryn Mawr, reaching Harcum just as the night watchmen were making their rounds. They let me in and I tiptoed up the stairs to my room and to bed, filled with shame and confusion.

Everything I "knew" about Jews was bad—that the Jews killed Jesus, that Jews were miserly, that Jews gypped and cheated everyone. Me, a Jew? I didn't want to be like that. I felt dirty enough after he molested me, and when Dad called me a "dirty little Jew," he took away what was left of my self-esteem. I hated myself . . . I wished I was anybody but me!

I never told Mom what Dad did to me that night, but when I went home for Christmas vacation I asked her, "Why did you marry my father? Why didn't you tell me he was Jewish?"

"I loved him," she answered, "and you must be as proud of his family as I am of the Ware family."

My mother had met my tall, dark, and handsome father, Walter Lytton, when they were both in college, he at Cornell and she at Smith. His father, Henry Charles Lytton, had put himself through college before joining the Union Army. After the Civil War, he opened a dry goods store in Chicago. The business prospered and expanded, eventually becoming a department store called the Hub, later known as Lytton's, which rivaled Marshall Field's in prestige. It was there that my father created the "bargain basement" and the "working man's suit."

That's the suit with two pairs of pants, one to wear to your job, and one to go to church in. My grandfather was now well known in Chicago as the dean of State Street merchants. His wife, my grandmother, Rose Eva Lytton, was the daughter of the legendary Sailing Wolfe, the seventh generation of her family in America, and president of the Chicago chapter of the Daughters of the American Revolution. Isobelle, her sister (my great aunt) was the mother of Bernard Baruch.

Dirty little Jew indeed. I decided that if Ware, Henry, and I were Jews, we'd be the best Jews in the world.

CHAPTER 2

NEW FACES

That winter, Ware attended Yale as a freshman, and Henry left for Chicago. Mother decided to move to New York, and took an apartment at 1111 Park Avenue for herself, Nancy, Bobby, the nurse, Dad, and me. I was sent to the French School for Girls on 86th Street, between Fifth and Madison.

It was there that I met Jane Swope, a beautiful girl full of fun, and we became best friends. Jane was the daughter of Herbert Bayard Swope, the executive editor of the New York *World*. Mrs. Swope, like her daughter, was a great beauty. They entertained lavishly, both at their Park Avenue apartment and at their summer home on Long Island, and, happily, they included me.

Practically every weekend during the summer, there would be fabulous parties at Lands End, the Swopes' lovely home at Sands Point on the Long Island Sound. The Swopes were absolutely the most fabulous hosts, and their guests were as fabulous as they were—Irving Berlin,

Oscar Levant, William S. Paley, the Marx Brothers, Clifton Webb, Heywood Broun, and Dorothy Parker and the rest of the Algonquin Round Table were regular visitors. All the great newspapermen and bigwigs from Washington were there, and they were mad to play croquet on the great lawns of the estate, which they did every afternoon.

It was a fascinating time to be alive. There were no Concordes, no freeways, no computers, no TVs, no cell phones, but people always seemed to have something to say. They dressed for dinner, gave huge parties, and were passionate about the theater, books, radio, opera, and the art of witty and intelligent conversation.

I went to see Anna Della at the Great Northern Hotel. I told her I had to get away from home because of my desire to get a job in the theater and sing. She advised me to write the Shuberts. At the time, Lee Shubert and his brother J. J. Shubert were the only producers putting up revues and light operas on Broadway. I wrote for an appointment, and was asked to come to Mr. J.J.'s office.

Although I was scared to death, I was determined to audition. The well-dressed J. J. Shubert sat behind a huge desk. "Sit down," he said as he smiled and took off his horn-rimmed glasses.

"So, you want to become an actress, Teddy?" Shubert continued. I saw my letter in his hand. "And, you live in Belle Haven, Greenwich . . . Why, that's very near my home in Mamaroneck. It's beautiful out there in the country right now, isn't it? But, tell me, why do you want to go on the stage?"

"Because I want to sing, and I thought that you might give me that opportunity," I replied. "I can dance, too, and I'm sure I can read lines." I stopped because Mr. Shubert was already ringing for his secretary.

"Is John still here?" he asked when the door opened and she came in.

"No, sir," she replied. "He left at three."

"Well, young lady, can you play?" he asked, turning to me. "I'd like to hear you sing. There's a piano over there." He pointed to a fine old baby grand in the corner.

"I can only play one song, sir, and not very well, but I'll sing it for you if you wish . . . Or I can come back again another day." I hoped he'd say "fine," but he didn't, so I bravely went to the piano, sat down, and sang.

After singing the entire chorus of "What Is This Thing Called Love?" Mr. Shubert gestured for me to stop. "Well done, Teddy," he said. "I'm going to give you the opportunity you asked for. Come back in two weeks and sing for Eddy Mendelson, our director. If he likes you, I'll put you in the revival of *Arms and the Maid*, a musical opening in October in Atlantic City."

I was thrilled. "Oh, Mr. Shubert, thank you!" I exclaimed.

Two weeks later, I sang for Mendelson. Two months after that, I was singing my heart out in the revival of *Arms and the Maid*. And two weeks after that, Mother and Dad, thinking I was too young, showed up and took me back to Greenwich. Mr. Shubert was so kind when I had to leave. "Don't be sad, my dear," he said. "You did very well. Come back and see me after the holidays."

My singing career really started in the summer of 1932, when Elsie Taylor (Mrs. W. R. K. Taylor Jr.) of New York had the brilliant idea of corralling a group of society girls from New York and Connecticut to appear nightly, singing with Jack Denny's orchestra on the Roof Garden of the Waldorf Astoria hotel.

We were in the worst of the Depression; most hotels and restaurants were half empty. This had never been done before—no debutante had ever sung with a band. It was not only fun for the girls but good for the

Waldorf. Elsie believed that because we were pretty and had talent, we would bring in the social register crowd. She thought they'd be anxious to see "their own" perform. It worked.

We were each paid $25 per week. Every evening we dressed in our most glamorous gowns. Lois Elliman, Timmy Dobbin, Gloria Braggiotti, and I arrived at nine, each with our escort, sat at the table next to the orchestra, had dinner on the house, and danced until our particular number was played. Then up we'd go to the bandstand and sing our song. Mine was "Lazy Days." It was fun, and every college friend of my brother's vied to be my partner for the evening. It cost them nothing but the price of gas to drive down from Yale, or up from Princeton, to wear a dinner jacket, have supper on the house, and dance till dawn.

Although no one knew it, I was the only girl living on that $25 a week. The others still lived with their families on Park Avenue or in River House. I was sharing an apartment with two sisters, Olive and Vida McClain, on the ground floor of a dingy, scary-looking brownstone walk-up at 36 West 75th Street, a half block from Central Park West. At the time, this was considered to be a dangerous area. When I came home late at night, I'd have to make a dash from the main entrance down a long, dark, paint-chipped hallway to our door. The man who lived in the first apartment off the corridor would sit on his bed in the dark, with the door half open. As I passed by, he'd reach out and try to grab me, but I was too fast for him.

Olive modeled at Saks Fifth Avenue, and Vida was a dancer at Radio City Music Hall. We each paid $5 a week for a living room, bedroom, bath, and kitchen. I had the use of a dresser and chair, and slept in a single bed right under a huge window overlooking the back alley filled with trash. It was summer, and we had to leave the window open to catch

whatever breeze might come our way, no matter how bad it smelled. The heat was unbearable. I remember lying naked on my bed in the dark, looking up into the night sky filled with stars, thwarted from sleep by the mating calls of a million cats. This didn't seem to bother my roommates, who shared a double bed at the other end of the room.

I had never been on my own before, but I learned fast that first morning, when I walked into the kitchen and started to pour myself a cup of coffee. I was told I had to buy my own, that I was not to use their bread, butter, eggs, cereal, juice, or coffee! At first I was hurt, but then I realized times were tough. It was the Depression—jobs were scarce, salaries low, and no one could afford to share. Watching these two sisters manage on so little taught me a great lesson—how to survive on $25 a week.

When the Roof Garden closed after Labor Day, I had to look for work. Determined to get another singing job, I marched off to Broadway to the music publishing house of Feist.

Feist was at 49th and Broadway. I walked up a flight of stairs and into their huge, crowded reception office and asked the man at the desk for their latest songs. He looked at me as if I were from Mars. "Where are you singing, kid?"

"The Waldorf Roof," I replied. Apparently this was the right answer.

"Mickey!" he yelled.

A little guy came out of a rehearsal room, walked up to me, and said, "Hiya, kid, what song do you want, and what key do you sing in?"

Not knowing, I smiled and said, "Any key you have . . . I just need songs." So he grabbed a few sheets of music and I followed him into his room.

Within minutes, he discarded Feist's latest numbers, saying, "These aren't for you. Let's hear you sing this." He started to play "Something

to Remember You By," that lovely song made famous by Libby Holman. When I finished, he turned and said, "That was swell, Teddy. Will you come on my show tonight and sing this song?"

I didn't know what show he was talking about, but I of course said yes. That's how I started singing professionally, with Mickey Addy on his radio show at station WPCH. He kept me on for months, singing solos and duets with Phil Reagan, a handsome Irish New York City policeman with a gorgeous tenor voice.

In due course Anna Della introduced me to Leonard Sillman, who was about to put on a revue on Broadway called *New Faces*. Sillman had produced a show called *Lo and Behold* on the West Coast at the Pasadena Playhouse, featuring a cast of talented young unknowns (Eve Arden and Tyrone Power among them). Now he was intent on doing the same in New York. After I sang for him, he turned to Annie and said, "You're right . . . she's got the voice. Sexy, too . . . No experience . . . but I'll use her!" He gave me a kiss and signed me to a contract.

It took Leonard a year and about 130 auditions for prospective backers to get *New Faces* to opening night in 1934. Even though it was the Depression and people were dying from cold and hunger, there was a serious theater shortage on Broadway—there were no theaters available to rehearse in, and no place where auditions could be held. Lee Shubert allowed Leonard to use his theaters in the morning—but not the stage. We would be called to audition for a potential backer at 10 A.M. in whatever theater was free, but instead of being onstage, we'd have to perform in the cold, ugly downstairs lobby, right in front of the men's and ladies' rooms. This went on for months, but all of us in the cast, which included Henry Fonda and Imogene Coca, were faithful to Leonard—bonded together by hope.

While waiting for *New Faces*, I still had to eat. In the winter of 1933, I got a job as a salesgirl at Atkins on 57th Street. I had to, because I was supporting myself and had to be ready to rehearse whenever Leonard called. I never took a penny from my mother from the day I left home and moved in with the McClain sisters.

By this time my brother Ware—newly graduated from Yale—and I had rented an apartment at 156 East 54th Street. It had one bedroom, a bath, a kitchen, and a living room with a dining alcove. It also had a doorman and an elevator man—that made me feel so elegant. I don't recall where our furniture came from, but my guess is that it came from the house in Belle Haven. I slept in the bedroom and Ware slept on the sofa bed in the living room. Once a month, Lulu, Mom's retired old housekeeper, would come in and clean. We loved Lulu and she loved us, and we three had fun working together.

The apartment cost $150 a month, which Ware and I split. By this time he was working for the Lennon and Mitchell advertising agency. I had finally gotten a job singing with an orchestra at the Merry Go Round, a nightclub not far from where we lived.

I STARTED EVERY evening at the Merry Go Round at 7:30, and never got home before two in the morning. Nick Bates, the owner, looked like Mayor Fiorello LaGuardia, and paid me $75 a week. The smoky club was jammed each night with people who drank too much. The bar was an actual carousel, and it moved very slowly, around and around. I sat on the bandstand with the orchestra. They played loud, and the dance floor was small and overcrowded. Sometimes men would hand me a bill as they danced by, saying, "Sing this song for me, baby." I always gave the money

to the orchestra leader, who only rarely divided it up with the other five in the band. He never offered any to me.

An angel finally appeared in the guise of Elsie Janis, the "sweetheart of the AEF" (the American Expeditionary Forces in World War I—the doughboys). Elsie, a dear friend of Leonard's, listened to the show's plight, asked the cast to audition, and was delighted. She called Charles Dillingham, one of the theater's most accomplished producers, to come and see us. He, too, was enthusiastic, so enthusiastic that he came out of retirement and agreed with Elsie to produce us. At long last Leonard Sillman's *New Faces* was finally in rehearsal!

We opened at the Fulton Theatre on March 15, 1934. As the curtain went up on the opening number, all of us were onstage with our backs to the audience. As we turned to show our "new faces," the roar of applause greeting us was so loud that the conductor had to stop the orchestra until it died down, just so we could sing. And sing we did.

Looking up at us from the front row on that marvelous opening night were America's Sweetheart Mary Pickford, Katharine Hepburn, author and conservationist Louis Bromfield, Libby Holman, and Tallulah Bankhead, smoking a very long cigarette. We later heard she never stopped smoking, but she did scream and laugh and loved the show, as did the others. When the curtain went down after the finale, the entire audience rose to its feet, whistling and applauding. *New Faces* was a hit—Leonard said later that there were twenty-nine curtain calls!

The revue played to full houses every night for six months. When President Roosevelt and the U.S. Fleet sailed into New York Harbor at the end of May, there we were, on a tugboat Leonard had chartered to greet him. With *New Faces* flags flying from every part of the tugboat, we

caught our president's attention. FDR waved to us from the deck of his flagship, the USS *Indianapolis.*

Mother loved the show, too, and invited the entire cast out to Greenwich one Sunday for brunch. Hank Fonda, God love him, endeared himself forever to Nancy and Bobby by playing hide-and-seek with them out on the lawn, and hiding from them in the dog house. It was a great day.

As more parties were given for us, we became known as the "Kids from *New Faces.*" I got a job singing after the show each night at the Gotham Hotel's supper club.

Later that same year, Leonard put on another revue called *Fools Rush In.* We opened on Christmas night, 1934. The show was great and the audience loved us, but by then our fate had been sealed. The critics had been invited to review the last rehearsal, and they crucified us. William Brady, our producer, put up the closing notice immediately. Instead of giving up, however, Leonard started hunting for backers.

Everyone in the cast did, too. I had become great friends with another member of the cast, Betzi Beaton. One night before the evening performance, realizing we only had one more week before closing, Betzi and I had dinner at an Italian restaurant two doors down from the Playhouse Theatre. Sitting up at the bar, having a bowl of soup and a sandwich while telling our sad story to the barman, I noticed that there were no other diners in the restaurant. Nevertheless, there were voices coming from behind a huge screen that ran across the back of the room.

Naturally inquisitive, I asked, "Who's back there?"

"My boss," the barman said, "and his buddies."

At that I got down and walked over to the screen, jumped onto a chair, and peered over. Six men looked up from their spaghetti. "Hi," one said, smiling.

I knew he must be the boss. I smiled back and said, "Hi, are you the owner of this restaurant?"

"Yeah," he said with a nod, then rose and came around the screen.

"I'm Teddy Lynch," I said, getting down from the chair. "I didn't mean to interrupt you, but I'm singing in the show next door, and they're going to close it in a week if we can't find enough money to keep it going . . . so I wondered if you might come and see a performance and, if you liked it, you and your friends might put up some money. We have a little, but we need more!"

I stopped because he was kind of smiling, looking me over and liking what he saw. "Why are you girls out beating the bushes for your producer?" he asked. "Why isn't he?"

"Oh, he is," I insisted, "and so are all the other actors. But there's so little time left . . . Will you come? Please . . . it's a great show, eh, Betzi?!"

I turned to my friend, who was sitting like a princess on the barstool, and said, "This is Betzi . . . she is absolutely the most beautiful and outrageously funny comedienne on Broadway . . . She's in the show, too, and you'll love her."

"Hi," Betzi said, smiling her most beautiful smile. And with that, the boss of that dear little Italian restaurant was hooked.

He came two nights later, with his entourage, saw the show, and afterward invited the entire cast for dinner at his restaurant. But he gave us no money. The day we closed, a chauffeur drew up in a black limo, got out in front of the theater, and came over to me as I was waiting for a cab. "Miss . . . you know my boss likes you very much. He wants you to come to Florida . . . with us."

I stared at him, so shocked I couldn't answer.

"Will you?" he went on. "He is very important, you know. He can

get you a job there." He leaned closer and whispered, "You know who he is, dontcha?"

"No," I said, shaking my head.

"He's Lucky . . . Lucky Luciano!"

My God, I thought.

"You can drive with us," the chauffeur said, as if this would be reassuring.

"In that car?" I pointed to the limo.

"Yes, it's a great car, bulletproof, too."

"I'm sure it is . . ." I replied. "But really, I can't. Thank you just the same, and please thank your boss, too. You see, I'm already booked, starting in two weeks at the Embassy Club . . . I'm singing with Henry King and His Orchestra. Tell your boss that Alice Faye is heading up the floor show and she's great . . . You come and see us, too, before you leave."

The chauffeur shook his head. I'm sure he wasn't looking forward to giving Mr. Luciano the bad news. "Too bad," he said. "It's so beautiful and warm in Miami."

As he spoke, I could feel the Miami sun's rays beating down on me. I wished for a second that I was the kind of girl for this part, but I wasn't. Moments later the chilling winds of winter reminded me that I'd better start walking home. There were no taxis in sight.

Heading back to the apartment, I wondered what Mother would say if I told her Lucky Luciano, the famous gangster, had invited me to go to Florida with him. I did tell her years later, when he was being deported to Italy and his face appeared on the front page of the *New York Times*.

She was appropriately horrified. "You knew him, Teddy?" she exclaimed. "How?"

CHAPTER 3

DEBUTANTE SINGER

I opened at Al Howard's Embassy Club, way over on the East Side, exactly two weeks after *Fools Rush In* closed, and sang with Henry King's orchestra. It was the dead of winter, 1935. The crowd there was mixed, with tables of Broadway celebrities next to tables of foreigners, and an occasional society foursome looking very out of place.

One night Al asked me to sit with friends of his. At the table, the waiter held out my chair. "Champagne?" he whispered in my ear.

"Coke," I replied.

When Al promptly kicked me under the table, I realized that was the wrong answer. I turned to the man next to me and said, "I've changed my mind. May I have champagne?" At once a bottle of Dom Pérignon appeared. The man edged closer to me and proceeded to tell me all about himself. I guess he assumed I'd be spending the rest of the evening with him. I was saved by the orchestra, which had just started to play my

number, "Stormy Weather." "I'll be right back," I said as I dashed to safety on the bandstand, never to return.

I was taking a risk. Any young girl who defied the rules of those who owned clubs like the Embassy could get herself into big trouble by refusing to go out with an important customer—especially if he was a backer.

I can still see Al sitting at a table each night, way at the back of the restaurant, surrounded by a group of men in tuxedos, who were rumored to be gangsters, and only smiled when the floor show began and Alice Faye appeared. She was blond and beautiful. I thought she had a great voice. Rudy Vallee thought so, too. He was mad for her!

I remember the night Alice stopped me after I finished performing. "Teddy, dear," she began, "I'm sorry to be the one to tell you this, but Al has asked me to let you know that you are through as of Saturday night."

I was stunned! I knew I was singing well. Henry had even spoken to me about doing some recordings with him. I must have looked forlorn, because Alice patted my hand. "Teddy," she said, "it's awful and I'm so sorry. It's not because you aren't good. You're great, kid. But it seems Al has been pressured by one of the backers to let his girlfriend sing with the band, and he can't say no, the bastard!" With that, she ran to meet Rudy.

I stood there, hardly able to stop the tears. But by the time I reached the apartment, I decided it didn't matter. I was not going to spend another minute feeling sorry for myself or angry with whomever it was who got me fired. I just had to get another job, and fast.

After about two weeks with no luck, I began to get scared.

My brother Ware, determined to help keep my spirits up, suggested we go out on the town for fun. Off we went, stopping first for a

drink at the then famous bar at the Weylin Hotel at 40 East 54th Street, where cabaret artist Guy Rennie was appearing. When I told him what had happened to me, Guy grabbed my hand and pulled me hurriedly through the lobby of the hotel to the new Caprice Room, which hadn't even opened yet—it was soon to be one of New York's most prestigious supper clubs. There, rehearsing a number, was a dance team, with Latin bandleader Enrique Madriguera at the piano.

"Rico!" Guy called out, at the same time pushing me into the room. "Heard you're looking for a singer. This is Teddy, Teddy Lynch, one of those debutante singers. She was in *New Faces*, and she'd love to sing for you."

Well, that's how it happened. Enrique needed a singer. I needed a job. I auditioned, and in a New York minute I was engaged by him at $100 a week to sing with his orchestra. But more than that, I was to be part of the floor show. When the lights dimmed and the orchestra started to play, I stood under a baby pink spotlight and sang the chorus of "Two Cigarettes in the Dark," while the dancers, their cigarettes aglow, whirled about the room, interpreting the song.

I got a call from Betzi Beaton, who was about to open in the Ziegfeld Follies. She wanted me to meet her for lunch at the Algonquin before she had to dash to the costumer's for a fitting. We hadn't seen each other since *Fools Rush In*. Anna Della joined us, and we three hardly ate. There was so much catching up to do!

Betzi was now living in a one-room apartment in the hotel, and suggested I move in, too, since Ware and I had lost our lease. She told me that Frank Case, who owned the Algonquin, was a family friend, and would make a special price for her and I if we took an apartment together.

I thought it was a great idea, and within a month we were ensconced

in a neat first-floor apartment, right over the main entrance on 44th Street. Our strategic location gave us an uninterrupted view of everyone coming and going. Friday at noon was the best time to see celebrities. If we saw someone special come in, we'd check our makeup, dash down the first-floor stairway to the lobby, and hastily walk to the Oak Room, where our friend Raoul, the headwaiter, would seat us at the table to the left of the doorway, so we could see and be seen.

The Algonquin was far more than it appeared to be from the outside. Entering through those creaking revolving doors, one half-expected to find a second-rate hotel. Instead there was an inviting lobby, with comfy chairs and huge leather couches. To the left of the front desk were the famous Algonquin dining rooms. To the right, behind a curtain, was a humming switchboard, where operators took messages for the famous. And there were always famous people in residence—John Barrymore and the great contralto Marian Anderson were on our floor. Frank Case gave her a piano, and from time to time we could hear her vocalize, very softly. Then there was the famous Round Table, where Alex Woollcott, Heywood Broun, Robert Benchley, Franklin P. Adams, Alfred Lunt, Charles MacArthur, George Kaufman, Moss Hart, and Dorothy Parker would meet.

Of course, there was the cat and the lobby was her home. And who can forget the funny old elevator that seemed to crawl up and down the floors behind gilded latticework, and the grandfather clock, which stood right in front of where Miss Bush sat. Miss Bush was a fixture at the Algonquin. She sat behind the curtain, hair piled high, perched atop a throne like a queen, overseeing the busiest switchboard in the city. From her command post she handled John Barrymore's calls to the West Coast, made sure that Marian Anderson got her tea with honey, and saw

to it that Damon Runyon reached Rose Bingham, Walter Winchell's girl Friday, for an important charity show appearance. A one-woman Central Intelligence Agency, Miss Bush pretty much ran the Algonquin. She oversaw incoming and outgoing everything, including love, money, and the inside scoop on what was really going on in the hotel—with staff and guests alike. It was not unusual for Betzi and me to come dashing in breathless to get our latest calls from her. Miss Bush would also happily take care of calls from men we didn't want to speak to, redirecting them out into infinity.

CHAPTER 4

BAILEY

I was meant to open at the British Colonial Hotel in the Bahamas for a six-week run and had taken the train from New York to Miami, where I caught the ship from Miami to Nassau.

I went to Paradise Beach every day to swim and lie in the sun. I sang every evening in the show, then was free to do as I wished the rest of the time. I had fun, because the hotel was filled with many friends of mine from Greenwich and New York who were on vacation. Most evenings they came to hear me sing. Then we danced till midnight. One moon-lit night we all went skinny-dipping in the hotel pool, which was a no-no. The hotel security guards were called out by the management, and I didn't want to get caught. Fearing I'd be reprimanded (or worse) if I was found, I quickly grabbed my clothes and raced to my room.

Jean Donnelly knocked on my door the very next morning, bearing exciting news. She told me that, after I'd left, she had introduced her friend Fred Stein to my friend Betzi Beaton, and it was love at first sight.

From the moment they met, they were inseparable. I searched her face for signs of a broken heart. "Don't worry, Teddy," she said. "I wasn't in love with him anyway. What I need now is a room. I can only stay till next weekend."

"Then stay with me," I said, pointing to the twin bed. "It won't cost you anything."

"Okay, good night," she said. And with that, she slipped under the covers and in moments was fast asleep. When she awoke, we talked about the great romance. Jean was excited and more than a little proud that she had played matchmaker for these two extraordinary people. Fred, so brilliant, dark, and handsome, was completely smitten with the beautiful, blond Betzi. "Now someone has to introduce someone to me," she said petulantly.

I laughed. "Okay. You might meet that someone at Paradise Beach. Come on, get dressed, let's go. There's a boat leaving for the island every half hour!"

By the time Jean had to return to New York, there *was* someone for her—a very tall Cuban boy from an extremely wealthy family. There was someone for me, too. He was a handsome, blond, blue-eyed Adonis, Bailey Balken by name, and he was wildly anxious to get me away from the rest of the crowd. A Williams graduate, he was divorced and now part of the New York scene. He'd been vacationing in Nassau and was in the audience the first night I appeared at the British Colonial . . . and every night thereafter, sometimes with others, most times alone, and always wanting me to go out with him.

Finally, we met one morning at Paradise, had lunch, went for a swim, raced each other out to the raft, and spent the rest of the afternoon just catching up on our lives "before Nassau." One morning very early, we

sailed to an uninhabited island about a mile away. We spent the day exploring and had a picnic lunch on a little knoll under a palm tree. I felt he was more than special. In fact, I felt such a closeness with him that I told him about what Dad had done to me. Then, like a couple of natives, we went swimming naked.

When I told Jean about it, she was wide-eyed. "Oh my God, Teddy! You *are* crazy! One doesn't go swimming naked with a man one doesn't expect to have an affair with! And then what? You did it?"

"Well, not really," I replied.

"What do you mean 'not really'? Either you did, or you didn't!"

"We didn't . . . I mean, we didn't go the whole way," I said. "I felt he understood me. When I told him what Dad did to me and how horrible I felt when he called me a 'dirty little Jew,' Bailey just kissed me, held me, and said 'forget it.' "

Her eyes narrowed. Jeannie had already figured out what happened. I stopped and took a deep breath. "Okay," I said, "I'll tell you the truth. Yes, we *did* make love, and it was wonderful! Maybe it wasn't love, but it was just the most exciting experience I've ever experienced. He's very sweet and kind. He wants me to live with him!"

Jean sprang to her feet. "You can't, Teddy! You're a lady!"

"No, I'm not! I'm a woman, and I think it's about time I lived like one."

"You can't, not in the world you were brought up in. *Think* of your mother!"

"*You* think of her!" I shot back. "I'm not in that Greenwich world anymore. I have no plans . . . only dreams."

"Well, I pray you wake up before you get too involved and get your heart broken."

And with those friendly words of advice, Jean left. I finished my six-

———

week engagement at the hotel, singing each night, swimming and sailing each day in the sunshine with Bailey, and becoming much too romantically involved. Was this love? I was beginning to think so, since Bailey was so adamant about staying together that he was now suggesting we get married.

When summer arrived, Betzi and Fred were on their honeymoon. I was still living in the apartment at the Algonquin and started studying with the young composer and songwriter Gene Berton while I was dating Bailey. I had finally introduced Bailey to Mother before she left for the Vineyard with my little sisters. He was surprised when she suggested we wait at least six months before marrying. The idea of his having been recently divorced didn't please her.

On the other hand, my mother's ultimatum didn't please him, either. He didn't want to wait. "Come live with me," he begged.

"You know I can't, not now," I said, secretly wanting to. "When I get back from singing at the Wardman Park Hotel in Washington next week, we'll go up to the Vineyard to Wild Acres, and you'll see where I grew up. We can sail and swim at South Beach."

"We can't make love there."

"We can make love *here* . . ." I replied, and in minutes I was in his arms.

About a month later I got a message from Bailey asking to meet. We were supposed to go out on a date that evening, but whatever it was, it couldn't wait. I was so excited to see him. He was sitting on my couch when I walked into my apartment. I ran to kiss him. He leaned forward and tried to clear his throat. "I don't know how to say this, Teddy," he said, looking up at me, "but . . ."

"But what?"

"But . . . I can't marry you!"

I went cold. I put out my hand, but he didn't take it. He just kept looking at me.

"Why? Are you still married?"

"No. It's not that."

"Then what is it? Are you ill? Dying from some disease . . . or . . . don't you love me anymore? Is there someone else?"

"No. I love you, Teddy," he spoke softly. "But . . ."

"But what?"

"It's just that I can't marry a girl who has Jewish blood in her veins."

I looked at him, not believing what I was hearing. "But you knew this, Bailey. You knew this when we first met. Remember, I told you . . . we were lying on the beach, telling each other everything."

"It was different then. We weren't in love."

"*I* was." I turned away from those memories, the memory of our affair. I struggled to stifle my tears.

"Think," he began, "think of what might happen to a child . . . if we had one."

"Don't worry, Bailey, we won't now."

"I love you, Teddy. Can't we go on as we are? I don't want to lose you . . ."

"*You just did!*" I said. And with that I picked up a carafe of ice water from the coffee table and hurled it at him, drenching him from the waist down.

"Damn you, Teddy!" he yelled, then turned and ran out of the apartment, dripping water all over the floor and down the stairs to the lobby.

I closed my eyes and stood there, the empty pitcher in my hand, my heart breaking, knowing that for Bailey I was only someone to have fun with, but not good enough to be his wife and the mother of his child. I

shuddered at the realization that Hitler just crossed the Atlantic and had invaded the American home and my life.

I put down the pitcher, walked over to the window, looked out, and saw Bailey. He was still dripping as he got into a cab, which quickly disappeared down 44th Street, taking him out of my life. Only then did I burst into tears.

CHAPTER 5

PAUL

After what happened with Bailey, I went up to the Vineyard to stay with my mother and sisters at Wild Acres. Wild Acres was Mother's summer home. Not far from Thorncroft, my grandparents' estate, it was a 125-year-old farmhouse that she had remodeled into a charming, inviting home. Neither the house, nor my family, nor the Vineyard's brilliant blue skies lifted my spirits. Desperately sad, I walked on the beach, played with Nan and Bobby, and listened to a band concert in the village. I was waiting for the right moment to tell Mom about Bailey, but when we were finally alone after the girls were in bed, she broke down and told me she was divorcing Dad. I was stunned by the news. It was Dad's drinking, of course. I was afraid for her, and for Nancy and Bobby, who were as protective of Mom as I had been at that age. I was worried about their being alone.

I could see how unhappy my mother was. My broken heart would have only added to her sorrow, so I returned to New York keeping my

troubles to myself. I stood on the deck of the ferry, waving good-bye to those three little faces smiling bravely up at me from the dock. They made me even more determined than ever to work harder and become successful, so that I could be of help. And as soon as I reached New York, my prayers were answered. I was asked to sing at the Club New Yorker.

I started rehearsing. I didn't dare allow myself to think about Bailey, or to speak of him to anyone, not even to Ware or Jeannie. He was a taboo subject, until Jeannie broke the ice. "You don't know how lucky you are," she said. "I told you he was a creep, not worth your little finger."

"Just wait," Ware chimed in. "Someday you'll meet the man who not only loves the body, but the voice, the charm, the character of the girl."

"Find him for me!" I pleaded, laughing.

Then I met Paul.

THAT FIRST NIGHT that I met Paul, at the New Yorker with Betzi, Fred, Jeannie, and Ware, once Jeannie had explained that "oil" was not a stage show but gasoline, Paul suddenly turned to me.

"I just struck a new field in Oklahoma, Teddy, so let's all go to Elmer's and celebrate right now!"

"It's too late for us, Paul," Betzi cut in. "Couldn't we make it Sunday?"

"Fine with me!" he replied. "Ware, what about you and Jeannie?"

"Sunday's perfect!" they answered.

"And you, Teddy, will you still join me tonight?"

I glanced over at Betzi. She nodded with a smile.

I looked back at Paul. "Yes," I said, "I'd love to."

As we said our good-byes, I took Paul's arm, stunned by the suddenness of it all. We walked down the spiral staircase and out into the night.

"Elmer's" was the nickname for El Morocco for those who frequented the New York nightclub world. When we arrived, it was obvious Paul was well known there. Passing the famous zebra-striped banquettes, we were immediately greeted by owner John Perona, who quickly signaled a waiter.

As if by magic, a bottle of Dom Pérignon and a tray of caviar followed us to our table—which was nowhere to be seen. Waiters soon appeared, carrying our table aloft. They placed it in a corner of the dance floor, there being no more room anywhere. We were quickly seated as the waiter popped the cork with a flourish. Paul smiled and lifted his glass. "Here's to a girl with a lovely voice. And I'm going to tell her what she should do with it, but first—let's dance."

His words startled me. What did he mean? I had no time to think, because he had quickly led me onto the dance floor, and was holding me as if he never wanted to let me go. The floor was so crowded that the other couples just stood and swayed to the music. So did we. I closed my eyes and let my body respond to his. I was in the arms of a stranger, but I felt I belonged there. For one mad moment, I wanted to belong to this man I knew nothing about, who had already tried to take possession of my future artistic plans, and who was now taking possession of me.

After the band stopped playing, we stood there a moment. *What must he be thinking? Does he feel the same way I do?* I wondered. I looked at him; he smiled. I turned away, trying to hide my thoughts and feelings from him, but I could tell that his eyes were reading mine. We sat down and I took a pack of cigarettes out of my purse and put one to my lips. He lit it. I closed my eyes as I inhaled. I blew the smoke out slowly and up into the twinkling lights. I knew he was watching me, that he found me desirable.

"Betzi tells me you're from Greenwich," Paul said, "that you studied in Paris, that you were both in the same show on Broadway. Before she married Fred, the two of you shared an apartment at the Algonquin Hotel."

"I'm still there," I said.

He looked straight through me with those very blue eyes. "I want to know more about you," he said.

"But we've talked about me all night," I replied. "It's your turn, Paul. I only know you're Betzi's friend from California. You produce oil for cars, you just arrived here in New York, you love to dance, and you are *very* persuasive in telling *this* girl, a perfect stranger, what she should do with her career. Now, please, tell me about *you*!"

He smiled. "Why don't we have supper tomorrow night, Teddy, after your performance, when we have more time? You must know I want to see you again, and then we'll talk about me, all right?"

I nodded yes and walked out of El Morocco on a cloud. When we arrived at the Algonquin, Paul escorted me into the lobby. As I entered the old elevator, I saw him stop and smile as he watched me disappear . . . And suddenly I realized I didn't know his last name!

Arriving at my apartment I found this note under my door.

Teddy, You certainly made a great impression on Paul! I've never seen him so attracted to anyone as he was to you tonight. Hope you had fun.

Call me tomorrow,
Betzi

All the next day I kept thinking about Paul, about his wanting to see

me again—and so soon—and about what I felt when I was in his arms. Damn! I wished I could talk to Betzi, but she wasn't home. Older men kind of scared me. He was probably only about forty, but he seemed so wise.

"Oh, Teddy," I told myself with a sigh, "just be yourself. That's who he wants to know. You: Miss Teddy Lynch, the glamorous debutante singer of the Club New Yorker . . . who is really a scared young girl, afraid that if he finds out who she really is, he'll never call again."

CHAPTER 6

VERSAILLES

The night after I met Paul, I saw him again in the audience at the New Yorker, sitting at a table all by himself. The minute I finished, he was beside me, smiling and applauding with the rest of the crowd. "You were great, Teddy," he whispered. "Come . . . let's go to Versailles."

It was always flattering to a girl to be taken to Versailles. It meant your escort wished to show you off. Versailles was the best of New York in the 1930s—the city at its most exciting and glamorous. Its walls were decorated with murals of the great palace. Crystal chandeliers, gleaming white linen tablecloths, sparkling silver, and elegantly dressed waiters in scarlet uniforms added to the illusion that one was living in the days of the Sun King, Louis XIV.

The Beautiful, the Social, and the Would-Be-Seen flocked here for fun and publicity. When we arrived, it was jammed. Harry "Puttin' on the Ritz" Richman was to appear within the hour. Because it was his opening night, the club was a madhouse, but the doorman easily recog-

nized Paul. We were ushered right in, past others who were waiting, and escorted to a banquette close to the stage.

Coming in from the bar area was Hope Hampton—a famous radio personality on the show *First Nighter*—draped in diamonds, all in white, with a young man at her side. She led the line, and was shown without delay to a ringside table. There, too, was the nightclub hopper and asbestos heir Tommy Manville, black shirt, white tie, with one of his eleven wives. Gypsy Rose Lee, who had already made the difficult transition from burlesque stripper to actress, saw me and waved hello, as did Cornelius Vanderbilt Jr. Columnists, including Walter Winchell, Ed Sullivan, Dorothy Kilgallen, and Leonard Lyons, were all there, taking notes, as were Cholly Knickerbocker (Maury Paul) and Nancy Randolph.

Once we were seated and had ordered our supper, Paul turned and looked at me. "You were great tonight, Teddy, and I wasn't wrong. You're young, beautiful, and talented, even more than you realize and . . ."

"Paul," I put my hand out, "please . . . You promised we'd talk about *you* tonight, remember?"

"Yes, I did, didn't I? Well, where shall I begin? With my ancestors?" He smiled. "Their name was Getty. They came from Gettystown, Ireland. The sons of John Getty left Ireland for America at the end of the eighteenth century. There were three of them: John, James, and William. John, a mercenary soldier, probably fought in Paris during the French Revolution. He eventually opened a tavern in Cresaptown, Maryland. I was told that when he was seventy, he married for the second time, fell off a horse after a drinking bout, and froze to death! James had a better fate. He eventually bought land in Pennsylvania, where Gettysburg stands, thus forever naming the famous battleground of the Civil War."

"How fabulous! You're part of our American history!" I exclaimed.

"We all are," Paul said. "You, too, I'm sure."

"What happened to William?" I asked.

Paul laughed. "No one really knows. He just disappeared someplace in the wilds of Kentucky."

"Oh, poor man."

"John Getty, my grandfather, was only a small farmer, but my father, his son George, worked his way through college, became a lawyer, and at forty entered the oil business. As for me, I went to UCLA, then to Oxford and, in between semesters, I worked in the oil fields."

"And now you're a producer, drilling your own oil wells," I said.

He reached for my hand. "Shall we dance before the floor gets too crowded? We can talk more later."

Again I was in his arms, he was holding me close, and it felt right. We didn't speak, we just danced as a thousand questions whirled through my head. Suddenly he stopped and looked at me. "This Gene Berton you spoke of . . . is he really teaching you?"

"Yes, and I'm making a recording of some of the songs next week."

"I want to hear them."

"You shall," I replied. "I'll even give you one. My German isn't very good yet, but the words are so tender and the melodies are divine."

Paul smiled. "That's a perfect description of German lieder. I can't wait. Come, let's eat!" We made our way back to the table, where a waiter in a scarlet uniform had just arrived with our food.

Harry Richman, still the great performer, excited the audience with his age-old songs. The show ended with six beautiful half-naked show-girls parading around, followed by Richman singing "Too Good for the Average Man" from the Rodgers and Hart hit show *On Your Toes*. The

applause was thunderous and, as it died down, I looked over and realized Paul was not looking at Harry or the girls, but at me. I blushed.

"You're very sweet, Teddy, and very tempting in that lovely dress."

"It's from Macy's French shop," I said proudly. "I buy all my evening clothes there. I love the color purple, and satin catches the light, so I kind of shine when I wear this out in the spotlight."

"It's not the dress; it's the girl *inside* the dress," he replied warmly. "You shine in or out of a spotlight, my dear. It's an innate quality, something you were born with that just shines."

"Thanks, Paul, and thanks for this wonderful supper. I didn't realize it, but I was starving."

"I'm glad it pleases you. In fact, I'm amazed and pleased that you have such a healthy appetite. Most girls I take out only pick at their food."

"Most girls are afraid they'll get fat," I answered. "It's the fashion today to be thin as a rail."

"Keep on eating, Teddy! Your figure's divine, and as for me, I'm happy to have found a girl who likes her food as much as I do. I'm going to ask you to dine with me every night, for as long as I'm in New York."

I stopped eating, my fork in midair. "And how long will that be?" I asked quickly, perhaps too quickly. I didn't want him to go. The thought of Paul leaving when he had only just arrived took me by surprise—as did my reaction. After all, I'd only seen him twice, but there was already this *something* that I felt, and I knew he felt it, too! It was an attraction I had not believed possible between strangers—till now. Then I heard that little voice inside my head. *Dreamer, wake up!* it said. I sighed.

"What's wrong?" Paul asked. "I heard you sigh."

"Oh! I was just waiting for your answer."

He wasn't fooled. "No, Teddy, you were a million miles away. You

don't have to dine every night with me. I'm sure there's a long list of suitors just waiting to take you out. And if there's someone special, I'll understand." I shook my head no.

As he helped me into a cab, Paul said, "I'm going to England soon. I'm not sure of the date, but I'd love you to be there when I am."

I looked at him in amazement, but said nothing.

"You could sing at the Dorchester Hotel in London," he continued.

"How could I possibly sing in London, Paul? I'd have to go there and audition."

"No, you wouldn't," he said. "I can guarantee the job."

"Not unless you own the Dorchester."

"I don't own it, but the owner is a personal friend. I'm certain he would book you on my recommendation. It would help your career to appear abroad. And when you come back, you'd have added a dimension to your career."

"Thanks, Paul," I said, realizing he was testing me, "but I have all the dimensions I need right now." I turned away.

"You'd be more in demand . . ." I heard him say.

"I'm in demand already . . . I'm booked solid," I said. "There are a lot of girls trying to get my job at the New Yorker, but the management likes me, so I'm not really worried." I felt myself grow cold. What kind of girl did he think I was? "You'd better take me home, Paul. I have to work with Gene in the morning, and it's almost two thirty now!"

"Tomorrow is Sunday!" he protested.

"That's the only time he has to work this week," I explained.

"But won't you still come to the Plaza tomorrow evening? I'm staying there. And don't you remember? I've invited Betzi, Fred, Jean, and Ware for cocktails and dinner to celebrate. We'll meet about seven o'clock in

my apartment, then go to the Persian Room. Emil Coleman's orchestra is playing. You don't perform on Sundays nights, do you?"

"No."

"Good. Because I really want you to be with me."

The cab sped down Sixth Avenue. I was sitting as close as I could to the door on my side of the car and was rather silent when Paul said, "Please say you'll come, Teddy. I know they are all looking forward to seeing you." As he spoke, he took my hand in his. "My God! You're cold . . . you're shivering! What kind of an evening wrap are you wearing?" He felt it. "It's too light!"

"It's gold cloth," I said.

"That's not warm enough."

"It's pretty," I said.

"You are really something, Teddy," he said, laughing. "I know you wore this because it goes with your purple gown, but you must never jeopardize your health for your career. Here." He put his arms around me and pulled a frigid me close to him. It felt so good to be held, to be in the arms of someone who really cared. We stayed that way until my shivering stopped.

"Are you warmer now?"

"Yes, thank you."

"Then don't move." I didn't. "Will you come tomorrow night?"

"Yes," I said. And with that, he leaned down and kissed me all the way to the Algonquin.

CHAPTER 7

ONE FIFTH AVENUE
AND THE STORK CLUB

On Sunday morning I rehearsed my songs with Gene Berton, but then I spent the rest of the day trying to find the perfect dress for dinner. I was really nervous when I reached the Plaza, but was excited when Paul said how lovely I looked.

He introduced me to his friends, Ruloff (Rully) and Sunny Cutten. When Ware, Jean, Betzi, and Fred arrived, we all went down to the Persian Room. After dinner, I danced with Rully, Ware, Fred, and finally Paul.

"I've been wanting to dance with you all evening," Paul whispered as he took me in his arms. "And now the evening is almost over!"

"I know," I said, thinking the same thing, "but I should go home soon. I'm recording a new song with Gene in the morning, and I want to do my best."

"I want you to do your best, too, and you will, I'm sure." Again he

held me close, and we danced the last few minutes without speaking. When the music stopped, we walked back to the table. After saying good night to the Cuttens, Ware, and Jean, I left with Betzi and Fred, who dropped me off on their way back to their home in the Village.

Just as I was going to sleep, Betzi called. "Darling," she said. "I think my friend Paul Getty is completely captivated by you. The entire time we were dancing he talked only about how independent you were, how principled, courageous, stubborn, and talented! What about you, Teddy? How do you feel about him?"

"Oh, Betz," I sighed, "I don't know. He seems to see right through me and it scares me. He's been telling me what I should do to have a more fulfilling career, and I seem to want his approval. I wonder why. It's strange—from the night you introduced us, I've felt a great attraction, but maybe I'm dreaming!"

"If that's how you feel, Teddy, I'm glad, because he *is* definitely interested in you, not only as a woman, but as an artist."

Later I could still hear Betzi's last words, "Don't forget Teddy, voice or no voice, you're someone special—and he knows it!" I smiled, thinking he was someone special, too!

When I hung up the phone, I walked over to the dresser, opened the drawer, and pulled out a lovely French handkerchief embroidered with the phrase *"Qui ne risque rien, n'a rien"* ("Nothing ventured, nothing gained"). Paul was saying the same thing, telling me what he thought was best for me to do with my career: "Attempt the impossible. Reach out for what you want." His advice and encouragement made me want to keep trying.

As soon as Gene and I had finished recording, I raced to see Paul at the Plaza, where he was waiting for me. "Come on," he said, "I have one

of those Liberty record players in the apartment. We can listen to your recordings there."

I watched him as he listened. I didn't say a word. I just sat and tried not to be noticeably nervous. It seemed to me that he was agreeably surprised. As the first song reached its climax, a smile crossed his face. After the second song, he turned to me. Before he could speak, I muttered, "Was it all right? I mean . . . I can do better."

"You'll do even better after you really study, but by God I *was* right about your voice! The quality *is* there! I believe you can do anything. Don't doubt yourself." He was watching me. "You look sad, Teddy. Are you crying? My God! Those *are* tears!" He came over and put his arms around me.

"I'm just emotional, Paul, that's all, *and* grateful."

I was so happy to be in the arms of a man who might open a door to a world of music and art that I never dreamt could be mine. So happy that I just leaned up and kissed him. And like a bolt of lightning, that simple kiss erupted into the most passionate desire, a craving to wrap myself around this man and never let him go. I wanted to be as good a singer as he said I could be, to do what he said I should do to further my career . . . but at the moment, none of that mattered. Suddenly his mouth was on mine, and he was kissing me like I had never been kissed before—ravenously, hungrily.

I looked up. He was still holding me, studying my face. Then he smiled and said, "You are an enchanting, unpredictable young lady, Teddy Lynch, but before I fall completely under your spell, let's go eat."

It was early, so we dined in the Oak Room of the Plaza. I don't remember what I ate, but I do remember the way Paul looked at me—as if he knew right then that we were going to become lovers. I felt his desire from across the table, as though he already possessed me. This

man had reawakened my longing to try for the best. More importantly, by the way he responded to me, he made me realize what a captivating young lady I really was.

Bailey had taken away my self-esteem. Paul gave it back!

One of Paul's and my favorite luncheon and pre-theater dining places was 21. Celebrities were never annoyed by the press, and could dine quietly without being stared at. I believe Louis Sobol was just about the only journalist who frequented the place, because the owner, Jack Kriendler, made a point of protecting his clients, who included the Duke and Duchess of Windsor, Eddy Duchin, Thomas Dewey, Carrie and Orson Munn, the William Rhinelander Stewarts, and many others. Kriendler was an aficionado of things American West. He displayed his silver saddle under glass in the den-like lobby, hung his great collection of Remington oil paintings there, and was always the most elegant, charming of hosts to Paul and me.

The fact that Paul and I were dating was not unknown around town. Our names appeared in the gossip columns of the day, sparking curiosity among Mother's friends. Some of whom, women with wagging tongues, would try to find out more. "Louise . . ." they'd whisper, "I see your daughter Teddy is going around with Paul Getty. Why, *he's* the catch of the year."

Mother would nod wisely and smile her beautiful smile. "And Teddy is quite the catch, too, you know," she'd reply.

I paid no attention to the gossip columns, for I had just signed a contract with Victor Gilbert, manager of the very posh mirrored club room at One Fifth Avenue. It was one of New York's most envied singing gigs. To get ready, I was working every day with Gene Berton, learning new songs and loving every moment of my life.

In October 1935, I followed Dorothy Lamour into "No. One" after she left for Hollywood. I starting singing twice nightly to a full house accompanied by two great pianists, Joe Lilley and his partner. (Years later, Joe became the head of the music department at RKO.) Gilbert was pleased with me, and asked that I stay on for two more weeks. Paul was in Los Angeles, visiting his mother, so he missed the show.

Sherman Billingsley, owner of the famous Stork Club, came in one night, heard me, and asked that I sing at his club with Nat Brandywine's orchestra during the coming Easter season. And, boy, did I accept—I was thrilled.

Sherm was as starstruck as the people who came to his club to see the stars. The name "Stork Club" had come from Walter Winchell, whose column announced the forthcoming birth of many celebrities' children by saying, "The stork was about to visit the So-and-So's." And as the Stork Club, it was to become the most famous club of its kind in the world.

When Sherm came out of the Midwest, gave up the drugstore he'd run, and took over the spot at 3 East 53rd Street, he hoped to attract the crowds by making it *the* place where everyone who was anyone would want to be. Other clubs, including El Morocco and Versailles, made up the nighttime circuit for those on the town, and that included some two hundred nationally recognizable names. The Stork quickly became part of this circle.

Shortly after it opened, Sherm asked a young adman if he would like to pick up a little extra in the way of food and drink, impress his date, and be out every night. That young man was my brother Ware, who immediately answered, "Why, sure, what do I do?"

"You know everyone who is anyone," Sherm said. "You're social,

and you know the thugs from the top names. Just sit at a table near the entrance within sight of Frank, the maître d'. You may bring a date, but no dancing, all the champagne and food you choose. When a person stands at the door, waiting for a table, Frank will look to you. If you nod, Frank will let him in. If you shake your head just slightly, he'll say, 'There is no room.' " Ware's frequent appearance at the Stork Club soon gave him the reputation for being a big spender.

Then he suggested something that came pretty naturally to a man in the advertising business. "Why not put up a rope, Sherm, a red rope? Then, when people arrive, they can't rush right in. Frank will stand there and, if you want the party inside, okay. If you don't, it will be easier to hold them back."

"But sometimes the room is empty," Sherm said.

"You'll be using what we call the psychology of scarcity. When something is hard to get, people only want it the more." Being banned from the Stork Club became a fate worse than death to those who cared, and the red rope was the hangman's noose to the aspiring who might have offended.

Under the personal direction of Sherman Billingsley, I opened at the Stork Club on March 4, 1936. In the lobby there was a large studio portrait, picturing me in the traditional heavy-lidded look of the day. Preparation included all the publicity Sherm could dream up. Cholly Knickerbocker and Nancy Randolph had announced it in their society columns.

My opening night was a smashing success. The red rope was up. The three hatcheck girls were ready, and so was I. From backstage, I watched the incoming crowd as they proceeded down the long walk past the bar. Their faces were eager, almost apprehensive. Would they get a ringside

table or be sent to a far corner and have their evening ruined? Would they be included among the "in" crowd, comprised not only of the well-to-do, but also of the flashy? Would they be seated among the glamorous society drifters—debs, actors, heads of state, bogus gamblers—who made the columns?

The club was full, and then some. Sherm packed them in as if he expected they would eat with one arm, sit sideways at their tables, and only breathe occasionally. Soon the throbbing music would begin, and the oh-so-elegant would rush, push, and elbow their way to the floor to grab a few inches of dance space. I would step up to the microphones in front of the band and sing my first number.

"Just One of Those Things" was a favorite of mine. Determined to be heard, I gave it all I had. Then, as Nat began the strains of my next song, "Begin the Beguine," something happened that had never before happened at the Stork. People stopped dancing. They actually stopped moving. They stopped clinging to one another, looked up at me, listened, and then started to applaud. From that night on, I was no longer just a vocalist with a band. I was a full-fledged attraction.

Paul had taken a large table—among his guests were Barbara Hutton, her husband Count Reventlow, the Ruloff Cuttens, Prince David Mdivani, Virginia Sinclair, Cornelius Vanderbilt, the Orson Munns, and Daniel Sickles and his wife. After my set, Paul proudly came to escort me back to join the others. (Entry in my diary: *I opened at The Stork. Paul there! Home at four! Will read reviews tomorrow . . .* Entry the next day: *Reviews the best . . . thank you, Nancy and Cholly. Lunch with Paul at the Plaza. Be on time.*)

And so I sang my heart out every night at the Stork for the next six weeks at a salary of $350 per week. Then to my surprise, Sherman sent

me a note asking whether I'd consider renewing my contract to sing there for another six weeks. I didn't know how to answer. His note-sending across the room was typical. He would be two tables away from someone and, rather than stand and go to them or interrupt their conversation, he'd send a waiter with his scribbled message.

It so happened that Paul was with me when I got the note, and I asked him what I should do. "I think it's about time you got a raise, Teddy. Ask for more money. I'll make a bet with you. If Sherman doesn't give you twice what you're making now, then I will."

"No, you won't, Paul," I said.

"He won't hesitate," Paul replied. "You are worth it."

"He's been so nice," I hedged.

"And you've been so nice to him, too. Look at the quality of the people that you've brought into the club, and look at the business! Put a value on yourself. Do it."

I took out a purple pen with purple ink. In my heavy strokes with great flourishes, many exclamation points, and several underlinings, I wrote, *Sherm . . . Thanks. I'd love to sing for you for another six weeks. You've been so kind . . . but from now on it's got to be DOUBLE . . . OR NOTHING!! O.K. Love, Teddy.* My heart raced.

We waited. I sipped my drink. Paul reached for my hand and we watched as Sherm took my note from the shuttling waiter, glanced briefly at it, and wrote something on it.

The waiter returned, carrying a bottle of champagne and my note. "On Mr. Billingsley," he said, "with his compliments." Then I read Sherm's scrawling *YES* across the face of my demand, and I sang there for another six weeks at twice the money.

About a month later, as I walked into the Algonquin one afternoon,

a jubilant Betzi was in the lobby. Without even saying hello she said, "I've got something to show you." And with that, she opened a copy of the *Journal American* to Cholly Knickerbocker's society column. I read, agog. "You see?" Betzi said.

"Wow," I said. "Me?"

"Yes, you, Teddy. There it is in black and white. Paul and you being together all the time hasn't passed unnoticed. The gossip and society columnists keep on top of those in the spotlight . . . and that means you two."

> A year ago, Paul Getty first came to the attention of Gotham Society, unimpressive and modest looking, and there was nothing about the youngish man with hair slightly reminiscent of a lion's mane to think here was a real oil multimillionaire out of the West. And to his credit, let it be said, Paul Getty made no attempt to help "Cafe Society" discover his all too solvent condition. But when Teddy Lynch, who possesses a superb voice, started chanting hot numbers and torch songs at Sherman Billingsley's "Stork Club," it looked like L*O*V*E, and the matchmakers are predicting wedding bells.

CHAPTER 8

ENGAGED

Paul met me after my performance at the Stork and we went to El Morocco. As usual it was mobbed, but owner John Perona greeted Paul effusively and immediately found us a table. I noticed that our entrance had caused quite a stir. Heads were turning—we were being watched and talked about. I don't think Paul noticed; he seemed to be only looking at me.

When we were seated and the waiter had finished clearing the table, suddenly Paul said, "Tell me about him!"

"Who?" I asked.

"That someone who broke your heart, hurt you, so that now you're afraid to ever fall in love again. True, isn't it?" He was watching me.

"True," I managed to say, "but then, he wasn't honest."

"Don't you think sometimes people are afraid to tell each other the truth about themselves because they might lose that person?" Paul asked.

"I suppose so, but in my case, I told him all about myself before we

became lovers, then when we were about to marry, he said he couldn't because of what I had told him."

"What did you tell him?"

"What I would tell any man I was in love with or hoped to marry."

"Is it that important?"

"Yes, I think so."

"So tell me."

I looked at him. "Why?"

"Because I care for you very much. I see in your eyes a certain sadness, even when you smile, and I find myself wanting you to be happy. Whatever it is, Teddy, dear, it can't be that bad . . . besides, I'm older and wiser than you." He smiled. "And perhaps, if you tell me, I'll know you better and can help."

And so, looking straight ahead, not daring to meet his eyes, I told him what my stepdad had done to me when I was a little girl, the shock of being treated in such a horrendous way. His saying that somehow "I deserved it because I was a dirty little Jew, like my father." It was still painful in the retelling, all these years later. "And I didn't want to be a Jew, because I'd been told they killed Jesus. I couldn't tell Mom what he did, because she loved him. And anyway, he'd warned me that she would believe him, not me."

Turning to Paul, I then told him about Bailey and Nassau. "I fell in love and told him everything. We became lovers, talked of marrying—we even told my mother. Then one afternoon he said, 'I love you, Teddy, but I can't marry you because you have Jewish blood, and I don't want a Jewish baby, but I don't want to lose you, either.' 'Well,' I said, 'you just did!' And then I threw a carafe of water at him. I cried when he left, not for him, but for our world!"

For a minute, Paul didn't speak, then he reached for my hand. "Teddy, dear, thank you for telling me, but don't be sad anymore. I wish you hadn't had that experience as a child and, as for Bailey, he doesn't know what he's missed. You were already way beyond him when you met. He could never have caught up. Just think"—he paused as our eyes met—"I would never have known you. As for being part Jewish, be proud. They're great people. Whoever your ancestors were, I'm sure they were refined, intelligent, gifted. I would like sometime to meet your father. Does he live here?"

"No, Chicago. But my grandfather, Henry Charles Lytton, is here. He has an apartment on Fifth at Seventy-Seventh, and a home out on the island. He is ninety years old, a remarkable human being. He owns the Hub in Chicago."

"That big store on State Street? I've shopped there. Can we call him, Teddy? I'd like to meet him."

"Why, Paul?"

"Because he's your grandfather, that's why. And I want to meet your mother, too."

"The Christian side?" I said, laughing.

"Yes, Teddy."

"She's beautiful, and so are my sisters, Nancy and Bobby."

"I'm sure they are. Who else is there?"

"Henry, my oldest brother. Yale graduate, very serious, lives in Chicago. Doesn't approve of my singing in nightclubs."

"Well, Ware does, and I like him. He is very protective of you."

"I know, we're very close. But why are you asking me so many questions?"

"Because of my feelings for you. You're so young and full of expecta-

tions . . . and you have a right to be. Every woman does . . . to love, to be loved, to be married, to have children. I don't want to hurt you, ever—so I need to tell you how I feel, and you *need to know* about me."

"What is it that I need to know, Paul?"

"I've been married four times, divorced four times. I have four sons and, because of my bad record as a husband, I don't believe I should ever marry again. It just wouldn't be fair. Strange, isn't it? Here I am, wanting you in my life, and at the same time telling you I'm a poor candidate for a husband. Long before we met, I swore that, no matter if I fell in love with the most beautiful woman in the world, I'd never marry again."

For the longest moment, I was stunned. I looked at Paul. He looked uncomfortable, but he had at least told me the truth about how he felt, and I was glad of that. But what was I to say in reply? I took a deep breath. "Thanks, Paul, for telling me," I said finally, "and thanks for the encouragement about my singing. But I guess we shouldn't see each other anymore. I've never been married, never had a baby, and I've not even reached anything near the top in my career. But . . . you've done it all"—I hesitated—"*four times already.* So it's absolutely insane for us to be together, because I do want all those things you said every woman has a right to—all those things you've already had."

I got up quickly. As I left the table, I looked back at him. "Besides," I said, "I'm a very beautiful woman, too." And then I ran out of El Morocco.

Paul caught up with me at the door. I was crying. We got into a cab. He held me in his arms, and I couldn't resist his kisses. I was in love. We drove through Central Park for what seemed like hours. Somewhere between the Fifth Avenue/72nd Street entrance to the park and the exit at the Central Park Zoo, Paul's face lit up. "Darling, I've got it!" he

exclaimed. "We can get engaged. I've never been engaged before . . . and I love you, Teddy. Will you?"

"Would I? How do you say yes in a hundred ways?" I was in heaven.

To say I adored the man would be an understatement. I really loved him, wanted to please him, to learn from him, to catch up with his brilliant mind, but how could I? One thing we had in common, though, was our love of work. Paul used to say he never saw anyone try as hard as I did to accomplish whatever I set out to do.

"You work as if your next meal depended on it," he would say. It did, for I supported myself!

Paul surprised me one afternoon by saying, "Let's go pick out a ring!"

It was exciting. We stopped at Tiffany's, then Cartier, before ending up at Paul Flato's, the "jeweler to the stars." Flato was the first designer whose work was considered comparable to European masters. We were both captivated by a particularly beautiful square-cut diamond, about six or seven karats.

Knowing you are loved by the one you love is the sweetest thing in one's life. The weeks following that crazy cab ride through Central Park are filled with the happiest and most exciting memories. He loved me, that was for sure. I loved him, too, and gave myself to him completely, with no regrets.

Of course I told Betzi, Ware, and Jeannie, but no one else, not even Paul's mother. Understandably, she would have had a stroke on learning he was engaged and planning to marry yet again, for the fifth time. I did put a call in to my mother, who immediately invited us both to come visit her on Martha's Vineyard, where she and my little sisters were spending the summer.

We planned to go as soon as I closed at the Stork Club, but until

then, for the next few weeks, Paul and I began to see New York together. Everything seemed so new, so much more exciting than it did before I'd met him!

We bought matching little stuffed Donald Duck dolls together, one for him, one for me. He took me to the opera, to Broadway openings, horse shows, prizefights, political rallies, and the Botanical Garden and the Aquarium in the Bronx. Being with Paul was like being in a whole new world. At night it was his custom to meet me after my last show, or we'd meet for lunch at places like Armando's, Le Coq Rouge, Mon Paris, or 21.

One afternoon, we drove out to Ridgefield, Connecticut, about a two-hour trip from Manhattan, to Rully and Sunny's spectacular home for dinner. Sunny gaily showed us around their enormous colonial estate in the foothills of the Berkshires and, after a delightful evening, we left.

Driving through the countryside, we stopped for a moment, off the road overlooking the Hudson River. It was nightfall and the fragrance of flowers surrounded us. Paul turned and said, "Teddy, dear—you seem to be in another world, like a fairy princess, enchanting and beautiful. I'm afraid I have fallen in love with you."

"Don't you be afraid, Paul. I am."

He took me in his arms.

CHAPTER 9

MARTHA'S VINEYARD

I wanted to introduce Paul to Martha's Vineyard, the island off Cape Cod, that had been such an important part of my childhood. We drove up along the New England coast in his car until we reached Woods Hole, where we took the ferry across the fifteen or so miles to the Vineyard. As the boat rounded the buoy and headed in toward the wharf, the smell of pine trees and bay brush carried across the hot, still water from West Chop.

To starboard we passed a colonial mansion, then considered the showplace of the island. "That's Thorncroft," I said as I pointed it out to Paul. "That's Uncle Herbert's summer home when he's not running around at the stock exchange. My grandfather, John Herbert Ware, built it in the 1920s, and the entire family has been coming here ever since. I feel I grew up here, on this island, in this sun."

"It's a magnificent mansion," Paul said.

"It's just 'coming home' to me," I replied. The Vineyard to me meant

magical summers of faded blue jeans; hot summer days in a Wee Scot (that's a sailboat) in a Vineyard Haven Yacht Club race; a gritty beach picnic in the dunes at South Beach with clams, lobsters, and corn on the cob and a roaring driftwood fire; the snapping off of Coke bottle caps with a fifty-cent piece when some idiot had forgotten to bring the opener; and fierce sunburns that almost ruined the night at the Yacht Club Dance.

As the ferry inched toward the dock, we glided by the yachts, all white and shipshape, and tiny children, in their rowboats or dinghies, waved greetings to us.

Driving up island, we turned off at Lambert's Cove Road, and drove through miles of oak woods and scrub pine. We passed waving grassy fields and luscious green lawns. Suddenly before us stood a rambling island house, all white, with freshly painted green shutters. This was Wild Acres, Mother's summer home. We got out at the little cutting garden near the patio and carried our bags to where my two beautiful blond sisters, Nancy and Barbara, and my mother, in a sparkling white dress, stood beaming at the door.

Paul's room was charmingly done with a spool bed and antique prints, multipaned windows and wide floorboards. The room was on the second floor, with a view overlooking the tiny duck pond, and beyond that, Vineyard Sound toward the Elizabeth Islands.

After an enjoyable family dinner, the girls went with their nurse for their evening walk on the beach. Mother, Paul, and I went to a movie at the Eagle Theatre in Oak Bluffs. We bought popcorn from Darling's candy shop and walked across the circle to the Flying Horses, the oldest merry-go-round still working in the nation. We tried for the brass ring for a free ride but didn't catch it.

The next afternoon, Paul and I drove up island to the famous Priscilla Hancock's to buy her luscious homemade chocolates. Then we walked South Beach in our bathing suits and wondered if there were notes in the bottles drifting ashore. The surf was high, but Paul went into it in a rush. I followed him, if only to prove I wasn't scared, but I found myself being carried out by a strong undertow. Suddenly helpless, I lost my footing. Paul's hand grabbed mine just in time. With a sudden strong pull, he broke through the next wave, with me in tow, and we fell laughing on the beach together.

Lying there in the warmth of the sun on this deserted beach, with only the gulls watching us, he reached over and pulled me to him and, in spite of the sand, beguiled by the smell of the sea and the taste of salt water on our bodies, we made love.

We lay there for what seemed like a long, long time. Finally opening my eyes, I saw he was watching me and picking off several little ants that were running up my arms. We both started to laugh, and it flashed through my mind how scandalous it would have been if the police or lifeguards had suddenly appeared.

We dressed, then drove home slowly across the sandspit and the beach to Vineyard Haven, with its shipyards, the ancient Seamen's Bethel, and the side-wheeler ferry at the dock, waiting to take tourists away from this fantasyland. Then we drove up to West Chop to visit other members of my family, tanned beyond belief, busy having fun, one and all with sun-bleached hair. Like my mother, the other descendants of John Herbert Ware all lived near Thorncroft, the main house. Paul met them all—Betty Bassett, Jack Ware, and my cousins—those two stalwart six-foot-and-more von Colditz boys, who even then gave promise of conquering the world. It wasn't long ago that one of them, Herbert von

Colditz, built his own sailboat in Holland and sailed it, under sail alone, across the Atlantic, bringing his family to call on me in California after a trip through the Canal to the Pacific.

That evening after dinner, Paul, Mother, and I sat out on the sun porch facing the Sound, and watched a beautiful day turn slowly into a magical night. We could see the gulls flying over the sand dunes to their nests in the cliffs beyond and small sailboats heading homeward, their sails catching the freshening breeze, with spinnakers bulging out. We could even hear the voices and laughter of those on board as they sped past.

A perfect Vineyard day was coming to an end. How I loved it, and how I longed to stay there and never leave the peace and the unique privacy of Wild Acres . . . the green lawn leading down to our private beach . . . the view of the mainland in the distance . . . the barn at the entrance to our road, where my brothers and I had held dances and parties every summer as we grew up . . . the adorable playhouse that my sisters practically lived in. I turned to Paul and asked, "Do you really like *our* island?"

"It's perfect," he answered. "And Wild Acres is a great tribute to you, Louise. I hope you will let me come for a visit again."

"Not without me," I said. Mother smiled. I decided to leave them together, so I excused myself and ran upstairs to kiss my sisters good night.

Of course, they wanted to know all about Paul . . . and especially his silver car—a sleek DeSoto Airflow. It looked like a bullet, and they couldn't wait to go for a ride. The next morning, he took them on the road through the woods leading to our house and amazed them by steering the car with only his pinkie on the wheel. To this day they have never forgotten.

———

Later, when I joined Paul, he told me that Mother was not too happy about my marrying a man twice my age, who had been married four times and divorced four times.

"Your mother is really quite right to object, since you are so much younger and have never been married before. And of course, my record isn't that good, but I told her I love you and would like us to be engaged, since I have never been engaged before . . . and I asked that she approve."

"Did she?"

"Yes," he said. "She did," and then he laughed. "You know, when I asked her to tell me what she thought you would need for an allowance to run a house . . ."

"But, Paul, we aren't going to have a house," I exclaimed, "not yet. We're only going to be engaged."

"I know, but I wanted her thought."

"So?"

"'Well,' she replied, 'it depends on where you are going to make your home. If it is a New York apartment, that's one thing, a log cabin, another.'" As he told me this, he smiled a very understanding smile and said, "Teddy, I realized right then that your doll of a mother would never interfere. She is a great lady."

On our last day, we rented a small sailboat in Edgartown, slipped out of the harbor, and sailed over to Chappaquiddick Island. "Someday we'll come back here, Teddy," Paul said. I knew he loved his own California beach and this was a new experience for him . . . a test for me, too, because had Paul not liked the island lifestyle, I might have been slightly turned off. I was so happy he liked *my* island.

That afternoon, we drove to Menemsha, a fishing village with fresh lobsters and clams. Nestled into the surrounding hills, the quaint com-

munity of small graying summer homes was known for its picturesque fishing fleet. We walked out to the Coast Guard Station at the end of the dock. As we walked, shells crunched underfoot. "Let's try the clams," he said, and we made a beeline for the clam bar, where we each finished off twelve little necks on the half shell.

"And now?" Paul asked.

"To Gay Head." Gay Head was the Indian reservation where the harpooner in *Moby-Dick* came from. We headed for the cliffs topped by the huge lighthouse at the end of the island. We climbed, digging our toes into blue, black, red, and yellow clay. Time and the pounding surf had finally worn away most of the colored clay into the sea, which stretched below. Paul bought a clay ashtray from an Indian. He also presented me with a ninety-eight-cent beaded ring . . . "Till Flato's is ready," he said.

At sunset, we drove home to a feast Mother had prepared. We left Wild Acres the next morning, and I fought back tears as we said good-bye to my beautiful mother and adorable, teasing sisters. We hurried to catch the first ferry to the mainland, then drove to New York.

On the way, I noticed Paul made notes occasionally in a little book. Though we were together constantly, he never discussed his business with me, and I knew little of his wealth and power. It was only later that I discovered that each corner where he had made a notation was the future location of a Tidewater Oil gas station.

CHAPTER 10

SUTTON PLACE

Several weeks later, while having dinner at the Louis XIV Restaurant in Rockefeller Plaza, Paul told me he was planning to leave soon for London on business. He wanted to take some of my records with him. He had met the great Wagnerian opera singer Kirsten Flagstad, had told her about my voice, and had asked her advice.

She immediately recommended that he contact the world-renowned singing teacher Madame Blanche Marchesi, in London. She was the daughter of Mathilde and Salvatore Marchesi, who were the famous teachers of Nellie Melba, Etelka Gerster, and Sybil Sanderson, the beautiful singer from California who was acclaimed as the "Girl with the Eiffel Tower Voice."

"So, Teddy, I was planning to see her and will ask her to listen to your recordings."

I realized that Paul was serious, and suddenly I was scared that no matter what *he* thought, maybe I didn't have the true vocal ability for a

career in concert or opera. Nevertheless, by the time Paul was ready to sail for Southampton, he was loaded down with my demo recordings. That very night, out at dinner, Paul took my hand and slipped the real engagement ring onto my finger. He gave me a great big kiss and said, "Now, darling, it's official. We're engaged."

I looked down at the ring and whispered, "It's more beautiful than when you picked it out."

"You chose it, too, Teddy," Paul said. "Are you pleased?"

"Pleased?" I laughed. "I'm ecstatic . . . elated . . . delighted . . . delirious . . . with joy . . . and I'll never take it off. Never. I swear."

"Good." Paul smiled, and then called for the check. "Come on, Teddy, I have another surprise for you. We can't be late!"

He hailed a cab. After a short ride across town, we pulled up in front of a huge apartment house on the East River: Number 1 Sutton Place South, right on the corner of 57th Street. There, we were met by the resident manager, who escorted us up to the penthouse. At the doorway, he handed Paul the keys.

We crossed the threshold into one of the most exquisite apartments in the city of New York. From the marble-floored entrance hall, we walked through a music room and into a drawing room at least forty feet long, with a high, gilded ceiling and elegant French furnishings. On one wall hung a seventeenth-century Beauvais tapestry. Opposite was a great marble fireplace flanked by two French doors. The doors led out to a terrace; I later found to my amazement that it ran around the entire penthouse. I could circle the whole block from 57th to 58th Street without leaving the apartment.

Although it was ten in the evening, every room was lighted, as if we had been expected. On the coffee table in front of the couch, facing the fire-

place, was a champagne bucket with a bottle and two glasses, just waiting.

As we walked through the rooms, he told me he was no longer at the Plaza, that he'd leased the penthouse from the Hon. Mrs. Frederick Guest (Amy, daughter of American entrepreneur Henry Phipps), and had moved in that morning. "Do you like it?" he asked.

"Like it? Of course I like it! It's fantastic, but aren't you going to be lonely living here by yourself? It's so huge."

"Not if you are with me."

"Paul, you know I can't do that. What would people say?"

"What they say anyway."

"Yes, but . . ."

"I know . . . but your mother . . ."

"And *yours*, and society."

"But we are engaged."

"Yes, but only as of tonight." I looked at the ring on my finger, sparkling in the moonlight. "Darling, it's *sooo* beautiful," I said. "And I'm so *proud* of it."

"Well, I'm proud to be marrying the granddaughter of Henry Charles Lytton," Paul replied, putting his arms around me.

My mouth dropped open as I looked at him. "What did you say? Why did you say that? You don't even know my grandfather. Maybe you wouldn't like him."

"Oh, but I do! I met him yesterday."

"You . . . ? You mean . . ."

"I mean, I decided to call on him, and I did. In fact, I went up to see him at his apartment, and we had a most interesting talk. He is a brilliant businessman, remarkable for his age—ninety-one, isn't he? Thinks I might be good for you."

"Oh, does he? Did you tell him you've been married four times?"

"Yes."

"And divorced four times?"

"Yes."

"What did he say to that?"

"That *you* will be good for *me*!" This made him smile. "He was pleased that we are engaged. Of course, he doesn't approve of separations, therefore he thinks it unwise for you to study in London. Thinks you can study here. Still, he admires your spirit and courage in making a career for yourself, and wishes you well."

"He was a singer himself when he was young."

"I know. A baritone. Still has a great speaking voice. And, by the way, he invited us to come out to Roslyn for lunch any Sunday. Shall we go?"

I could only nod, for I was still in shock at what Paul had said—that he was "proud to be marrying the granddaughter of Henry Charles Lytton." After what Dad and Bailey had done—and why they'd done it—it meant the world to me to hear Paul say those words. It was all I needed to make me accept who I was and no longer be afraid or ashamed.

From the terrace, the view of the city in every direction was astonishing, especially at night. And, in the late 1930s, the buildings, though not so high or close together, still resembled a jungle of sparkling lights. We stood looking down at the East River, watching the ships head upstream until they disappeared under the 59th Street Bridge, which connects Manhattan to Queens, or downriver, past the tip of Manhattan and the Statue of Liberty, leading out to sea.

All at once, I became aware that the roar of the city traffic had been muffled by sweet music drifting out to us from the drawing room. "That's the new Muzak system I had installed. Isn't it great?" Paul said.

Muzak was a novelty then—not yet in every airport, elevator, and public restroom—and very fashionable.

"Come, Teddy," Paul said. "Let's dance." I followed him inside and into his arms and we twirled around the room, ending up on the couch in front of the marble fireplace, which Paul had miraculously lighted. I remember as if it were yesterday that I leaned back and closed my eyes for just a moment and then heard a cork pop and the sound of two glasses being filled. There was Paul, offering me a glass of champagne and saying, "To us, Teddy. I'm happy. Are you?"

I nodded, took the glass and drank not only one, but two and a half glasses of champagne. Then, with the firelight and sweet music filtering through the room, and his arms around me, I fell sound asleep.

I awoke to his kisses on my mouth, my breasts, my whole body. I was completely naked. He had undressed me and was now studying me. "Darling . . . you are beautiful," he said as he inspected me, his fingertips gently caressing my lips. "Even when you're asleep," he added, smiling.

We'd been together before, but this night was extra special. We were engaged, and I was totally in love with this man and wanted so much to please him.

In our first years together, Paul, in his early forties, was as demanding and passionate as I. Strong and well built from years of weight lifting and working out with Nat Pendleton on the beach at Santa Monica, he had developed his body into that of an athlete, and was proud of it. But it was also his mind, his sensitivity, that aroused me. I could never say no to this man.

I tried to protest, but he coaxed me into his bed and we made love the old-fashioned way, making me forget all but the knowledge that we were one.

We slept curled up, spoon fashion. In the morning we had breakfast in his pajamas, he wearing the bottoms and me wearing the top. We ate shredded wheat and milk (all we could find in the kitchen). Then we walked around the entire terrace in the midday sun, showered, and went back to bed.

How I ever got out of that apartment the next day without being seen by the stodgy other residents, I'll never know.

CHAPTER II

NASSAU

Late one afternoon, in November 1935, I was in my apartment at the Algonquin when Jeannie knocked on the door and staggered in carrying two huge Saks Fifth Avenue boxes. "I've been with Paul for the past two hours!" she said, gasping for breath and dropping the boxes on the floor. "He wanted me to bring them to you at once."

I looked at her. "What are they?"

"You'll see," she said. "Open them up."

"Are you kidding me, Jeannie?"

"No. Come on, get some scissors . . . hurry."

Out of those two boxes came one gorgeous mink coat and one long ermine stole. For a moment, I couldn't believe my eyes . . . but there in the tissues was his card, *Teddy . . . to keep you warm. Love, Paul,* written in his boyish handwriting.

"He asked me to meet him to pick out a present for you," Jeannie explained, "so I have been trying on fur coats all afternoon at Bonwit's

and Saks, and these were the prettiest of all. God, am I tired!" With that, she walked into the bedroom and threw herself on the bed.

"Jeannie," I called out, "I can't accept these. It's not right. I'm not a kept woman. Anyway, my mother would die if I did, so take them back."

"Not I," came the tired voice of my good friend. "*You* take them back . . . or get Saks to call for them. I'm exhausted. Anyway, I think you should keep them . . . think of next winter."

"Well, I hate to have to tell him."

"Then don't take them back . . . after all, you're engaged."

"It's still not right. I can borrow his car, accept books, lunches, dinners, flowers, theater tickets, but I can't accept fur coats . . ."

"Still, you go to bed with him, no?"

I looked at her. "That's mean of you."

"But it's the truth."

"Yes, it's the truth, but I can't help it. I love him."

"Okay, Miss Proper Face, order me a stiff drink and I'll return them to Saks."

Before leaving for London, Paul had a grand piano put in the apartment so that Gene and I could practice. On his arrival in London, he immediately called on Madame Marchesi. Afterward he phoned me from the Dorchester and relayed their conversation in an excited voice. After listening to your recordings, Marchesi had said, "I can see your young lady has charm and taste in her selection of songs. She is knowledgeable about what she sings, but her whole voice needs to be smoothed out, so she can move unnoticeably from one register to the next. I cannot predict, however, if she is operatic material. Besides a voice, one needs dedication, perseverance, and character. However, there is that something there in the quality of her top register that I like, and if *I* like it, it's good."

"Then, will you take her as a student?" he asked.

"Yes, send her to me."

And with that, my future was sealed! For a moment, I was silent, not really daring to believe what Paul had just told me. Then I heard him say, "Darling, did you hear me? Aren't you excited that this woman, who is one of the greatest teachers in the world, has accepted you?"

"Oh, yes, Paul, I am! Only, I just can't believe it. Thank you from my heart for doing this."

"Well, I knew I was right about your voice from the first night I heard you. So start planning. You have time. She can't take you until January. I'm off to Switzerland on Sunday for meetings. I miss you, Teddy. Do you miss me?"

"Yes. You know I do."

"Bye, darling."

"Bye, Paul."

The minute I hung up the receiver, my whole being was flooded with doubts. Could I really do it? Could I just drop everything I'd worked so hard to accomplish, go to another country . . . and study to become an opera singer? Suppose I failed . . . What would Paul think of me? *He is so used to success.* Would he still love me? And how long would it take? Maybe years! *But . . . he believes in me! I must try . . . even if I fail. If I don't try, how will I ever know if I can do it?*

My furious conversation with myself was interrupted by a phone call from the manager of the British Colonial Hotel in Nassau. He was begging me to return for a two-week engagement—at twice what they had paid me before. Seems some singer had disappointed them and it was a real emergency. I needed time to think about Marchesi, and I needed the money. So I went.

CHAPTER 12

MATTERS OF LIFE AND DEATH

After returning to New York, I resumed working with Gene Berton. Paul was once again in Europe. I hadn't heard from him by phone for almost a week when he called from the pier of the French Line. "I'm here. Get ahold of Gene and meet me at the apartment at once." There was something mischievous in his voice. In less than an hour, Gene and I excitedly arrived at Sutton Place.

Minutes later, Paul arrived. I flew into his arms. He greeted Gene, walked to the piano, took out a sheaf of notes, and said, "Darling, these describe Marchesi's method. I took ten singing lessons from her, so that I could show you."

I looked at Paul, shocked! I couldn't believe that this very busy man actually had taken time out from his important business meetings to study with Marchesi, but he had.

"Now, Gene, play these chords and I'll show Teddy how this first exercise goes." Then Paul took a big breath and, as Gene struck the first

chord, Paul sang "Aah" in a very deep, rich baritone . . . changing to "Eee" as the scale went up and returning to "Aah" as it descended to its original starting point.

He repeated the exercise several times, then hurried to show all of them to us. "Teddy, Marchesi says these exercises will strengthen your lower and middle registers, so that there will never be a noticeable break between them, nor between the middle and top. She also said, 'Don't ever force your voice.'" He took my hand, and I reached up and kissed him.

What a wonderful thing he'd done. What love . . . but now I really had to make a major decision. Probably the most serious decision of my life . . . not only to do with my career, but also with Paul. Again the questions raced through my mind: How long would the lessons with Marchesi take? Just what would be involved? Was I really ready to plunge into a lifetime study of serious music? Should I give up a career as a popular singer, which was now just opening up for me? Shouldn't I just stay right here in New York and continue to live in a world I already knew . . . the well-worn track between Fifth Avenue and Broadway? And what about my friends and family, whom I so dearly loved? Could I leave them? Could I give all this up to try a new medium of expression? And in a foreign country?

I once again thought of the words on that French handkerchief: *"Qui ne risque rien, n'a rien."* Suddenly I was aroused by Paul's deep, reassuring voice. "Well, Teddy, if you think you understand how to practice Marchesi's method, you and Gene get busy. I'll catch up on some telephoning."

Our eyes met . . . My decision was made. I just knew I couldn't disappoint him. From then on, with Gene at the piano, I began working every day. I realized immediately that these exercises were really helping.

With the holidays approaching, I planned to see Mother, my sisters, and Ware, be with Paul and, after the new year, get ready to leave for London.

Then I found out I was pregnant.

The minute the doctor told me, I realized that I wanted that baby, and I wanted so badly to tell Paul about it. I told Jean and Betzi, but then I didn't tell Paul . . . I couldn't. When I saw him again after I'd been to the doctor, we met at Sutton Place, and sat on the couch before the marble fireplace. We were alone, and it was so good to be together again after my trip to Nassau and his time in Europe. I wished I could stop the clock, freeze time. I was a girl in love, in the arms of a man who said he was madly in love with me, and I wanted to stay that way forever.

We were so happy the way we were . . . We were engaged and planned to get married in a year, but I didn't want this to be the reason. There have always been stories of men forced to marry girls because they are pregnant; I had a sense that these marriages didn't last. I didn't want that to happen to us.

But that wasn't the only reason. According to the rules I was brought up with, I had overstepped what was considered correct behavior. I had given myself to him before marriage. Oh yes, we were engaged, but we had not set a date. Now, finding myself pregnant and not married, I felt how large the gap was between being engaged and being married. "Rules must be followed," I told myself, "or one has to take the consequences."

I also believed that if I told him, I'd destroy our plans. Here was a brilliant, creative, vital man in the midst of building his oil empire. Because he'd been intrigued by my voice, he had encouraged me, had found me the teacher Marchesi, and had arranged for me to go study with her . . . and now here I was pregnant.

———

Two days after he'd arrived, Paul was to leave on the Super Chief for Los Angeles to see his mother. He phoned me early in the morning to say good-bye. That afternoon I asked Jean to go with me to a doctor's office on the west side of Manhattan near Riverside Drive. I went through a procedure to terminate the pregnancy. It was horrible, and I still remember everything about it to this day, including the nurse and the room where it took place. The whole thing was wrong, frightening, and I don't believe I ever got over it. Dr. Schwartz had told me I would feel nothing, which was a lie. Most of all, I remember my great sorrow at what I'd done, but I was young, and I was truly afraid it would wreck our relationship . . . What a fool.

Afterward, I took a taxi back to the hotel and went to bed. But I was awoken by a message from Paul, saying he had decided not to leave and would pick me up at eight o'clock that evening for dinner. I begged Jean to phone him and say I was ill, that I had a bad cold. (Paul hated bad colds. All his life he used to literally run from people who even started to sneeze.) But somehow or other, he told Jean it didn't matter . . . he wanted to see me. I guess that's when she broke down and told him what I'd done. In less than an hour he came charging into my apartment, dragging a doctor with him. He was so worried and frightened for me. "Why did you do this, Teddy? How could you? My God, you might have died! Doctor, is she all right?"

I looked up at him and started to cry. "I just couldn't tell you, Paul. I mean, you would have had to marry me now."

"What are you talking about? I'm going to marry you anyway."

"Yes, but we can't yet. You told me the other day that Ann's lawyers were holding you up, saying your divorce papers would not be final till next year."

"Darling, I'm sure Ann can handle this. She is already in love with Doug Wilson . . . and told me so when we had our meeting at the Plaza. She wants to marry him. Teddy, why didn't you trust me?"

He was on his knees beside my bed, kissing me, right in front of the doctor. Finally, he left the room. The doctor took my temperature and asked a few questions. Going out the door, he turned and said, "You don't need me, young lady. He does."

Later, Paul ordered dinner to be sent up for us, then sat by my bed until I fell asleep. He finally left, but only because Jeannie reassured him that she would stay the night.

During the following week, Paul came to see me every day . . . sent flowers . . . brought books for me to study, to inspire me . . . operas . . . stories of famous singers. It made me smile to think of the many subjects he brought up in his effort to teach me. "No matter how much I try," I said, "I'll never catch up to you, Paul. You speak five languages fluently. You read Greek and Latin (my worst subject in school). You know so much about so many things. You're like the Book of Knowledge, or some shooting star I long to follow . . . But I can't, because, by the time I arrive at where you were a minute ago, you've gone on."

This made him laugh. "Teddy, you speak like a child sometimes. I'm really not so far ahead of you. I'm just older. I've studied all my life, and I find it tragic when I think that no matter how much one studies, one can never know it all. Try as we might, there is just not enough time in any of our lives . . . and there's so much to learn. Still, you and I have lots to talk about: art, music, books, plays . . . And we have each other. That's the most exciting subject of all!"

At the end of the week, Paul left for the coast, and I began working again with Gene on the songs I planned to sing at One Fifth Avenue. I

also went out to Greenwich and stood by my mother when she got her divorce from Dad.

It wasn't long thereafter that Paul called me from California. "Have you heard?" he asked. "Has anyone called you about your dad?"

"What is it, Paul?" I said.

"I heard it over the radio, on the six o'clock news. The police found your dad. He killed himself . . . hung himself at his hotel, right across from the Algonquin. I'm so sorry, Teddy, so sorry for your mother and sisters."

"Oh my God . . ."

"And, darling, you didn't know this, but he had borrowed money from me. Do you think that might have contributed to his doing this?"

"What are you talking about?"

Apparently, Frank had been at the Vineyard on one occasion when Paul and I had visited Mother. After that, he'd phoned Paul, gone to see him at his apartment, and asked him for a loan of a thousand dollars.

I knew nothing about any of it. "Paul, I'm sure what he did had nothing to do with borrowing money from you. He's tried to kill himself several times before—including one time in the barn at Wild Acres. Mother had to climb up a ladder and cut him down. He was half dead, but he survived. That was bad enough. What was worse was that Bobby and Nancy saw everything. Frank must have been terribly unhappy about himself. Once the Depression hit, he wasn't ever really able to make a living. And he just couldn't stop drinking. And when he drank, well . . . Oh, dear. I must call Mother at once."

"Is there anything I can do, Teddy?"

"Thank you, but no, Paul. There's nothing you can do."

CHAPTER 13

MARCHESI, 1938

On Thanksgiving Day 1937, Paul invited Mother, my sisters, and Ware to lunch with us at the Cotillion Room in the Pierre Hotel. We were amazed to find ourselves the only people being served in this magnificent room. Our table was right in front of one of the huge windows overlooking Fifth Avenue. My sisters kept getting up and standing at the window, their faces pressed against the glass, thrilled to be able to watch the Macy's Parade go by at such close range.

During lunch, Paul surprised us by saying he had just bought the hotel, but that wasn't his only announcement. He said that because Ware had done such a great job handling publicity for the Museum of Natural History, he had invited him to become head of public relations for the Pierre. Ware was happy to accept.

The Pierre was—and still is—an elegant hotel that stood forty-two stories high on the corner of Fifth Avenue and 61st Street, overlooking Central Park. Having fallen into bankruptcy with the Depression, its

suites were half empty, there were no patrons in the Cotillion Room, and it had a bar no one could find. Even in its run-down condition, as soon as Paul saw it, he realized its potential. He also realized that it was a bargain. Built in 1930 for $15 million, Paul paid $2.5 million for it.

The changes he made after he took ownership turned the Pierre into one of the smartest hotels in the city, on a par with the Plaza, the Sherry-Netherland, and the Ritz. At Ware's suggestion, a new door was installed on the corner of Fifth and 61st, making the bar accessible from the sidewalk. Soon everyone who was anyone became regulars of the Cafe Pierre. The once-deserted Cotillion Room became the most sought-after spot in the city for dinner dances, coming-out parties, and charity galas. Suddenly, reservations became hard to come by, as Hollywood stars and the cream of society from around the world flocked to the hotel. At last, the Pierre came into its own.

Around Christmastime, Mother gave an engagement party for Paul and me at her home in Greenwich. She was planning to take my sisters out to the coast for the rest of the winter, and wanted to do this for me before she left. I suppose it was kind of old-fashioned, considering we didn't expect to be married for a year, but Mother thought it the right thing to do. All of our closest friends, among them boys I'd dated in my childhood, came to meet Paul, "the mystery man" from California.

Among the guests was Bill Gaston. Originally, he was a friend of Betzi and Fred, then Betzi had introduced him to Jean. Now Jeannie was mad for him. Bill was everything she'd dreamed of in a man. He lived on an island in Maine in the summer, and in an apartment overlooking the East River in the winter, and roamed the world in between. He was handsome, rugged, intelligent, charming, and a rebel, like Jean. We were all happy that she was so in love, even though we weren't too sure

about Bill. A Harvard man from a good family, he'd already been married twice. Both of his exes were actresses. He had a bit of a reputation for playing the field, and I didn't want Jeannie to get hurt.

Bill was an old friend of Paul's, too, and the day of Mother's party, Paul, Bill, and Jeannie drove together to Greenwich. As Jean told me later, the three were talking politics most of the way. All of them were staunch Democrats, and Paul said he wanted to be of use to the Roosevelt Administration. Bill, who was a great friend of James Roosevelt, suggested that Paul might be an excellent ambassador to Iran, but Paul wasn't interested. Somewhere along the Merritt Parkway, Paul changed the subject. "Bill," he said, "do you think I'm doing the right thing, marrying Teddy?"

Bill started to laugh. "Friend, you better make up your mind right now, because we're only ten minutes away from Belle Haven." I was shocked when Jeannie told me this—I never realized how close I was to being dumped. I guess Paul suddenly got cold feet. Luckily it was temporary.

I thought it was great that Mother was taking Nancy and Bobby to California for the winter. After Dad's suicide, a change of scenery and some warm, sunny weather would be good for all of them. As Paul and I were leaving that night, he asked Mother where she and the girls were planning to stay. "Laura Isham, my cousin, has invited us to spend the first two weeks with her," Mother replied. "That will give me time to look for a house to rent. Laura has a very old, rather magnificent house on Bellefontaine Street in Pasadena, built by the famous Greene and Greene architects."

"Well, I have a house at Wilshire and Irving boulevards in Los Angeles," Paul said, "near Hancock Park. It's empty, needs furniture, and I'd

be happy for you and the girls to stay there. Be my guests, of course, if you wish to decorate it. Naturally, just send the bills to my office."

"Thank you, Paul, but I don't think—" Mother began.

"Don't say no, Louise," he cut in, "till you see it. You might like it."

The result of this offer was that Mother did go to see it. She took one look at its grandeur, its twenty-two rooms, its tennis court and gardens, and decided to take a small house in Pasadena instead. She did write Paul a thank-you note. Years later, it was the one used by Billy Wilder as Norma Desmond's house in *Sunset Boulevard*.

As soon as Mother; my sisters; and Pat, our Irish terrier, had left for the coast, I started preparing to go to England. I made arrangements to give up my apartment, put things in storage, and read up on transatlantic crossings. I had saved enough money, I thought, for a month's stay in London. One wintry afternoon in early January, Paul and I met at the Plaza. Instead of going into the hotel for tea, however, we took a carriage ride. Drawn by a very-slow-moving horse, we toured Central Park with its now snow-covered lawns. The swans and ducks had gone, leaving a thin layer of ice on the lakes and ponds. Snow lay lightly on the walkways, marked by footsteps of children, who had been playing with sleds and making the year's first snowballs. I sat close to Paul under a blanket supplied by the liveried driver, whose silk hat sported a bright red rose. His back was a huge, black silhouette against the white background, and he held his head down as he let his ancient horse walk slowly along the familiar route. It was an enchanting, still afternoon in the New York we had come to love.

We huddled closer, hypnotized by the steady clip-clop of the horse's hooves. We were alone together in a city of millions. Paul finally broke the silence. "Teddy, dear, I've been thinking about you and your trip, and

I'm a little worried about you going to England alone. What would you say if I asked Jeannie to go, too? I'd feel much better knowing there was someone with you."

I looked up at him and smiled, thinking what a terrific idea it was. What fun it would be to have Jeannie with me, dashing around London when I wasn't studying! I didn't answer him right away. My first thought was of Jeannie. She was in love with Bill Gaston. How could I ask her to leave?

"Paul," I finally said. "You've done enough already . . . I'll be fine."

"Damn it, Teddy, why are you so independent? Don't you know I planned to pay for your lessons and your apartment? After all, I got you into doing this, and we *are* going to be married."

"But we aren't yet, Paul, so stop planning. Just come over as soon as you can, so we can be together. As for Jeannie, I'm sure she'll say no. She's in love."

On February 4, 1938, with my passport in hand, I stood on the upper deck of the SS *Europa* as she edged her way out of her berth into the frigid, murky Hudson River. It was a midnight sailing. Bells were ringing and the ship was ablaze with lights. Paul, Ware, Betzi, and Fred were all waving and calling good-byes to me from the pier. But no Jeannie. I guessed she was with Bill. I wanted to wave back, but I was holding tightly to my passport with one hand, and trying to hold on to the huge bouquet of red roses that Paul had thrust into my arms as he kissed me good-bye. With the crowd waving to their loved ones, I was pinned against the rail and couldn't move. So I just screamed "Bye!" until my byes became sobs.

As we slowly headed out to sea, I took a big breath and, turning away from the rail, bumped into Jeannie. I couldn't believe my eyes, but there she was, standing right next to me.

———

"Paul arranged it. He wouldn't let me tell you," she yelled over the noise of the crowd.

"What about Bill?"

"I can't think about him right now. I'm too excited about going with you."

"Oh, Jeannie, so am I. I can't believe Paul did this." We both started laughing and hugging each other in a little dance around the deck. After throwing kisses to the twinkling New York skyline slowly receding in our wake, we went to find our cabin.

The *Europa* was a German flagged ship, and one of the fastest in the north Atlantic. Years later, my friend Sandy Gould would tell me that the hairdresser on board in the ladies' salon was a famous Nazi spy. Sandy's father, a federal undercover agent, was the one who had broken the code and caught her. Had I known it at the time, I would have died of shock, since she was the one who did my hair on gala night.

On our arrival in London, we checked in at the Grosvenor House Hotel. I phoned Paul to say I had arrived and planned to call on Marchesi the very next day. On February 10, 1938, I stood before the door of her house at 75 Lancaster Gate. As I rang the bell, I wondered if she would really accept me. The door opened almost immediately, as if someone had been waiting inside. Indeed, someone was. There stood a small Italian woman with long black hair, dark brown eyes, and an ample figure. On seeing me, she cried out excitedly, *"Madame, l'americana è qui."* I knew then she must be Zenia, Marchesi's maid. Carrying my *Tosca* and *Carmen* scores under my arm, I followed her into the foyer. Beyond, I heard the rich, mature voice of Marchesi, coming from what I presumed was her salon.

"Come in . . . come in, my child, and welcome."

Standing in the center of a well-furnished room, aided by a cane, was an elegant lady who reminded me of Queen Victoria. Marchesi was dressed in a black gown with a full bodice of lace, covered with many medallions and other awards, over which she wore a bright green shawl. Around her neck was a velvet choker, and I noticed she wore many rings and a brooch. Her abundant light-gray hair was piled high on her head in the classic Victorian style. She had great elegance about her, and an aristocratic air. Her portrait, a charcoal by John Singer Sargent, hung on the wall over the fireplace behind her. I was fascinated.

She was elderly, yet there was a sparkle of youth in her eyes as she smiled and said, "So you, my child, want to sing opera. Well, we shall see. Take off your hat and let me look at you. Yes, Paul was right. You are very beautiful. He is so in love with you." I smiled shyly, thinking how Paul must have talked about me to her. "Let us see whether you also have what he said you had—those beautiful golden notes."

I watched as she slowly moved toward the piano, upon which stood silver-framed, signed photos of Liszt, Brahms, and many crowned heads of Europe. I moved to give her my hand.

"Don't touch me!" she almost screamed. "I can manage. Now, turn around, please."

Before doing as she asked, I saw that she walked in great pain. Whether from illness or extreme weight, I didn't know.

"I hate ugly things," she said. "Old age is an ugly illness. Now come, let us sing."

I handed her my two scores. "Place them over there, my child. We might get to them in two years." Feeling deflated, I put them down on a table, almost upsetting an autographed picture of Puccini.

"Now, come over to the piano," she said, striking the first note. Her

elegantly shaped hands, classic in contour and quite young looking, captured my attention.

"Now, take a breath and let's use the diaphragm."

As I was about to start, a chill of excitement ran through me. I realized I was actually standing in the same position at the same piano where Nellie Melba and other famous opera singers had stood when they studied with Marchesi's mother. Paul said that when he was taking his ten lessons with her, she had told him how, as a child, she had hidden under this very piano to listen, while the great Brahms played his music for her mother. I felt so humble.

Then she said, "Take a big breath and control it, my child. Now, let me hear you say 'Ah.'" She urged me on, a smile of interest on her face. When I reached the last note, I stopped and looked at her. She studied me for a moment, and then said, "I shall be honored to have you as a pupil."

"Oh, thank you, Madame, but do you really think I have the voice to sing opera?"

"Yes, I do," she said. "You have a lovely dramatic quality, and you will make a magnificent operatic coloratura contralto."

When the session ended I stood on her doorstep, stunned and disappointed. *Coloratura contralto.* My voice, according to her, was much lower than Paul thought it would be. "You are a dramatic soprano," he had always said, as had Gene Burton. I walked home feeling sad. If she was right, I would never be able to sing *Tosca.*

Brokenhearted, I called Paul in New York and relayed what Marchesi had said. "Study with her, Teddy, darling. Stick it out for the moment. I still think she has your voice misplaced, but maybe we are both wrong and you really are a contralto. After all, she is the great Marchesi."

Less than a week after arriving, I found a charming, furnished flat just right for Jeannie and me in the nicest part of Mayfair. It was on the top floor of Chesterfield House on South Audley Street. I quickly settled into a routine. Every morning, I walked across Hyde Park to Lancaster Gate. From ten to noon, I sang with Marchesi. Then, after lunch, I studied with Miss Squires, who came to the apartment and sat at my little rented piano. We worked all afternoon on the roles and arias—I had so much to learn: the languages, the music, and the repertoire. When I thought of all my friends having fun going to parties, dating, traveling, marrying, and having babies, I was tempted to give up and go home. But I stayed and studied and hoped and prayed that I was doing the right thing.

Shortly thereafter, I wrote to my mother to tell her what great progress I was making, and to let her know that Paul was due in London in a matter of weeks. In the meantime, I was studying every day to be ready to sing for him. I expected to have several roles under my belt so I could audition for a small part at Glyndebourne or Salzburg before going back to the States. That was my dream.

As soon as Paul arrived, we knew that, despite months of separation, we were still very much in love, even if the path of love did not always run smooth. One evening, after attending the opera, Paul invited Lady Glamis and her daughter, Nancy, and some others to supper with us at the Ritz. The music began while we were being seated, and Paul turned to Nancy and asked her to dance. I was shocked, and more than a little insulted. I thought he should have asked me, his fiancée, first. I was furious.

I hardly spoke to him during the rest of the evening, but in the taxi going back to my apartment, where he was to drop me off, I cried, "This

is it! The end." And with that, I took off my engagement ring and threw it at him. He looked down at the floor of the cab, where it lay sparkling.

Slowly, he picked it up, examined it, and then, holding the ring in his hand and putting his arm around me, said, "Teddy, dear, I love you very much. But you must understand that in England, according to protocol, one always asks one's guests to dance first, especially when they are of the royal family."

"Well, American families are pretty royal, too. And when we go to a dance, the boy asks the girl he brought to dance first. So, when you're with me in England or anywhere, I expect you to ask me to dance first." He didn't answer, just smiled. I was still pouting. "And anyway," I continued, "I don't think an engaged man should act that way."

Paul started to laugh. Suddenly, I realized how ridiculous I was, and I laughed, too. He stopped me with a kiss.

The taxi driver, who looked like he had just stepped out of Madame Tussauds wax museum, turned and said, "Can I be of any help to you, Govn'r?"

By this time, we were in each other's arms, and he could see Paul was doing quite well all by himself.

CHAPTER 14

WAR CLOUDS

Soon after this, Paul received a wire calling him to the continent on business. He left for Paris, then went on to Zurich, Rome, and Berlin, arriving back in London in time for the auction of the Mortimer Schiff collection, which Christie's had placed on sale in June.

Mitchell Samuels, a well-known art dealer and an associate of French & Company of New York, was in London, and it was he who helped Paul choose some fine pieces, mostly eighteenth-century French furniture, an exquisite Savonnerie carpet, silverware by Paul de Lamerie, and a desk by Molitor, created for Louis XV. Mitch was not only knowledgeable, but he became a trusted friend and adviser. In time, Paul was as well informed as he.

In July of 1938, Paul took me with him to the Colnaghi gallery, where he bought the portrait of James Christie, founder of Christie's, painted in 1778 by Thomas Gainsborough, in which Christie is seen holding a painting by Gainsborough, apparently auctioning it off. I found this fas-

cinating, and wondered why the Christie family had allowed it to be sold.

At the July 20 auction at Sotheby's, Paul bought Raphael's *Madonna of Loreto* for $200 and a portrait of Louis XIV by Rigaud for $725 from the collection of HRH Princess Beatrix de Bourbon-Massimo. Paul was one of the few people who believed the *Madonna* was a true Raphael, and after many years, the painting was declared to be an authentic work of the Master. This pleased Paul beyond words, not only that the value had soared, but that he had known from the beginning it was a true Raphael.

While Paul was in London, I went for my singing lesson each morning. Then we'd meet for lunch and spend afternoons at the Tate, the Wallace Collection, or at the Victoria and Albert Museum. I learned a great deal and was enchanted by the provenance of each work of art Paul bought or showed me. Each piece told a fascinating story of people who had lived, enjoyed, and used these objects in another time. *Which king had sat at this magnificent desk? Whose mistress had used this charming little side table of rosewood with the inlaid Sevres plaque?* They all joined in my mind with the operatic stories I was learning from Marchesi, so I couldn't help but romanticize them. Paul was enveloping me in a world of great music, paintings, furniture, architecture, and literature—all created by the great masters of their day—and I loved it!

One thing that surprised Paul that summer was the notable absence of buyers. Most who attended the auctions were Americans; others just came to look. People seemed preoccupied by events that were slowly developing in far-off places. War clouds were gathering across Europe, but that didn't stop Londoners from going to the theater or to the opera at Covent Garden. The nightclubs were jammed.

I wasn't focused on the pending war. I was in London to study. But I did listen to Paul and his friends when they spoke of what they felt was

inevitable, unless Hitler could be stopped. Germany had already occupied Austria in March, but none of them thought it would end there. Hitler seemed to be eyeing the Sudetenland in Czechoslovakia, but what country could stop him? Other than Germany, no one else had prepared for war. For the moment, the world just waited.

On July 24, I was awakened early in the morning by a phone call from New York. It was Gene Berton. He was so excited I could hardly understand what he was saying. Finally, I realized he was about to board the *Europa*, and wanted me to know that Paul had invited him to come to London and take some lessons from Marchesi, so he and I could work together later back home. What a surprise! Paul had not mentioned this to me. I thought it was pretty wonderful of him, and told him so.

Gene arrived, had his first lesson on Friday, July 30, then Paul joined us and listened approvingly to my progress. Gene stayed in London for two weeks, took twelve lessons, and left for the States on the *Europa*. I was grateful to Marchesi for working with him, grateful to Paul for the trip, and frightened to death by the realization that Gene, being Jewish, was on a Nazi ship. Fortunately, he arrived safely in the United States.

On August 20, Paul left again for more business meetings on the continent. He hoped to make an oil deal with the Arabs. It had been years since he'd decided it was important for his company to gain a foothold in the Middle East, where he was convinced great reserves of oil could be found. Someone had persuaded him not to pursue it, and he'd lost a great opportunity. *Now* he was determined to try.

The BBC radio and the newspapers were filled with news of Hitler threatening the world. London seemed to be preparing its citizens for a siege—we experienced our first "brown out." Each day, radio alerts warned that all civilians who could, should leave the city. Children were

separated from working parents and hustled off to families in the North.

Gas masks were issued—everyone in London was supposed to have one. Madame Marchesi refused. When the civil defense workers arrived at her studio, she turned them away. "I didn't wear one in the First World War," she declared, "and I refuse to wear one now." Most of Marchesi's students had left, but I still went to her every day.

I was walking home through Hyde Park. It was later than usual because Marchesi had asked me to stay for an early supper, and Zenia's spaghetti alla bolognese was too much of a temptation to refuse. As a result, I was only halfway home when it grew dark. I became a little frightened and started to run. I ran right into a tall man in a dark suit who seemed to have come out of nowhere. He was wearing a homburg and carrying a briefcase, which flew out of his hand, as did all of my music. He excused himself, speaking English with a definite German accent. I became terrified; my heart almost stopped beating. *What is this German doing in Hyde Park?* I thought. *And in such a hurry?* He looked me over, then quickly leaned down and started picking up my music.

"Young lady is a singer?" he said with a smile, as he handed me my scores.

"Yes," I replied as calmly as I could. "I'm an American."

"So . . . and I am Austrian. My name is Rudolf Lothar, and I am afraid I am lost in Hyde Park."

Thanking God he wasn't a Nazi, I asked him where he wished to go. "Lancaster Gate," was his response.

"I've just come from there," I replied. "Take the path to your right. You can't miss it. What number are you looking for?"

"Seventy-five," he said.

"Why, that's Marchesi!" I almost screamed.

"Yes! Her son is my best friend," he said, smiling.

"Well, Madame is my teacher."

"You are then a fortunate young lady, and good luck," he added, then picking up his briefcase he turned. "I must hurry . . . Good-bye, Miss America."

"Take care," I called out to him, and he was gone.

Marchesi told me at my next lesson that he had called on her with news of her son, Baron von Poppa. Lothar was the librettist of the opera *The Queen of Cyprus*, which he'd written with the composer Eugene d'Albert. She reminded me that she had already given me the exciting aria "Medieval Hymn to Venus" from that opera. How strange, our meeting in the park . . . I never saw him again, nor did she.

I reached my apartment just as Jeannie arrived back from visiting friends in Scotland, and was I happy to see her! We spent the rest of the night talking about the war . . . Was it really coming? Was it safe to stay in London? Suddenly she asked, "Where's Paul?"

"I don't know," I said. "He told me he'd call back in a few days. He was on his way to Switzerland, then Germany."

"How long has that been?"

"Almost a week."

"Teddy, you're mad. He probably can't get through to you. We'd better get out of here."

"No, Jeannie, if Paul said he'd call, he will."

And that night, he did. Over a poor connection, he shouted, "Teddy, get out of London! At once! I've a seat for you on the KLM flight leaving for Amsterdam at ten tomorrow morning. Get to that plane and get on it! I'll meet you there."

"But, Paul, there are no taxis."

"Then walk to the airport!" he ordered. "And get on that plane!"

"I can't leave Jeannie. She just returned from Scotland."

"Well, bring her with you. I'll get her a seat. Just come." He sounded frantic.

Luckily, the next morning we found a taxi, boarded the plane, and in a matter of hours were flying over the countryside of Holland with its canals, dykes, and fields of flowers. So many tulips . . . so much beauty . . . so peaceful . . . so helpless. It was hard to imagine, if war really came, how much terror and devastation this little country would suffer. Our plane arrived on time and I was in Paul's arms, safe again.

While driving to the Amstel Hotel in the center of Amsterdam, Paul told us what happened to him. He had been staying at the Hotel Adlon in Berlin, and had heard Hitler's saber-rattling speech at the Sportpalast. Right after that, friends warned him to leave Germany. He quickly packed his bags, paid his bill, filled the gas tank of his car, and headed for Holland.

Just before he crossed the border, several German plainclothesmen leapt onto his car, showed their badges, and ordered him to the police station at the frontier town of Bentheim. Paul was held there for hours. He was searched, as was his car and his luggage. Then he was released with an apology. "Times are unusual," the police explained. They sent him on his way over a mined bridge into Holland.

That evening we dined at the home of a charming Dutch couple, friends of Paul's. The entire conversation was, of course, war and the fear of it. Later that very evening, October 1, the news came over the radio that Hitler had marched unopposed into Czechoslovakia. No one knew where he would go next . . . nor could anyone stop him.

The underlying hysteria was incredible. One could feel it every-

where, yet the proud people of Holland were seemingly unafraid. The next morning, to keep Jean and me from being frightened, Paul took us to the Rijksmuseum, where we spent thirty minutes in front of Rembrandt's magnificent *Night Watch*. It was cold and windy when we walked together later in Rembrandt Square. The only movie house open was showing a German film, but we wouldn't see it. At dawn, we drove twenty miles to picturesque Volendam and Veendam, where Hollanders, dressed in quaint costumes, posed for pictures in front of their thatched homes. Paul presented each of us with a pair of wooden shoes.

Our last night at the Amstel Hotel, we dined with a crowd of happy and carefree young couples and danced to the music of a very American-sounding orchestra. After visiting Rembrandt's studio, we drove out of the city among hundreds of bicyclists on their way home from work. We headed for The Hague, then Antwerp, and finally Paris. By ten that night we were safely in a suite at the Hotel Lotti.

Paul took me to the Bal Tabarin, but Jeannie spent the evening on the phone, trying to get passage on the next ship leaving for New York. She'd figured out that it was Bill Gaston, not war, that she longed for.

That night is one I will remember forever. The Bal Tabarin was jammed with people who acted as though it might be their last night on earth. Fear seemed to sweep across the dance floor, but I felt safe when Paul took me in his arms and held me close. We didn't speak, just danced, and then he took me back to the hotel. Jeannie was gone, having left a note on my night table. She was on her way by train to Le Havre; the *Queen Mary* was sailing at dawn.

Paul and I ordered breakfast sent up, and I climbed into his bed. We were in the middle of a world gone mad with the threat of war. No one really knew what was going to happen, or when it would happen, but

everyone was certain that war was inevitable . . . and Paris was wild with rumors and predictions.

Three days later, Paul decided it was safe to return to England. I knew Paul was leaving soon for New York, but I couldn't go with him, much as I wanted to. I couldn't—I'd only been studying for eight months. I simply had to stay and finish that year with Marchesi. I felt honor bound. After all, I had been given a great opportunity by Paul, and I loved what I was doing. I wanted to be the best that I could be, not only for myself, but also for him.

I think Paul realized I was truly serious. I think he admired that quality in me, my determination to reach my goal. He himself set a great example, working sixteen or more hours a day, many times canceling dinners, dates, parties. Instead, he'd go back to his apartment or hotel room and work on a project through the night, or until his desk was cleared. I knew he hated failures, and I didn't want to be one.

He also hated tardiness, and transportation fascinated him. He noted exact times of arrivals and departures, and what trips were like. He couldn't understand why trains, ships, and planes issued exact schedules, and then were invariably late. He sailed on the *Normandie* in mid-October, but called me every day during the crossing. After he left, I think he missed me *almost* as much as I missed him.

CHAPTER 15

PAUL'S MOTHER

I kept working with Marchesi until I left for the holidays. I arrived in New York on December 22, 1938. Paul met me, and we drove immediately up to the Vineyard to be with my mother and my darling sisters for Christmas. Paul went on to the coast to be with his mother for New Year's, and to see his sons. I stayed with my mother and sisters for three wonderful weeks, and then joined Paul in Los Angeles. It was time for me to meet his mother.

Mrs. George Franklin Getty was in her late eighties when we first met. She was a woman of medium height and a strong personality. She was gentle, yet firm of manner, and she greeted me with the natural appraisal of a woman concerned with her son's happiness. She too had been married to a man obsessed with business, and I could see that she was hopeful that Paul had finally made a permanent attachment to someone he not only loved, but someone who loved him enough to put up with his way of life.

I believe it helped quiet her fears knowing we were only engaged and not yet married, and that I was seriously pursuing my own career in music. She smiled when I told her this, and when she smiled, her whole face lit up and her eyes twinkled—just like Paul's.

Several afternoons, we had tea alone together in her upstairs living room, and it was over tea that Mrs. Getty startled me by asking, "Has Paul mentioned your signing a prenuptial agreement before you marry?"

"No, he hasn't," I replied. "Why?"

"Because his lawyers have made it clear that it is necessary this time. You must realize you will be his fifth wife. In case you divorce, you will already know what to expect in the way of support."

"Oh, but Mrs. Getty, I've supported myself ever since I left home, and Paul has already given me all that I need—his belief in my accomplishing the goal I had already set for myself, long before we met."

"Then you will sign? I think it is important for you both."

"Then I will."

"Good," she replied, looking greatly relieved.

Mrs. Getty lived at the corner of Wilshire Boulevard and South Kingsley Drive in the same lovely English Tudor that she, her husband, and Paul had called home for many years. At our last meeting, she asked me to drive with her to the Getty beach house in Santa Monica, and then up the coast. We passed the Miramar Hotel, overlooking Santa Monica Bay, and drove down the ramp to the sea, with palisades on one side and the wide expanse of the blue Pacific before us. At the base of the ramp, a row of fine-looking houses hugged the curve of the shoreline all the way to Malibu. The whole scene was so beautiful I could only hope that one day I'd return.

Driving along, we spoke to each other as two persons who loved the

same man. I wanted her to know how much I cared for Paul, how much he meant to me. "Please, don't take my son from me," she pleaded.

I reached over and took her hand in mine. "I couldn't take your son from you, Mrs. Getty. What I want for both of us is to be here with you," and I leaned over and kissed her cheek.

We returned to her home, and as I left, she pressed an envelope in my hand. I slowly walked down the stairs and said good-bye to Paul's cousin, Ruth Richardson, who lived in the house with Mrs. Getty as her companion.

Once on the sidewalk, I opened the envelope. A check for $25 was enclosed, with a note. It read:

My dear Teddy:

This is just a small token of my affection and good wishes for you. Buy some little thing for yourself in New York. I am wishing only the best for you always.

My love,

Sarah Getty

Paul was waiting for me across the street in his fabulous green classic Duesenberg, with its mahogany and silver dashboard. We took Sunset Boulevard all the way to the beach. Then, just as the sun disappeared below the horizon, we turned south. As we passed his beach house, he pointed out the elegant homes of Marion Davies, the Jesse Laskys, the Sam Goldwyns, the Louis B. Mayers, and the Darryl Zanucks. This was the Gold Coast, as it was known in those days. Only a few of those grand estates remain today.

Suddenly, the lights on the Santa Monica Pier loomed up out of the

approaching darkness and, drawing nearer, we could hear the sounds of the organ coming from the merry-go-round grinding out the strains of "The Skater's Waltz." A mile farther on we turned seaward and ended up at Jack's at the Beach, a famous eating place.

After ordering dinner, Paul turned to me. "Teddy," he said, "there's something important I must discuss with you." His voice sounded so serious that for a moment I felt like a child who had misbehaved, and inwardly I panicked.

"What is it?" I asked defensively, wondering what I'd done. This made him laugh out loud and he leaned down and kissed me.

"Don't worry, darling," he said, putting his arms around me. "It's just that I want some very important people in the music world to hear your voice, and I've arranged for you to sing for them at the Temple on Wilshire Boulevard. It's the largest hall I could find. If you can fill that auditorium, you can fill any opera house in the world."

"When will I sing?" I asked.

"Tomorrow at ten in the morning."

At ten the next morning I stood dead center on a very large stage, looking out over miles of empty seats, and then at the faces looking up at me. In the center of the auditorium sat several formidable critics— Valentin Pavlovsky, accompanist for the great cellist Gregor Piatigorsky; Dr. Edouard Lippe, Nelson Eddy's voice coach, who had once told Paul he would be delighted to train me before I chose London; four members of the editorial staff of the leading music journal *Musical America*; several important men from the music department of MGM; and California's greatest impresario, Lynden E. Behymer.

I took a breath, nodded to my accompanist, tried to remember everything Marchesi had taught me, and smiled once at Paul. Then I began to

sing "Non piu di fiori," a beautiful aria from Mozart's *La clemenza di Tito*. When I finished, I knew I had done my best and I walked off the stage.

There was a long moment of silence—too long, I thought—and then my critics burst into enthusiastic applause. Paul, businessman that he was, addressed the group. "Gentlemen," he asked, "do you agree with me that she is concert and operatic material?"

The "yea's" were unanimous and wholehearted. Then Paul asked, "Do you agree with me that she should return to Marchesi and prepare her repertoire?"

"Indeed! Indeed!" was the response.

Well, that definitely did it. Paul was jubilant as he put me in his car. I was excited, too, excited that I had done well, and that I hadn't disappointed him. Thank God for Marchesi . . . and thank you, God.

Paul leaned over, kissed me, and said, "Teddy, dear, you were terrific, and I'm so proud of you."

"You are?" I turned and looked at him. His eyes said it.

"You know I am . . . and that was a truly difficult piece. They loved you . . . and so do I. Are you hungry?" he asked as he put the car in gear.

"Always," I replied and we both laughed.

"Then let's go to the Brown Derby and have breakfast."

Seated in a secluded booth, Paul hurriedly ordered, then started to tell me more. MGM wanted to test me right away. Dr. Lippe had said, "Tell her to prepare her roles."

"Mr. Behymer assured me that when you are ready, he will arrange your concert," Paul continued. "Darling, when you drill for oil, you may know that it is there . . . *but* the big question is . . . how much is there? You don't know till you drill and see it pouring up out of the earth—a tremendous gusher. Well, I've always known, since the first night we met,

that your voice was beautiful. It had a certain warm, luscious quality. And you sang with such feeling that I felt you would make a fantastic Carmen or Tosca. Still, I never was sure it was strong enough to fill an opera house. But when you sang this morning in that immense auditorium, sang with such power and authority, I knew I was right . . . you could do it. As Pavlovsky said, you were a tour de force. So, you see, you are on your way!"

"Do you really think so?" I asked.

"Yes, I do," he answered.

"Well, then, I must go back to London right away. There's so much more I have to learn, and so little time."

"But *not* yet," he said vehemently. "You still have to see the California desert. Palm Springs is so beautiful at this time of year, and I want to take you there. So don't leave, darling, please!" His voice was so persuasive I almost laughed, but I really wanted to cry, because I too wanted to stay with Paul and have fun. After all, I'd been in California for such a short time. We drove to Palm Springs in his divine Duesenberg, top down under a full moon, with the most wonderful, soft desert wind blowing my hair all around.

We arrived at the Desert Inn just before midnight. Leaving our luggage in the suite reserved for us, we walked through the gardens, so fragrant with desert flowers, and I marveled at the spectacular palms standing like sentinels along the paths. Returning to our suite, we found a table filled with chicken sandwiches. A bottle of champagne had been placed right beside the couch in front of the fireplace, which Paul immediately lighted. It was a night I shall never forget. We ate, made love, then fell asleep after making plans to be married at Herstmonceux Castle in England when Paul came over in the spring. We went swimming, lay in

the sun, had breakfast in town, then drove to Idyllwild up in the mountains. It had snowed there the day before, and it looked just like a picture postcard of Maine, with its log cabins and pine trees. For the next few days and nights, except for Paul's business calls, we cut ourselves off from the world.

Then Paul drove me to the railroad station in Pasadena, where the Santa Fe Super Chief was waiting to take me on my first leg of the long trip back to England. I had a stateroom, with bags and music piled high. Paul kissed me twice, stood in the doorway looking at me, then came back and kissed me again. "I love you," he whispered. "Don't forget that, and be a good girl." He smiled and was gone.

As the train pulled out of the station, I had a premonition of danger. I felt, even though we had made plans, that I might never see him or my homeland again. I had a sudden desire to stay, a struggle between the woman in me and the singer. Paul and I were always meeting and leaving each other. It seemed endless, yet there was this drive in me that I knew Paul admired. He, himself, gave up everything and everyone for what he felt he had to accomplish. That came first, even before love. It wasn't his fault. Hard as it seemed for me to leave him, I had to do what I set out to do. But I did it for love!

Traveling from California to England was not a plane ride in those days. The Super Chief took me as far as Chicago, where I changed trains and boarded the 20th Century Limited to New York. In New York, I embarked on Paul's favorite ship, the SS *Normandie*, bound for Southampton. Certainly travel had a glamour, an excitement not felt today. There was always the thrill of boarding, the quick search of the passenger list for friends, the invitation on the first night out to join the captain's table for dinner, the movies, morning walks on the deck, the dancing, the

parties, and the hours to catch up on one's reading. But traveling alone, leaving the one you love, even though it would be for only a few months, seemed to take forever.

As soon as I arrived in London, I phoned Paul to say "I miss you," and that I'd taken a flat at Eresby House in Rutland Gate. I also wanted to catch him up on my social life. "I was invited to dine at the home of Baron Frédéric d'Erlanger, an old friend of Marchesi who lives in a magnificent house directly across the park from where I now live. He is a very elegant, older gentleman, also the composer of the ballet *Les Cent Baisers*. His brother, Baron Emile d'Erlanger, and his nephew, Baron Leo, were invited, too, so I was the only girl at the dinner table. It was a first for me, having a liveried manservant stand behind each chair while we dined. Then off we went to Covent Garden to hear Lotte Lehmann in the role of the Marschallin in *Der Rosenkavalier*. She was sensational. Afterward we had supper at Quaglino's—remember, you took me there last year? After dancing one dance with Leo, they drove me home promptly at midnight, in Baron Frédéric's Rolls."

"Stop, Teddy dear," Paul said, laughing. "You should have written all this to me. It's extremely interesting, but, darling, just think of your telephone bill. Remember, Eresby House charges are added on top of the outside long distance charges."

"Well, Paul," I said, realizing he was right, but terribly excited, "I just wanted you to know who I was going out with."

"I'm glad to know, darling, and I'll never be jealous as long as you date men in their eighties. In the meantime, go to bed, young lady. Tomorrow, *I'll* call *you*! Bye."

For the next month, I earnestly obeyed Marchesi and studied the roles she had given me. I sang the part of Cherubino from *Le nozze di*

Figaro, remembering that Marchesi was adamant that Cherubino's aria "Voi che sapete" must be sung as Mozart had written it. She reminded me that in Rossini's époque, singers started slurring from one phrase to the next. "It is bad taste to do this with eighteenth-century songs," she declared, then added, "When you are singing a beautiful high note, never push. Enjoy it. When singing Charlotte's aria 'Va! Laisse couler mes larmes' from Massenet's *Werther,* the singer must never be so emotional as to bring herself to tears. It is for *your public* to cry."

Much as I loved studying with Madame Marchesi, and much as I had learned from her and grown as a singer, for me there was still the problem of where she had placed my voice. She was sure I was a mezzo-soprano, not a soprano, which meant that the roles I most wanted to sing would always be out of reach.

CHAPTER 16

MADAME CAHIER

After attending the Mozart Festival at Glyndebourne, the phone rang. It was Paul. "I want you to join me in Rome, to meet Madame Sarah Cahier. She is a famous contralto and now teaches. Marian Anderson recommends her. I want Cahier to hear you sing, and give us her opinion as to the correct placement of your voice. Oh, and be sure to let me know the train, the date, and the hour of your departure from London. I'll meet you. Bye, sweetheart."

Within a fortnight, I left London with a promise to see Madame Marchesi when I returned. I notified Paul of the date and hour of my departure, the number of the train and of my compartment, and took off on the Simplon Express for Rome.

As the train roared into the station at Milan and came to a screaming stop, I looked out the window at the crowd on the platform and looked into the faces of those boarding the train, and those waiting to wave farewell. Faces! Some happy, some sad—all of them faces of strangers to me.

Suddenly I felt so alone—and just as suddenly, I looked into the face of a man I knew. The man I loved. Paul!

Seconds later, he rushed into my compartment and in minutes (or so it seemed), the porter banged on the door and shouted, "Roma!"

Madame Cahier lived in an apartment on the second floor of a palazzo owned by Prince Massimo on the Corso Vittorio Emanuele. A gracious, rather small and slender lady in her late sixties, with graying, reddish-brown hair, she met us at the head of the marble steps.

"Paul Getty, what a pleasure," she said, as he took her outstretched hand. Looking at me, she smiled and said, "So you are Teddy . . . come in."

We followed her into the immense drawing room, and within minutes were seated and served tall tumblers of cool lemonade by a young Italian girl no older than fourteen, dressed in white, who noiselessly made her way in and out of the large room, her bare feet almost dancing across the marble floor. She made me wish I were barefoot. I then presented Madame Cahier with a gift, a kit she had asked me to bring her from Harrods in London, which was supposed to stop a person from smoking cigarettes.

It wasn't long before we learned Cahier was an American, born Sarah Walker in Nashville, Tennessee. Having married Charles Cahier, a Swede, I immediately nicknamed her Madame Notebook, the English translation of the French word *cahier*. She had studied with the great tenor Jean de Reszke in Berlin, and had sung leading roles in Dresden, Munich, Paris, Berlin, and Copenhagen, as well as at the Metropolitan Opera in New York. She told us she would be in Rome only for a few more months, as her desire to return to America was overwhelming, now that war seemed imminent.

"But, my dear Teddy, let me hear you sing now. You have come a

long way for my opinion, and we are wasting precious time speaking of a war you and I can do so little about. Our business is to bring beautiful music to the world . . . so let us do a few exercises first to warm up the voice. We'll be ready for a song or aria when my accompanist Hans arrives."

Hans Hasl, a delightful and very handsome young Viennese who played the piano beautifully, arrived a few minutes later. I sang an early Italian song, then the aria "Bel raggio lusinghier" from Rossini's opera *Semiramide*, which had originally been written for the contralto voice.

Paul and Madame Cahier sat at the far end of the room, facing the piano. When I finished singing, Cahier rushed over to me, took my hands in hers, and said, "*Brava*, Teddy, that was beautifully done. I'm astonished that you have the ability to sing the fioritura passages with such agility. This is a wonderful tribute to Marchesi. She has given you a fine foundation. Your voice is 'even' from the lowest notes to the top, but I cannot understand why she has classified you as a mezzo-soprano. Although your lower notes are rich and warm, I find your top register thrilling. Perhaps at this point in your development she did not want you to force the top, but I definitely think you are a soprano."

In seconds Paul moved to the piano. "That's just what I've always said about Teddy's voice. A mezzo-soprano doesn't have the thrilling high notes that she has, and that's why I have always been convinced she is a soprano in the making."

Cahier smiled a knowing smile. "Paul, you obviously sense a voice as well as you sense oil! If you both agree, I will work with Teddy until I leave for America, agreed?"

"Agreed!" we answered.

She then showed us through her apartment and said, "In the mean-

time, unless you prefer to stay in a hotel, Teddy, you may stay here with me in the other wing. Would you like to see it?"

My private quarters were exquisite. The bedroom was two stories high. My bed was an enormous, ornate piece of furniture covered in luscious white velvet, and the headboard, gilded pipes of what was once part of a church organ with two gilded cherubs holding white velvet drapes from ceiling to floor, which, of course, was of white marble. The bathroom, fit for a princess, boasted an enormous tub. Over it, at one end, knelt a lovely nude Venus statue, holding an alabaster jar from which poured the water. At the end of the hall, French doors opened onto a very private terrace with a little fountain, a round table, several chairs, an umbrella, and an inviting chaise longue. It was soon to become my perfect, quiet, open-air study hall. Below was the Piazza Navona, where ancient Romans had once held their chariot races.

An ancient fountain with a deep well stood in the center of the courtyard and doubled as our refrigerator, where two young little Italian girls, Silvia and Maria, kept our milk and butter cooling there from the heat. They lived below, with the *portiera*—the gatekeeper, or concierge. I was fortunate that the girls were very talkative when serving me breakfast each morning. Since they didn't speak English, their conversations helped my Italian tremendously. I found it absolutely fascinating to have to ring a bell for the *portiera* to let me onto the grounds of the Palazzo Massimo after a certain hour. She'd have to open a little door within a door, right in the middle of the huge bronze main door facing the street. It was kept open all day, but meticulously closed and bolted after nightfall. It gave me the strangest feeling of living in the Middle Ages.

Paul took a suite at the Hotel Excelsior on the Via Veneto. We spent each day together, after my lessons with Cahier. We walked through

Rome, rode through it, danced through it, wined and dined in it. We shopped, visited the Vatican, stood in awe before the *Apollo Belvedere*, and strained our necks in the Sistine Chapel under Michelangelo's magnificent ceiling. We drove a little rented car down the Appian Way, stopping for fettuccine and wine at the tiny restaurant opposite the entrance to the catacombs. We then followed a flickering candle in the hand of our priestly guide, and made our way through the musty tunnels, where the early Christians hid. Whenever we came upon the skeleton of some martyr, I'd reach for Paul's hand.

To me, one of Paul's most attractive qualities was his delight and ability to surprise people. One day, as I walked into his suite at the Excelsior, he calmly announced, "We are about to be carved in marble by Pier Gabriele Vangelli, a great sculptor whom I have just met."

"When?" I asked.

"Right now," he replied.

"Where?"

"In here," he said. "In the bedroom. It has the best light."

We walked into the bedroom to find it had been already transformed into a sculptor's studio. Sunlight from the open window shone on a huge chunk of gray clay resting on a movable tripod. The floor was covered with a tarp, and a vigorous man, undoubtedly Vangelli, dashed back and forth, muttering to himself as he watered down the clay and began molding it with his artistic hands.

"Darling, may I present Signor Vangelli," Paul said.

With that, Vangelli excitedly took my hand in his wet one and kissed it. "Mademoiselle Teddy, I will capture your rare beauty for eternity." Then in his broken English he said, "Donta move," and slowly he walked around me as if to memorize every detail of my bone structure. Turning

to Paul, he pointed to my face and with passion cried, "*Il naso è perfetto.* You are a fine patrician beauty, I will capture it."

This made me laugh, but I managed to say *"Grazie,* signore." After two weeks of us posing, he finished the first models of us in clay, the likenesses remarkable. Next he made plaster casts of our heads. Finally, we chose the Carrara marble out of which Vangelli would chisel his final work.

A month later, standing in an unheated, undecorated, shedlike work-shop on a plank floor worn by time and usage, rain beating down on the skylight roof, Vangelli, with a great sweeping gesture, removed the canvas coverings from his completed work . . . and we stared at our faces in marble.

They were striking. "Paul, your likeness is fantastic," I said.

"Well, yours is magnificent," he replied. "Vangelli, you've truly cap-tured her beauty." Laughingly he turned to the sculptor and added, *"Il naso è perfetto."*

More than seventy-four years later, Paul's marble bust can be seen just inside the entrance to the Getty Museum in Brentwood, California, while mine sits on the floor of my living room—where I left it after the last earthquake—next to my piano in my home in Venice, California.

Dolly Mills de Mastrogianni, wife of a famous music critic in Argen-tina, came to hear me sing one afternoon. Being part of the social and musical circles of Rome and knowing Cahier was leaving for California, she insisted that I sing for Maestro Julio Moreschi. "Your voice is beau-tiful and he will continue to prepare your repertoire and roles for the opera." Cahier agreed and, when she left, I moved to the Ambasciatori Hotel, across from the Excelsior and the American Embassy on the Via Veneto, then dashed over to No. 11 Lungotevere Anguillara in Traste-

vere to the studio of Julio Moreschi, which was next door to the house in which "The Immortal Dante" had lived.

Julio Moreschi was the son of one of the last great singers of the nineteenth century, a male soprano. He had sung as a member of the Cappella Sistina, and was a man devoted to pasta, the art of singing, and his love of people. Short in stature, with a sweet face and a huge smile, he greeted me at his doorway, dark-rimmed glasses hiding the gleam within his eyes. After hearing me sing, he pronounced me a soprano.

Soon after this, Paul, Vangelli, Moreschi, and I had dinner at Alfredo's. The great maestro of the restaurant, Alfredo di Lelio himself, stood before us in his chef's hat and starched white apron, and in his hand was the large fork needed to mix the pasta. Then, in tune with his musicians, Alfredo performed his magic and we feasted on his work of art, "fettuccine Alfredo." After Vangelli left, Paul turned to Moreschi, whose white napkin was still tied about his neck, his hand on the last of the wine in his glass, and asked, *"Quanto tempo chivolle?"* ("How much time will she need?")

Taking his napkin from his neck and applying it to his mouth, Moreschi answered, *"Non piu di tre mese"* ("No more than three months"). Then in French he went on, "I believe we can get her into an opera here to start her off. If she makes her debut in Italy, even in a small opera company to begin with, it would be good for her." Between the two of them, they made the decision that I should study at least for three more months, do some concerts, and maybe an opera. When I was ready, Moreschi could arrange it. An hour later, we left Alfredo's, Moreschi singing "Core 'ngrato" like no one since Caruso.

CHAPTER 17

MARRIED IN ROME

It was late August when Jeannie telephoned that she was in Rome to meet her new husband, who was due to arrive in a few days. I was amazed it wasn't Bill Gaston.

That evening Paul invited her to dine with us on the terrace of my hotel . . . the Ambasciatori. Seated next to us was Count Ciano, Mussolini's Foreign Minister (and son-in-law), and Joachim von Ribbentrop, Hitler's Foreign Minister. The presence of von Ribbentrop in Rome, amid other intimations of war, imposed a pall over every one of the otherwise carefree diners. Even our conversation took on a quieter tone and Paul noticeably hurried us through dinner. We left quickly. On the way to the elevator, he leaned over to kiss me good night and whispered, "Teddy, darling, be prepared to leave Rome. There are rumors of an all-out war and, if anything happens in the next few days, I want you out of Italy. Jean, too. She has a car, drive to Switzerland and I'll join you at the Victoria-Jungfrau in Interlaken. I have two meetings

here tomorrow afternoon that are very important. I'll take the train tomorrow night."

Very early the next morning, the phone rang. It was Paul, he said, "Go."

We left immediately in Jean's Fiat and drove to Villa d'Este in Lake Como. At sunrise the next morning, we took off for Switzerland. We drove over Monte Rosa, the Rhone Glacier, and the Furka Pass, up and down those narrow mountain roads. At nightfall a heavy fog set in, and, at 7,500 feet, one cylinder in the car went "poof." The lights went dim, and I had to get out and walk slowly in front of the car with our flashlight, leading the way for Jean to drive the precarious roads. It was scary, and at moments I couldn't see the road at all.

Fortunately, after a few miles the headlights of the car came back on. I jumped in and we continued on to Interlaken, thankful that the little Fiat had gotten us over the mountains and out of Italy before all private cars were confiscated. Even the Swiss guards at the border were amazed to see two American girls at such a late hour. Arriving at the hotel in Interlaken, we found that Paul had reserved a beautiful suite for us facing the Jungfrau. Jeannie and I each had a mug of hot, delicious Swiss chocolate, then climbed into our beds and fell sound asleep.

The following day, Paul arrived and was I glad to see him. He was pretty happy to see me, too. When I told him of our trip across the Alps, especially the part when I had to walk in front of the car with the flashlight, he said, "Teddy, you could have been killed. Those roads are icy and difficult, even in daylight. One wrong turn and you . . ."

"I know," I said, interrupting him, "but I thought you wanted us to keep going and not stop till we arrived at Interlaken, and that's what we did."

"And we made it," Jeannie added.

"Yes, you did, thank God," was all Paul could say.

Later, when we were alone, he took me in his arms and said, "Darling, please, be more careful. I don't want to lose you, and I almost did."

At dinner that night, Jean contacted her husband and left the next day to meet him. So there I was, alone in our big suite. Outside there was a full moon shining down on the snowcapped mountains. I opened the door to the terrace and stepped out. What a world greeted me . . . so clean . . . so fresh . . . so icy cold. I looked up into the heavens, took a huge breath, filled my lungs, and wanted to shout "Hallelujah." Instead, I took a shower, wrapped my fur coat around me, and tiptoed barefoot down the hallway of the hotel to Paul's room.

"I'm lonely," I called out as I knocked. He opened the door. I dropped my fur to the floor and stood there naked until he pulled me into his arms and into his bed.

"Teddy," he whispered, "you never, ever need to be lonely again."

I awoke at noon. I could hear Paul talking on the phone in the next room. There was a pair of his pj's on the chair beside the bed. I picked them up and went into the bathroom. I ran cold water over my face, swished some Lavoris around in my mouth, brushed my hair, put on the pj's, and quietly walked into the living room of the suite. Paul was still on the phone, but motioned me to come in and sit down at the table, where breakfast was waiting for me. He was speaking to someone in California. I wondered who it was until he said, "Good-bye, Dave, just send the papers to Rome." I knew then it was his lawyer.

He hung up, turned to me, and smiled. For a minute he said nothing, then, his eyes bright with amusement, he asked, "Young lady, tell me . . .

How are we going to get you back to your room without everyone in the hotel knowing you crashed here this morning at dawn, barefoot, and stark-naked under a fur coat?"

I looked at him. Was he teasing me, or was he serious? For just one minute, I couldn't tell. Then I answered, "It's a puzzle I'll have to solve, Mr. Getty, but I need your help."

"It's solved." He came over to the breakfast table, leaned down, kissed me, took me by the hand, and said, "We'll go together."

"You mean you're going to walk with me down the hallway all the way to my room? Paul, this is crazy. Can't we wait till nighttime?"

"No. Come on."

"Like this?" I said. "In your pajamas?"

"Yes," he answered emphatically. "But wait, I have something I must get in the closet." As he opened the door, I saw that it wasn't a closet, but a bedroom and there on the floor was my luggage. "I had it moved here this morning. It's better than walking down the hall, isn't it? Now, go put on some slacks and a sweater, and we'll go sightseeing before we leave for Grindelwald."

The little town of Grindelwald was at least two thousand feet higher than Interlaken, and was entirely surrounded by the Alps. The Bear Hotel was enchanting, reminding me of a gingerbread chalet, and our rooms looked directly out at the majestic Jungfrau. Paul decided we should stay there and wait for the threat of war to subside. The weather was perfect. We played tennis and swam, and walked through the green countryside, stopping to look at the grandeur of the snowcapped Alps, which gave out such a feeling of protection.

Late one night, Paul and I, a barmaid and a chimney sweep black

with soot, and a mountain climber and his guide sat in the bar having drinks and listening to the news broadcast from London. Suddenly, the commentator said, "A year ago this month, Hitler told the world that if Czechoslovakia does not give Germany the territory marked as Sudetenland, 'I will act by October first.'" The reporter continued, "Not one of us who listened to that speech can ever forget or forgive the famous words of this *so infamous liar* when he shouted, 'The Sudetenland is the last territorial demand I have to make in Europe.' Today, just one year later, Nazi mechanized legions moved into Poland."

We were stunned. It was September 1, 1939. Two days later, September 3, on Sunday afternoon, quietly, yet dramatically, over the airwaves came Prime Minister Neville Chamberlain's declaration, "Great Britain is at war with Germany." Later that same day came France's declaration.

We waited in Switzerland until Paul was certain that it was safe, then we took the train back to Rome. Italy was still neutral and Rome quiet, but there was tension and anxiety on everyone's faces. Hoping Italy would stay out of the war, I went back to Moreschi.

One warm evening in October, Paul and I were flying along the winding roads on our way back to Rome in a little rented car, after having spent the afternoon going through the excavations of the Emperor Hadrian's villa and roaming the Tivoli Gardens. I had a feeling of concern and told Paul. "Concern about what, darling?" he asked.

"About our friends in countries that are now at war."

Paul turned and looked at me. "Teddy, dear, I'm concerned about them, too, but I'm more concerned about us. We've got to make plans." He turned from me just in time to slow the car down to a near stop. A huge wine cart had suddenly appeared in the road before us. It moved slowly, a tiny oil lamp swinging at its back. Under the canopy, the driver

was sound asleep, but his tired, faithful donkey was methodically plodding along, right down the center of the road.

As we followed the cart, Paul continued, "I have to go back to America soon, and I know you want to stay here with Moreschi for another two or three months. In case anything happens, like war, I would feel safer about you if you were my wife. I know we had planned to be married at Herstmonceux, but that's out of the question now. So, darling, I've already set the wheels in motion for us to get married right here. I've talked to the Italian officials about it, and one of these days I'll just call you and say, 'It's today, let's get married.'"

"You mean . . . just get married?"

"Yes, just get married."

A month later it happened. The ringing telephone awakened me. It was Paul. "This is it," he said.

"This is *what*? It's only eight o'clock."

He repeated, "Teddy, this is it."

"*What* is it? What do you mean? Is Italy at war?"

"No, but get ready . . ."

"For what?"

"Darling, this morning we are going to get married."

"Wow." I jumped out of bed. "But what am I going to wear?"

"Just put on something and meet me right away."

"But, Paul, I haven't got the right clothes."

"Put on anything. They came through."

"What came through?"

"The papers permitting us to get married here, and that prenuptial agreement. We have to sign as citizens of the United States; the authorities here had to approve, too."

It was noon when we started for the Capitol of Rome. We had a law-yer and we signed the papers, but on the way, Paul stopped the cab while he dashed inside a jewelry shop.

When he came out, he said, "I bought a wedding ring."

"What happened to the one you bought from Paul Flato?"

"I don't know. It's in my luggage somewhere. I looked for it this morning. Couldn't find it, and we can't wait."

"Eccola . . . siamo qui," the cabbie said. *"E grazie,"* he added as Paul thrust a handful of lire in his hands.

The driver dropped us at the base of the famous grand stairway that led to the seat of the Italian government. At the top of the steps, to the right and the left of the balustrade, were two colossal statues of Castor and Pollux, standing beside their horses.

"This is the Piazzo del Campidoglio. Look at this huge statue of Marcus Aurelius on horseback. That building behind it with the clock tower is the Palazzo Senatorio. Just think, Teddy, Michelangelo was responsible for this entire magnificent square."

It was truly magnificent. I felt somehow I had seen it before and for a moment, as I stood very still, the sun shining on my face, I felt like I was one of the statues, too. The next moment, I was aware Paul had grasped my hand and was gently pulling me toward the entrance of the Capitol.

He smiled and said, "Come on, darling," and we walked inside and into the great hall where we were to be married. The Italian officials and our lawyer were waiting for us. They reaffirmed our citizenship and status, completed the necessary paperwork, and instructed us to take our seats—two huge chairs that resembled thrones, as if we were the emperor and empress of Rome. My heart began to beat faster. The cer-emony was not like we had expected, so we put ourselves in the hands of

the men who were there to instruct us in the Italian civil ceremony. I felt as if I was onstage, being given lines and cues.

"Here comes the magistrate," whispered Paul, as a very elderly, dignified gentleman in judicial robes entered.

"Who's the little fellow with him?" I whispered back. "And why is he dressed up in that ornate, bright blue costume? And why the epaulets, ribbons, and medals?" I laughed. "And that tricornered hat . . . It's so silly, and the sword . . ."

"Shhh, Teddy," Paul said. "Now remember, when the magistrate asks you questions, just answer *'Sì.'*"

When Paul placed the ring on my finger, the ceremony began. It was held in rapid Italian, and took about ten minutes. I dutifully said *"Sì"* to everything I was asked. Paul did, too. Then, with a great flourish, the little man in his epaulets and medals presented me with a leather-bound book, saying, *"Bella signora*, this is your family-to-be." I took it as graciously as I could, opened it, and saw that it contained spaces for at least twelve children.

"This is your *Libro Matrimonio*," the man said with dignity. Then he kissed me on both cheeks, after which the other officials hurried over and proceeded to do the same.

"Adesso voglio baciare la signora," the magistrate exclaimed, and kissed me.

"Me, too!" shouted Paul. Then he took me in his arms and kissed me solidly on the lips, to their wild applause. At that, the doors opened and two little girls ran in, quite out of breath, carrying armfuls of wildflowers, which they presented to me.

As we walked out into the beautiful sunlight, Paul said, "Teddy, dear, let's send your mother a cable and tell her we're married."

At midnight, we stood in the curve of the open French doors of our suite at the Excelsior. Beneath us was a great silence. All at once, peace was shattered by a bell . . . it was the telephone. It rang so loudly, so insistent, so demanding, it had to be important. A great fear gripped me. Was this the call that might mean Paul would have to leave for New York?

I suddenly felt cold, and wrapped my negligee tightly around me. We'd had such a fabulous day, it couldn't end like this. Over lunch, we'd spoken of where we would spend the next summer . . . a beach house by the sea. Next winter, the apartment in New York. Or wherever I was singing, or he was digging. And we had laughed and joked about the fact that now that we were married, maybe making love would have lost its charm . . . only to find out that very afternoon that married love was sweeter, more exciting, than ever before.

Paul answered the phone. I could see by his reaction that it was *the call* I had dreaded. We looked at each other . . . neither spoke.

I went to him. "Do you really have to go?"

He nodded.

"How soon?"

"Immediately, and you are coming with me."

"No, Paul, I can't. I have to stay two more months, as you and Moreschi agreed I should. Otherwise I'll never get beyond being a student. I'll never sing in opera like I want to, and like you want me to. I'll just be a failure."

"I love you, Teddy. I love your voice and I want you with me, but *you* must decide. In the meantime, please help me pack and then we'll get your things."

I started to cry as I realized that, much as we both knew I had planned to stay, I had never actually faced the fact that my decision

would have to be made this soon. I wanted to accomplish what I had started out to do—not just for myself, but because I wanted Paul to be proud of me. I was mindlessly stacking his books in a duffel bag when Paul came over, took me in his arms, and said, "Darling, I'm so proud of you. I love your courage, and whatever you decide, I'm all for it. But, until you make up your mind, Mrs. Getty, will you *please* dry those tears and join me for breakfast downstairs."

The next few hours flew by. I finally made the decision. I'd stay. The concierge got Paul passage on the *Conte di Savoia* leaving Naples the next morning. Arrangements were made for me at the American Express with the manager, Mr. Fornacca. We lunched between business calls to California, dined between business calls to New York, and then, as night fell, I drove with Paul to the railroad station, his luggage strapped precariously to the top of the taxi. Neither of us had time to think, we just rushed. The train, crowded with American tourists fleeing the country, was about to leave without him when we finally arrived and we both raced down the platform. With the warning whistles shrill in our ears, we reached the last car just in time. He kissed me good-bye. The porters caught his luggage. He turned back to me and smiled. I don't think Paul ever looked as good to me as he did at that moment. I was already agonizing over parting, and seeing myself alone again.

"Darling, I love you," he shouted over the noise, the steam from the train pouring out and up into our faces. I don't know whether he kept waving or not. I couldn't see through my tears.

As I turned from the departing train, I was met by a fast-running squadron of Mussolini's elite troops, the Bersaglieri. They never walked; they ran, their capes flowing.

Paul's train now gone, another arrived. The crowds, the loud hoot-

ing, and the noise of whistles made me feel even more alone and so scared that I ran through the station and hailed a cab. When I got back to my hotel room, I burst into tears.

It must have been at least two hours later when Paul called from Naples. "I miss you terribly," he said.

"I miss you, too, Paul."

"Good-bye, Teddy."

"Bye, Paul."

No sooner had I hung up the receiver than I placed a call to my mom in Greenwich. "Teddy, darling," she said, "we just received your cable. Congratulations. We're so happy for you both. Let me speak to Paul."

"He's gone, Mother."

"Gone where?"

"He's gone to New York."

"You mean he's gone and left you all alone in Italy?"

"I wanted to stay here."

"*You* wanted to stay there. Why, Teddy? Why?"

CHAPTER 18

SHATTERED DREAMS

The approach of war in Italy was not a sudden thing. It may be hard to understand in hindsight, but, in the early months of 1940, war seemed unlikely to those of us who lived in Rome. Even though there were shortages and groups of Nazis appearing in the city, war was something that was going on "somewhere else" . . . "it would end soon" . . . "it had to" and even if it didn't, we were sure "war couldn't possibly come to Italy . . . certainly not to Rome."

I didn't notice warning signs because I was still upset at having made the decision to stay and study instead of leaving with Paul. I kept telling myself, *He believes in me . . . He's given me this opportunity . . . I mustn't fail . . . If I do, at least I'm going to try my best.* I so wanted to make him proud . . . to please him. Foolish girl? Maybe. And so I spent every day studying. I'd write Paul of my progress, telling him there was no panic in Italy . . . that, as soon as I was ready and Moreschi made the arrangements, I was going to make my debut either in an opera or concert. "And

hopefully *you* will be here. Remember, you said you'd return? Or did you just say 'maybe'? Oh, darling, I do so hope you will . . ."

In America, it seemed the news of our marriage had already made the papers.

The *Daily News* wrote:

Romance bloomed from the first. When Teddy, one of the best of blue blood torch singers, was crooning into the mike at the Stork Club, Paul would sit quietly listening to her, his devotion so obvious no one was startled when their engagement was announced."

Another paper wrote: *"Paul has returned to New York to attend some urgent business, but Teddy intends to remain in Rome a while longer to continue her studies."*

From the *New York Journal* and Maury Paul's Knickerbocker column: *"Vivacious, talented Teddy Lynch became the bride of J. Paul Getty . . . in Rome."*

Nancy Randolph of the *News* wrote: *"Teddy is the isolated case of a debutante turned café singer, who could really sing. And friends, who recently returned from Italy, insist the singer is making great progress in her studies and should give music lovers something to swoon about when she returns. She is expected to be back soon to join Paul.*

Of course, I never saw those articles until years later. Had I . . . I might have burst into tears, because I was really heartbroken at not being with Paul. I never knew at the time that Paul was negotiating to sell oil to Russia while in Berlin. In fact, I can't remember ever asking him what he was doing, except I knew he was drilling for oil. What I *did* know was that I was heartbroken at not being with Paul.

It was terrible now living in Rome without him—his thoughts, his attention, his advice. I missed the way he looked when he looked at me, which sometimes made me feel like a child, sometimes like a woman. I guess this is the way one feels, if one truly loves. I did truly love him, and I damned myself for being so independent that I stayed on in Rome. All the time I was trying to cement an already exciting relationship by accomplishing what *he* thought I could do.

A tidal wave of reporters was waiting for Paul when the *Conte di Savoia* docked in the United States. He was surprised to find himself the most sought-after person on board. The press surrounded him not just because we had gotten married, but because of a major business deal Paul had been working on while in Europe. Reporters peppered him with questions about the deal he'd been negotiating to sell oil to the Soviet Union. Transportation in Russia was so bad that it was faster and cheaper to ship oil across the Pacific in tankers from California to Vladivostok than it was to send it from Russia's own Baku oil fields.

Two days after he landed, Paul left New York with Ware to celebrate Thanksgiving in Greenwich with my mother and sisters. He wrote to say how much everyone missed me. I missed them, too, Paul most of all. We had been so close, *when* we were close, even though there were weeks and even months when we were apart.

About a month later, not wanting to live alone, I moved from the Ambasciatori Hotel to a very quaint penthouse apartment atop a palazzo overlooking the Piazza Argentina. I shared the apartment with two other girls: Magdaleine Snyder, aide to Mr. Marquis, the American delegate and vice president of the International Institute of Agriculture, and Nedda Brunette, a secretary at the British Embassy. Each of us had our own bedroom and bath, and shared an artist's studio/drawing room with

a lovely terrace overlooking the ruins of the Piazza Argentina. We also shared Maria, an excellent cook and housekeeper. Once a week she would take possession of the terrace, undo her floor-length hair, wash and dry it, then put it back up on top of her head in time to make supper. She reminded me of Mrs. Danvers, the housekeeper in *Rebecca*.

In addition to my singing lessons with Maestro Moreschi, I decided to study the history and literature of Italy. I thought it would help me prepare for my roles as a singer. Remembering that Marymount, the Paris school/convent where I had been a student as a teenager, also had a branch in Rome, I looked it up and drove out on the Via Nomentana for a visit. Imagine my surprise to find that Mother Brendon, who had been the Mother Superior at Marymount in Paris when I was there years earlier, was now the head of Marymount in Rome. She greeted me with great warmth and, after a quiet talk, arranged with the headmistress for me to have private lessons each morning. They usually ended with a short visit in her lovely garden, along with cookies and a glass of milk. The school was housed in a beautiful villa on the Via Nomentana, formerly the home of an ambassador, and was directly across the street from the Villa Torlonia, the residence of Il Duce, Benito Mussolini.

Days now were not so difficult. I had my lessons, and I started memorizing roles, putting all my energy and thought into the characters I was to portray. But evenings were a torment. I was lonely for Paul. At first he'd call, telling me he loved me and missed me. Then, as time went by, he'd cable me. I still have all of his cables tied up in blue ribbons, along with his letters.

"Come home," he'd say. "Right now."

"I can't," I'd reply. "You know I can't . . . remember? We promised each other that you would come back when I was ready. Well, it won't

be long now, that's what Moreschi says." And that's what I was looking forward to . . . the day Paul would return and I'd be ready to sing—as a lyric soprano.

Some nights Moreschi would invite me to join his family and other students at the Cisterna, a simple little restaurant in Trastevere, where, after much fettuccine and wine, we would all sing. Ethi Junger, a beautiful coloratura soprano from Salzburg, was among Moreschi's most promising students. Madly in love with an English boy, Rodney Jennings, and unable to leave Italy for England, she managed to get permission to marry him by proxy (Moreschi stood in as the proxy).

On the day she married and received her British passport, she asked me to drive her to the German legation. On being presented to the German consul, Ethi took out her German passport and threw it on the floor, right in front of him, declaring, "Today I have married an Englishman. I am now a citizen of Great Britain, and I give you back your passport with joy. *Mein Gott*," she cried, "how happy I am to be free of you Nazis!"

And with that, she grabbed my hand and hurriedly pulled me out the door. I must say I was grateful they didn't shoot us.

One late afternoon, Moreschi asked that I sing for Maestro Bonaventura Somma, the leading director of the renowned choir of Santa Cecilia, who brought with him the directors of the Bari and Formia opera companies. I sang Mimi's aria from the first act of *La Bohème*, "O mio babbino caro" from the comic opera *Gianni Schicchi*, and "The Willow Song" from *Otello*. They were extremely pleased, and definitely agreed with Moreschi that I must study further, learn several roles, and make my debut in Italy if I could, before returning to America. Maestro Somma was adamant that I first do a concert tour. The group planned to meet within days to see what schedule could be arranged.

When they left, I raced out of Moreschi's studio to call Paul and tell him the good news. Running down the street, I was followed by my little clique—the impoverished and forgotten children of Trastevere, who listened to me every time I had a lesson. They would stand, rain or shine, on the sidewalk and applaud when I sang one of their favorite arias. They were always out there on the street, seemingly homeless, deserted by their parents. When I asked Moreschi's wife about them, she said very sadly, "Children of Jewish mothers who are illegitimate. They sleep in cellars, eat what people give them, and the government doesn't care."

But I cared, and they knew it. After my lessons, they followed me to the small café at the end of the street, where the buses stopped. After ordering hot chocolate for everyone, with their cries of "*Grazie,* signorina" and "*a domani*" ringing in my ears, I found an empty seat on the next bus, which swerved and careened across the Ponte Garibaldi to the Corso Vittorio Emmanuele, and dropped me off right in front of our apartment in the Piazza Argentina. I ran up all six flights of stairs just to get to the phone to call Paul.

After what seemed to be hours, the call went through and I could hear him saying, "Hello, hello . . ."

I was so excited to hear his voice! "Paul, it's me," I yelled. "I just sang, and they liked me."

"Darling!" I could hear the excitement in his voice (I loved his voice). "How marvelous . . . When did you sing? I can hardly hear you . . . tell me . . . what did you sing?"

"I sang three arias . . . about an hour ago," I yelled back into the phone.

"I'm so proud of you, Teddy! Tell me more," he said.

"I just finished telling you, Paul," I cried.

"Yes, but I want you to tell me again." He sounded happy.

"I won't till I hear you say you miss me, because I miss you, Paul, so much. Do you miss me?"

"What a question, darling, of course I do!" he said. "Now, write me the details of your audition. When will you sing? Because I want to be there, and maybe I can. You know I love and miss you, sweetheart."

"Well, I love you and miss you more," I said. And, as I spoke, we were abruptly cut off, and there I was in the dark of my room, holding a dead telephone in my hand.

I felt so let down, even though I knew he was proud of my progress and we were both so excited talking to each other. I think it was that word "maybe" that frightened me. When he left, he had been so positive that he would return in three months. What was it in his voice that caused me to doubt this now? Perhaps he couldn't return due to business, which for Paul always came first. And how could I blame him, for I had done the same thing months before when I had put my studying ahead of going home with him. I simply had to believe he would come back to me as he promised, if he could. I immediately sat down and wrote him the details of my audition, ending my letter with a little poem I composed in Italian . . . and sent it off the next day.

Paolo, torno presto, carissimo Amore
Non ti scordar di me
Ti voglio troppo bene
Per vivere lontano da te.
Paul, come back quickly, dearest love
Please do not forget me

I love you much too much
To live so far from you.

The following week, I was amazed to receive a long letter from Paul, written in Italian, which took me one whole afternoon to translate. Starting with *Mia Carissima Orsacchiotta* (My Dearest Teddy Bear), he went on to describe what he'd been doing. Apparently, he had stayed in New York far longer than he had planned, then went out to Tulsa, Oklahoma, and on to Los Angeles to see his mother and sons, George, Ronny, Paul, and Gordon. Deciding to visit Mexico City on business, he drove there with his cousin, Hal Seymour. After sightseeing and being entertained by the president of Mexico, the two drove to Acapulco, which was virtually unknown to North Americans at that time. The most famous landmark, of course, was La Quebrada, the cliff from which Mexican divers would plunge one hundred feet down into the swirling whirlpool below.

He also became enamored of the natural beauty of the land down the coast from Acapulco, an untouched forest and a beach called Revolcadero, its surrounding land owned by a tribe of Indians. He made an offer, bought the land, built a hotel right on the beach, and called it the Pierre Marques. He described the sand as so white and soft, the sea so blue and clear, and the waves so high that at times one could see giant sharks swimming right through them. It sounded wild to me and, oh, how I wished I could have been there.

Instead, I was seated at a table on the fashionable terrace of the Hotel Ambasciatori in Rome. It was June 10, 1940. Maestro Moreschi, our accompanist Hans Hasl, Ethi Jungar (now Jennings)—our Musetta—and the Greek tenor, who was to sing the part of Rudolpho with us,

were celebrating our last rehearsal before leaving on a little concert tour arranged by Maestro Somma. I barely nibbled my food; I was excited, for we happened to have ringside seats for "History in the Making."

As usual, Mussolini's son-in-law, Foreign Minister Count Ciano, was there. Beside him was an oddly striking, blond woman, clearly the wife of a German high official. Guests of the restaurant were accustomed to Ciano's presence. Still, they glanced nervously at him, because they sensed he was at that moment playing a major role in the threat of war, which was daily becoming more ominous. He left before we did.

Just an hour later, our little group stood in the Piazza Venezia, looking up at Mussolini as he addressed the nation. From his historic balcony, he shook his fist and shouted his declaration of war on France—still reeling from the blitzkrieg and all but defeated—and England, much beleaguered and now fighting alone. Il Duce had decided to get his share of the spoils after Hitler had made the kill. At first, most people around us just stared up at him, bewildered, some frightened, others disappointed. But the thousands of university students and young Fascists in the Piazza went absolutely wild, yelling themselves hoarse. Then, suddenly, as if on cue, they set off through the streets like hoodlums.

To avoid being trapped in the swarming mob, we ran to my little car, which I'd parked on a side street. As soon as we were all inside, I turned onto the Corso Vittorio Emanuele, only to come face-to-face with the demonstrators. They surrounded us, bombarding us with sticks, flags, paper bags, and a sort of confetti. Then they kicked the car and started rocking it to try to overturn it. That's when the Maestro stood up and yelled for them to stop. Realizing the car was our best weapon, I put my hand on the horn, threw the car into gear, and pushed the accelerator to

the floor. With a screeching start, the car lurched forward, throwing the Maestro to his seat. As we gained speed, the mob scattered.

Arriving at his studio, we were met by his child and his wife, who was crying hysterically, *"Julio, Julio, siamo in guerra."* ("Julio, Julio, we're in war.") To which he replied, *"Stai zitta. Calmati, amore."* ("Be quiet. Calm yourself, love.")

That night was frightening. Rome was blacked out for the first time. When the French planes flew over the city and the air raid alarms went off, we all ran down to the shelters. No bombs were dropped, but the buildings shook each time the antiaircraft guns blasted at the planes. Within the next few days, France had collapsed to the Germans but England carried on, alone. In Rome, we were isolated, our only concern our immediate safety.

In spite of this, I was still fired with the anticipation of our approaching concert tour when, three days later, Moreschi received the following message:

> Due to regulations issued yesterday, no foreign artists will be allowed to appear in Italy at this time. We deeply regret not being able to present the great talents of your students, but expect that this ruling will be lifted within the next few months, so please be patient and express to your students our sincere thanks for the privilege of hearing them and know that I shall do all in my power to arrange a future date for their concert tour and opera debuts. Sincerely, Bonaventura Somma.

When Maestro read the message to us, it was as if a special bomb had blasted my fondest hopes. Everything that was me—my dreams, my

hopes, my efforts—all had been with one thing in mind: to do what both Paul and I had felt I should and could do. This had been the only reason I had stayed in Rome—with the hard work, the exercises, the daily struggle to study and learn the roles—letting the man I loved return home without me. And now it looked like I'd done it all for nothing.

The war had shattered my dreams. There was nothing more I could do but go home . . . and yet, looking around the studio and seeing the same look of disappointment on the faces of the other students, I wondered whether I should not give up. Maybe Maestro Somma could still arrange a tour. He wouldn't have said so if he hadn't thought he could. It was a chance we'd have to take. That wonderful saying *"Qui ne risque rien, n'a rien"* kept coming to mind. So maybe, just maybe, if we didn't give up, we would soon be booked on a concert tour and be given roles in an opera. We just had to pray and wait, and that's what we did.

The next eventful few months moved swiftly. My roommates left Italy—Nedda for England and Magdaleine for America. I accepted an invitation from Ruth Ricci, an American journalist, to share her home on the Via Clitunno. Ruth had already applied for her exit permit from the Italian Dipartimento di Immigrazione, and recommended that I do so, too.

Although I planned to stay on with the other students, I decided to call on Signor Fornacca at the American Express Company on the Piazza di Spagna. He had always been so helpful to me. When I told him my plans, he suggested that I get my exit visa at once, even though I expected to stay in Italy until Maestro Somma arranged for the concert tour. "You're an American, Teddy," he said. "You really have nothing to worry about. America is not at war. But get the exit permit at once. Then go to the Swiss or Portuguese legations for visas to pass

through their countries. Then come back here, and I'll arrange for your passage."

Hurriedly, I headed for the immigration offices. The Dipartimento was crowded. After standing in line for a while, watching the relieved faces of those who had been in line ahead of me as they received their permits, I finally faced the officer in charge. I presented my passport and said, "I'm planning to leave Italy soon, and would like an exit permit, please."

He looked at me, then at my passport, and went into an inner office and closed the door behind him. I stood there, hopeful that with my exit permit I might still be able to make it back to the legations before they closed for the day. Then tomorrow I would see Mr. Fornacca, get my ticket, and arrange my itinerary.

The chimes of the large wall clock roused me out of my daydreaming, and I realized that it had been nearly a half hour since the officer had gone into that room with my passport. What was he doing? Why was it taking so long? I looked around. Only two people were waiting in line behind me. Just then the guard locked the main door and turned off some of the overhead lights. Obviously it was closing time.

Suddenly, the door opened to the inner office. The officer came out, handed me my passport, and said, "I am sorry, signora, but your permit has been denied."

"Denied? Denied why?"

With great finality he said, "Come back next week," and motioned to the person behind me to step forward.

I was stunned. I can't remember how I walked out of there, or how I got home. I do remember the fear that gripped me. Why had my exit permit been denied? Why must I wait till next week? Would I get it then?

Ruth had hers. Why was I singled out to be denied what was rightfully mine? With each question, my fear increased, so much so that when I arrived at the house, I grabbed the telephone. I had to talk to Paul. "Sorry," the operator said, "there is a five-hour delay on all transatlantic calls."

Disappointed, I said, "Okay . . . keep the call in. I'll wait."

A few moments later, there was a light tap on my bedroom door. I knew it was Ruth. She had just returned from Attilio's, the beauty salon in the Piazza di Spagna, her hair beautifully coiffed, ready for her trip home in a few days to join her doctor-husband. She was radiant. "This came for you today," she said, handing me a cable. It was from Paul. It read, *I love the voice, but I love the woman more. Come home at once.*

" 'Come home at once'? How can I, Ruth? The Italian officer refused to give me my exit permit today. He said, 'Come back next week.' "

Trying to calm me, Ruthie said, "Don't worry, Teddy. That's just a formality. You'll get it next week."

The telephone rang. Maybe my call had gone through. The operator said, "I am sorry, but on your call to New York, there is now a *nine*-hour delay."

"Okay," I said, "keep the call in. I'll wait."

"Come on, Teddy," Ruthie said. "Let's go out on the terrace and have our supper. We can hear the telephone from there."

The terrace was unusually dark. The sky was moonless and our hurricane lamp gave off only the barest of light, in conformity with the blackout regulations. Ruth was quiet all during supper. Suddenly she blurted out, "Teddy, I'm leaving tonight. I got the last seat on the train for Switzerland, and from there I'll take whatever transportation they'll

give me. Just so I get home to my Ricci." I was staggered by the news. She sensed it and said, "I'm so sorry to leave so suddenly, but please don't worry. You'll be leaving next week, I'm sure."

I wasn't reassured. There was something wrong. I couldn't define it, but I felt it. And now that I would be alone, I felt it more. At midnight her cab arrived as ordered. After wishing her Godspeed and watching the cab disappear in the darkness, I went up to my bedroom to wait for my call. I waited all night. The call never came through.

At dawn, I cabled Paul: *Due to regulations, concert canceled. Moreschi hopeful next month. If it happens, will you come? If not, will try to arrange to leave for home. Miss you, Mother, and family. Love, Teddy.*

My cable, I later learned, was deciphered at once as "Teddy is in trouble."

Beniamino Gigli, the great Italian tenor, lived directly in back of Ruth's house. Each morning, when Ruth and I had our coffee out on the terrace, we could hear him vocalizing. It was always a tremendous privilege, like having box seats at a private concert. The morning after Ruth left, I was having my breakfast out on the terrace, and as usual Gigli was vocalizing. But now I took no pleasure, no inspiration from hearing his beautiful voice. Instead, it had become a horrifying reminder that, "due to regulations," my own singing had been silenced. I not only agonized because I couldn't reach Paul by phone, I was also apprehensive about being in Ruth's big house by myself. Worried by the thought that my own country might somehow become involved in the war, I tried to drink my coffee, but I couldn't swallow. I telephoned Moreschi. "May I have a lesson, Maestro, right now?"

"You mean, this morning?"

"Yes, I want to sing. They can stop me from singing in public, but they can't stop me from singing with you."

That afternoon, Maestro and his wife persuaded me to take a very small penthouse apartment on the Janicolo Hill, to be closer to them. My former maid, Maria, came to take care of me, and I waited for the days to pass when I would return for my exit permit.

While I waited, I began to notice more Nazis on the streets of Rome. They were buying everything of value they could get their hands on. They swarmed the restaurants and the theaters, many of them in the guise of tourists. Their excessive buying, plus the reckless purchases of some wealthy Italians, made the shortages worse, and fed the black market. Though I can't say I really noticed this at the time. Although things were getting tighter for average Italians, I still didn't fully realize how serious the situation was because somehow Maria always managed to return from the butcher and grocer with enough for us to eat.

Exactly one week after I'd first appeared at the Dipartimento di Immigrazione, I stood face-to-face with the same officer. He said, "No exit permit today, signora," and walked away. For a second, I just stood still. I felt trapped. Again I was denied my exit permit without any explanation. Why?

I dashed back to my apartment, a lump in my throat, greatly concerned, and for the first time, very fearful. I opened the door and froze. My rooms had been searched. The drawers and closets had been opened and my things were strewn about. Someone had read all my letters from Paul. The phone was already in my hand and I was dialing the police when the door opened and Maria entered, her arms loaded with grocery bags. "Maria, I'm calling the police. Look what happened!"

Seeing the disarray of the apartment, she exclaimed, "Please, signorina, *un momento.*" She dropped the bags and dashed about, checking drawers and special places where she kept her few valuables. Finding them, she said, "Nothing stolen, signorina. It's the secret police. *Calmati.*"

Secret police? "Maria, what does all this mean? Today, for the second time, I was denied my exit permit with no explanation, and now *this.* Am I under suspicion of something?" Oh, how I wished that I had not been so independent and that I had gone home with Paul.

Me at age seven, in the "secret" garden at my grandfather's house, Thorncroft, also known as Henry Ware House, in Martha's Vineyard.

Thorncroft.

My grandmother Louise Stevens Ware.

A poster from the Stork Club, 1937.
(Photo by Herbert Mitchel)

A photo of me at the opening night party for Leonard Sillman's *New Faces* on Broadway, printed in the *New York Evening Journal*.

Teddy Lynch pictured at the Algonquin Supper Club as she tells A. K. Mills just how it feels to be an actress after she made her theatrical debut in a new Broadway produc- tion. Notables from th foregathered at the club tain to celebrate the play by Evening Journal Staff

Paul at Wild Acres in Martha's Vineyard.

Photo by a young George Hurrell.
I didn't like my fat stomach so I
penciled in a better line.

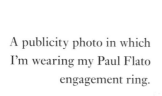

A publicity photo in which
I'm wearing my Paul Flato
engagement ring.

Paul's mother, Sarah Getty.

On the terrace of my
apartment in Rome,
with a friend and Maria,
my maid, who has made
us lunch, 1939.

On my terrace in Rome,
during the war, in 1940.
I'm holding an American flag
and the Donald Duck that
Paul gave me.

With Paul at the Beverly Hills Hotel on
my first trip home from Italy.

11 Out of Every 12 Night Club Marriages End in Reno, Society Reporter Finds

One of the latest cafe society romances to end at the altar is that of millionaire Paul Getty and Louise Dudley (Teddy) Lynch, society songstress, whose marriage in Rome has just been revealed. They are pictured in the Stork Club.

Failures Fail to Curb Enthusiasm, However

By HELEN WORDEN

NEW YORK.—Wedding bells may ring in night clubs but they play a sour tune. For every dozen cafe marriages, there are 11 crack-ups in Reno.

Do the boys and girls who are the major patronage of these fashionable jazz spots pay any attention to these matrimonial crashes, or do they like to take a gambler's chance and hope for the best?

After scanning the recent list of acknowledged and suspected night club romances, one would be inclined to the latter theory.

"Teddy" Lynch, the cafe society song bird, and Paul Getty, the millionaire oil operator, who first met at the Stork Club, cabled friends last Friday from Italy that they were married two and a half months ago in Rome.

Some Are Successful

Earlier in the week, Eileen Herrick and George Lowther, two of cafe society's most faithful standbys, declared, in spite of the objections of Miss Herrick's parents, their intention to marry. About this same time, Frederick Kugel and Marianne Ward, who have been holding hands at Armando's for several weeks, were married unexpectedly at the home of Marianne's sister, Isabelle, who met her husband, Robert Coogan, at an Armando dance.

The Coogans' marriage is one

Wealthy hotelman weds socialite singer in Europe

NEW YORK, Nov. 17.—J. Paul Getty, wealthy hotel operator, and Louise Dudley Lynch, socialite singer, were married in the American consulate in Rome last September 14, it was announced here today.

Mrs. Getty, formerly of Chicago, has been studying opera in Europe for the last two years. She was described here as being one of the first society girls to sing in a night club. Her mother is Mrs. L. Ware Lynch of Greenwich, Conn.

Getty is a large stockholder in the Tide Water Oil Co., the Pacific Western Oil Co. and the Skelly Oil Co.

SUN— 11/17/39

SOCIETY   23

Miss Louise Dudley Lynch Wed To J. Paul Getty at Rome Consulate

Mrs. L. Ware Lynch of Belle Haven, Greenwich, Conn., and Wild Acre, Vineyard Haven, Mass., has announced the marriage of her daughter, Miss Louise Dudley Lynch, to J. Paul Getty, son of Mrs. George F. Getty of Los Angeles, Cal., and the late Mr. Getty on September 14, in the American Consulate in Rome, Italy.

Mrs. Getty attended the Greenwich Academy in Connecticut, the Harcum School, Bryn Mawr, Pa., and Marymount, in Neuilly, Paris, France, and has been studying singing in London with Mme. Blanche Marchesi and with Mme. Cahier of the Palazzo Massimo in Rome, Italy. She is a granddaughter of

the late Mr. and Mrs. John Herbert Ware of New York and Chicago, and a niece of Mrs. Frederick C. Shorey of Montreal, and is a descendant of the Dudley and Perkins families, Colonial settlers.

Mr. Getty is a well known financier and patron of the arts, having exhibited his Rembrandt and Gainsborough paintings at the World's Fair of 1939. He lives at 1 Sutton Place South. Mr. Getty is connected with the Tidewater Oil Company, as well as the Getty Realty Company, sole owners of the Hotel Pierre.

Mr. and Mrs. Getty will return from Europe to the United States shortly and will make their home in New York and in Los Angeles.

Mrs. John D. Ryan to Be Hostess At Benefit for McMahon Shelter

Mrs. John D. Ryan of 3 East | other members are Mrs. Tho

Hotel Man's Marriage To Socialite Revealed

NEW YORK, Nov. 16.—(UP)—J. Paul Getty, wealthy hotel operator, and Louise Dudley Lynch, socialite singer, were married in the American consulate in Rome on September 14, it was announced here today.

Mrs. Getty, formerly of Chicago, has been studying opera in Europe for the past two and a half years. She was described here as being one of the first society girls to sing in a night club. Her mother is Mrs. L. Ware Lynch of Greenwich, Conn. Getty is a large stockholder in the Tidewater Oil Company, the Pacific Western Oil Company and the Skelly Oil Company.

"11 Out of Every 12 Night Club Marriages End in Reno":
Paul and me at the Stork Club, from an unidentified newspaper, 1939.

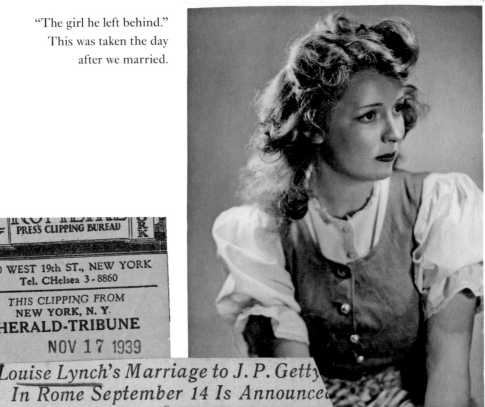

"The girl he left behind."
This was taken the day
after we married.

Louise Lynch's Marriage to J. P. Getty In Rome September 14 Is Announced

Bride Is the Daughter of Mrs. L. Ware Lynch; Ceremony at American Consulate

Mrs. L. Ware Lynch, of Belle Haven, Greenwich, Conn., and Wild Acres, Vineyard Haven, Mass., yesterday, announced the marriage of her daughter, Miss Louise Dudley Lynch, to Mr. J. Paul Getty, son of Mrs. George F. Getty, of Los Angeles, and the late Mr. Getty, on Sept. 14, in the American Consulate in Rome, Italy.

The bride attended Greenwich Academy, the Harcum School, Bryn Mawr, Pa., and Marymount, in Neuilly, Paris, France. She has been studying singing in London, England, with Mme. Blanche Marchesi and with Mme. Cahier, of the Palazzo Massimo, in Home, for the last two and one-half years. She is a grand-daughter of the late Mr. and Mrs. John Herbert Ware, of New York and Chicago, and the niece of Mrs. Frederick C. Shorey, of Montreal. She is a descendant of the Dudley and Perkins families, Colonial settlers.

Mr. Getty is a financier and patron of the arts, having exhibited his Rembrandt and Gainsborough paintings at the New York World's Fair and lives at 1 Sutton Place South, New York City.

Mr. and Mrs. Getty will return soon to the United States and will make their home in New York City and in Los Angeles.

Herbert Mitchell
Mrs. J. Paul Getty

Our wedding announcement
in the *New York Herald
Tribune*, November 17, 1939.

My teacher Madame Cahier calls me "highly talented" in the *New York Telegraph*, May 9, 1940.

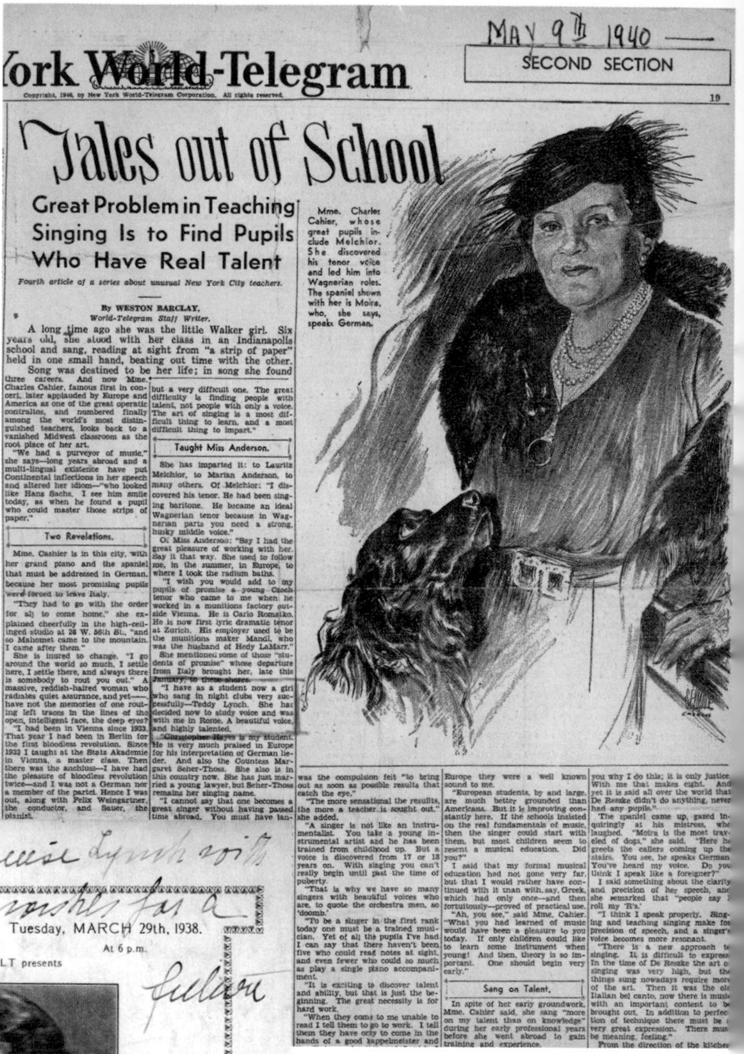

May 9th 1940

York World-Telegram

SECOND SECTION

Copyright, 1940, by New York World-Telegram Corporation. All rights reserved.

19

Tales out of School

Great Problem in Teaching Singing Is to Find Pupils Who Have Real Talent

Fourth article of a series about unusual New York City teachers.

By WESTON BARCLAY,
World-Telegram Staff Writer.

A long time ago she was the little Walker girl. Six years old, she stood with her class in an Indianapolis school and sang, reading at sight from "a strip of paper" held in one small hand, beating out time with the other.

Song was destined to be her life; in song she found three careers. And now Mme. Charles Cahier, famous first in concert, later applauded by Europe and America as one of the great operatic contraltos, and numbered finally among the world's most distinguished teachers, looks back to a vanished Midwest classroom as the root place of her art.

"We had a purveyor of music," she says—long years abroad and a multi-lingual existence have put Continental inflections in her speech and altered her idiom—"who looked like Hans Sachs. I see him smile today, as when he found a pupil who could master those strips of paper."

Two Revelations.

Mme. Cashier is in this city, with her grand piano and the spaniel that must be addressed in German, because her most promising pupils were forced to leave Italy.

"They had to go with the order for all to come home," she explained cheerfully in the high-ceilinged studio at 28 W. 56th St., "and so Mahomet came to the mountain. I came after them."

She is inured to change. "I go around the world so much, I settle here, I settle there, and always there is somebody to rout you out." A massive, reddish-haired woman who radiates quiet assurance, and yet——, have not the memories of one routing left traces in the lines of the open, intelligent face, the deep eyes?

"I had been in Vienna since 1933. That year I had been in Berlin for the first bloodless revolution. Since 1933 I taught at the Statz Akademie in Vienna, a master class. Then there was the anchluss—I have had the pleasure of bloodless revolution twice—and I was not a German nor a member of the partei. Hence I was out, along with Felix Weingartner, the conductor, and Sauer, the pianist.

... but a very difficult one. The great difficulty is finding people with talent, not people with only a voice. The art of singing is a most difficult thing to learn, and a most difficult thing to impart."

Taught Miss Anderson.

She has imparted it: to Lauritz Melchior, to Marian Anderson, to many others. Of Melchior: "I discovered his tenor. He had been singing baritone. He became an ideal Wagnerian tenor because in Wagnerian parts you need a strong, husky middle voice."

Of Miss Anderson: "Say I had the great pleasure of working with her. Say it that way. She used to follow me, in the summer, in Europe, to where I took the radium baths.

"I wish you would add to my pupils of promise a young Czech tenor who came to me when he worked in a munitions factory outside Vienna. He is Carlo Romaiko. He is now first lyric dramatic tenor at Zurich. His employer used to be the munitions maker Mandl, who was the husband of Hedy LaMarr."

She mentioned some of those "students of promise" whose departure from Italy brought her, late this January, to these shores.

"I have as a student now a girl who sang in night clubs very successfully—Teddy Lynch. She has decided now to study voice and was with me in Rome. A beautiful voice, and highly talented.

"Christopher Hayes is my student. He is very much praised in Europe for his interpretation of German lieder. And also the Countess Margaret Seher-Thoss. She also is in this country now. She has just married a young lawyer, but Seher-Thoss remains her singing name.

"I cannot say that one becomes a great singer without having passed time abroad. You must have lan-

Mme. Charles Cahier, whose great pupils include Melchior. She discovered his tenor voice and led him into Wagnerian roles. The spaniel shown with her is Moira, who, she says, speaks German.

... was the compulsion felt "to bring out as soon as possible results that catch the eye."

"The more sensational the results, the more a teacher is sought out," she added.

"A singer is not like an instrumentalist. You take a young instrumental artist and he has been trained from childhood up. But a voice is discovered from 17 or 18 years on. With singing you can't really begin until past the time of puberty.

"That is why we have so many singers with beautiful voices who are, to quote the orchestra men, so 'doomb.'

"To be a singer in the first rank today one must be a trained musician. Yet of all the pupils I've had I can say that there haven't been five who could read notes at sight, and even fewer who could so much as play a single piano accompaniment.

"It is exciting to discover talent and ability, but that is just the beginning. The great necessity is for hard work.

"When they come to me unable to read I tell them to go to work. I tell them they have only to come in the hands of a good kappelmeister and

Europe they were a well known sound to me.

"European students, by and large, are much better grounded than Americans. But it is improving constantly here. If the schools insisted on the real fundamentals of music, then the singer could start with them, but most children seem to resent a musical education. Did you?"

I said that my formal musical education had not gone very far, but that I would rather have continued with it than with, say, Greek, which had only once—and then fortuitously—proved of practical use.

"Ah, you see," said Mme. Cahier. "What you had learned of music would have been a pleasure to you today. If only children could like to learn some instrument when young! And then, theory is so important. One should begin very early."

Sang on Talent.

In spite of her early groundwork, Mme. Cahier said, she sang "more on my talent than on knowledge" during her early professional years before she went abroad to gain training and experience.

... you why I do this; it is only justice. With me that makes eight. And yet it is said all over the world that De Reszke didn't do anything, never had any pupils."

The spaniel came up, gazed inquiringly at his mistress, who laughed. "Moira is the most traveled of dogs," she said. "Here he greets the callers coming up the stairs. You see, he speaks German. You've heard my voice. Do you think I speak like a foreigner?"

I said something about the clarity and precision of her speech, and she remarked that "people say I roll my 'R's.'

"I think I speak properly. Singing and teaching singing make for precision of speech, and a singer's voice becomes more resonant.

"There is a new approach to singing. It is difficult to express. In the time of De Reszke the art of singing was very high, but the things sung nowadays require more of the art. Then it was the old Italian bel canto, now there is music with an important content to be brought out. In addition to perfection of technique there must be a very great expression. There must be meaning, feeling."

From the direction of the kitchen

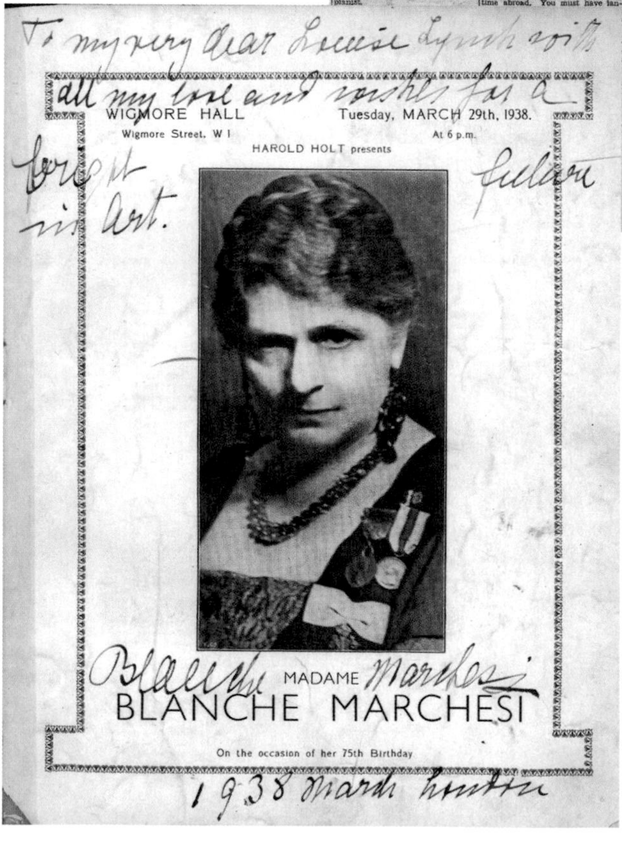

To my very dear Louise Lynch with all my love and wishes for a bright future in Art.

WIGMORE HALL
Wigmore Street, W 1

Tuesday, MARCH 29th, 1938.
At 6 p.m.

HAROLD HOLT presents

Blanche Marchesi

MADAME
BLANCHE MARCHESI

On the occasion of her 75th Birthday

1938 March London

My teacher Marchesi's last performance in London at seventy-five years old, 1938.

My journalist's passport, issued in Italy, 1940.

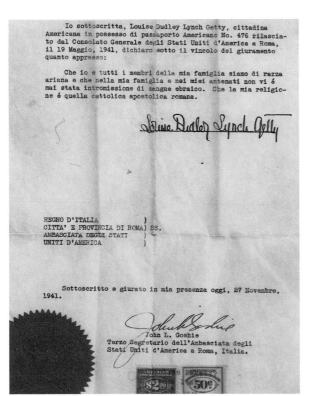

Signed declaration that I was of the Aryan race ("*razza ariana*"), issued by the State Department in Rome.

My lover Kostya.

On our way to the ship that would take us home. With Livingston Pomeroy, 1942.

In Siena under
house arrest, 1942.

In Siena, under house arrest with
fellow reporter John Cianfarra, 1942.

Secret police follow us
interned correspondents
across the Piazza del Popolo,
Editor and Publisher,
December 1942.

Paul being rushed by reporters on the *Conte di Savoia* after he made his oil deal with the Russians, November 23, 1939.

"Oilman J. P. Getty Sells to Russians," the *New York Mirror*, November 24, 1939.

26

"Liner with Diplomats Arrives from Lisbon": The Swedish *Drottningholm*, the ship that brought us home. I slept on the deck for most of the trip.

EWSREEL continued

PHOTO BY MORRIS GORDON

Home and Happy: Mrs. Paul Getty arrived from war-torn this week aboard the special diplomat-exchange liner —holm, and was met by her brother, Ware Lynch. A music student, she was caught in Rome by the declaration of war. Most of the liner's 908 passengers were as happy as Mrs. Getty to be here. They brought a general picture of gloom and war-weariness among civilians in Axis countries.

My brother greets me as I disembark the *Drottningholm*, *Newsreel*, June 7, 1942.

Mrs. Getty Tells Of Privations In Italian Jail

(Continued from page one)

troops, with fixed bayonets, stood guard at the gates. No one was allowed in or out. With no hope of seeking refuge in the embassy, I went home to pack, and then to the Foreign Press Club to learn what had happened to other American journalists.

Police Waiting at Home

I tried to get in touch with our charge d'affaires at his hotel, but could not get by the police guards, so I phoned my house for news. In a trembling voice my maid said "two gentlemen" were waiting for me, and after paying a few farewell calls on friends I went home and surrendered myself to two agents of the secret police.

They took me to the "Royal Questora" (police station), which was in great confusion, and I was put in a temporary cell until 11:30 p. m., when I was told I was to have a paying room for the night. By police car I was taken to the Mantellatte, the largest women's penitentiary in Italy. There, after being fingerprinted and having all jewelry, money, documents and cosmetics taken from me, I was ordered to follow a man and two trusties.

We passed through a maze of locked doors and finally into a high, dark corridor where fifteen women were sleeping on the floor. Opening one of the doors leading off the corridor, the trusties pulled out some evil-smelling, bug-ridden straw which they piled up next to the wall, and, with my coat for a cover, I was left for the night. It was bitter cold and damp, the prison being below the level of the Tiber, and I could feel the water trickling down the side of the wall near me.

Somewhere below us, I discovered later, were women in solitary confinement. They moaned all night long. I never understood how any one could possibly sleep in such a place, but as the days went by I discovered I, too, could sleep. It was the only refuge from one's thoughts.

"Mrs. Getty Tells of Privations in Italian Jail," the *New York Herald Tribune*, June 7, 1942.

Photo from my profile in *Time*, written upon my return.

Teddy Lynch started as a society crooner at Stork Club, Waldorf-Astoria and in musical comedies but discovered she was a lyric soprano and switched to opera in 1939. She went abroad to study, first in London, then in Rome where she found time for tennis (*above*) as well as music.

CHAPTER 19

PASSPORT TO FREEDOM

It was comforting to be awakened from sleep each morning by the sound of the church bells of Rome, but more than that I longed to be awakened from sleep each morning by the sound of the telephone bell and Paul's voice saying, "Hi, darling."

One morning the telephone bell did actually awaken me, and a typical American male voice said, "Hi. Teddy? This is Allen Raymond of the *New York Herald Tribune*, and I want to take you to lunch today at Caffé Greco. See you there at noon." And with that, he hung up.

But . . . how did he know I could make it?

Precisely at twelve noon, I dashed into Caffé Greco on the via Condotti. I stood for a moment, but before I even had a chance to look around the room, a voice at my side said, "Hi, Teddy?" It was Allen Raymond, a very handsome, very knowing individual with a great sense of humor and a marvelous, hard-hitting voice—a typical American newspaperman.

Swiftly he moved me through the crowded room to a table right

inside the second arch. After ordering for us, he said, "Have you ever lunched here before? No? It's world famous. Since 1760, Caffé Greco has been the meeting place of artists, poets, and writers of all countries. And in the next room, the walls are lined with autographed portraits of Byron, Shelley, Goethe, Keats, Gounod, Bizet, Berlioz, Wagner, Rossini, Mendelssohn, Schopenhauer, King Ludwig of Bavaria, and many other celebrities. In fact, we're sitting at the very same table where Shelley and Keats sat when they wrote poetry on the menu." Then, very pointedly, he said, "Teddy, I know you can sing. But can you write?"

"Well, Allen, with an apology to the great masters Shelley and Keats, I fearlessly admit, I write poetry."

"I'll drink to that," he said, "but Teddy, seriously. I want you to work for me. I want you to write a series of articles on the hardships of war-time living, as seen from the Italian woman's angle."

"Allen, I don't know much about that. Maria, my maid, gets everything we need."

"Well, find out how she does it. And what about Signora Moreschi?"

"I don't know. I never asked her."

"Find out what she needs, and why she can't get it. That will be your first article."

"Oh, Allen, I'd love to do it, but I don't think I should, because I'm expecting to get my exit permit. I desperately want to go home to my husband."

"Teddy, if you *don't* take this assignment, you may not go home for a long time. I already know you have been refused an exit permit. *Twice.* And who knows when you'll get it? If the United States becomes involved in the war, being an American, it would be even more difficult for you to get out—at all. You're in a tight situation . . ."

"Tight situation . . . Do you know that last night, when I came home, I found my apartment ransacked? Drawers opened, letters from Paul read . . . Nothing stolen, but everything thrown about. Maria said she was sure it was the secret police. Allen, why did they do that?"

"Teddy, it looks as though you're under suspicion."

"Suspicion. Me? But I love Italy."

"Well, so do we all. But there's a war going on. Naturally, you haven't completely realized it, because you've been devoting your life to music. You've been floating on that beautiful pink cloud. But you need protection, Teddy, and the only way to get it is to take this job I'm offering.

"It's this simple: you write the articles, I'll accept them. Then we can go to the American Consul and have your passport changed from 'Student' to 'Newspaper Correspondent.' This at least will furnish the maximum possibility that if America does enter the war, you can go home with the rest of the journalists. Just working in the office as my assistant would not give you the accreditation necessary to put you on the preferred list.

"Teddy, you naturally are wondering how and why I am involved in protecting your welfare. Well, here's the story. It seems your husband and your brother Ware became very concerned when they received your last cable in which you said you were 'trying to get an exit permit.' After discussing it at length, they decided that Ware would contact the *Herald Tribune* to see if the paper could arrange to put you on as a correspondent. The newspaper agreed, and yesterday, via coded conversation, our New York boss, Mrs. Grace Allen Bangs, told me what I have just told you. 'Put the new correspondent to work,' she said. So, Teddy, get busy now and write." Then laughing, he added, "No poetry . . . only facts. Here's a key to our office, and the address. Try to bring the first article to

me tomorrow afternoon. If I'm not in, just leave it on my desk. Now, let's have some coffee."

As he looked up to summon the waiter, he called out, "Norman!" And over to our table came a handsome, very confident-seeming man, Colonel Norman Fiske, U.S. military attaché. After Allen introduced us, Colonel Fiske said, "Teddy, I'm glad to meet you. A friend of your mother's, Ambassador Alexander Kirk, has been trying to contact you. He promised your mother that he would try to influence you to go back home. He left for America yesterday."

Allen interrupted. "Norm, don't worry about it. Teddy is going to work for me. With luck, we'll get her passport status changed. Let's drink to that."

As Colonel Fiske drove me to my apartment, in a strictly matter-of-fact voice, he said, "It is not really necessary that you worry about the possibility of your being tailed, but it is necessary that you realize that there are about fifty thousand secret police in Rome. In fact, look over here in the rearview mirror . . . there are two of them following us right now. Let's have some fun and try to lose them." He pushed the accelerator to the floor and we sped up the Janicolo Hill, leaving the little Fiat way behind. But when we reached the top of the hill and pulled up in front of my apartment, saying good-bye, up came the Fiat. "Start writing, Teddy," Norman said. "I'll take the gremlins with me. I'll call you . . . Good luck!" he shot back as the two cars raced down the hill.

The next afternoon at four o'clock exactly, I entered the Rome office of the *Herald Tribune* with my first article. Allen read my copy, his face completely expressionless. When he finished reading, he suddenly broke into a wide smile and said, "Damn good, Teddy. You're hired."

"Oh thank you, Allen, and bless you for saving my life."

In addition to news gathering for my articles, I continued to study faithfully with Moreschi, whose students had by this time dwindled down to a very few. His great Greek tenor had to leave when Mussolini declared war on Greece. Only Ethi; Signora Delphi Valiani, a beautiful Italian woman whose husband owned the restaurant in the Roma Termini, the city's main train station; Assia de Busny, a Hungarian movie star; and myself remained. The war had robbed Moreschi of his livelihood, and he was suffering, as were all the artists, painters, and scholars, for Rome was empty of gaiety, the people disheartened, and there were no foreigners who wished to study or to buy. All that was left was the daily sickening infiltration of the Nazis, who virtually took over the Italian government—their secret police everywhere.

Foreigners were not allowed to visit the seaside. As gasoline became rationed, only those of us who were close to the diplomatic corps could drive. The only way I could go swimming was to take the train to Ostia. But with all of this, on weekends, Moreschi and his little band of students made happy trips to Fregene and Frascati, where we had picnics and sang, before we returned to sad, empty, blacked-out Rome. Bit by bit, even the museums were closing, and there was no more open-air opera at the Baths of Caracalla. Our only contact with the evening glamour of Rome was our visits to see the moonlight shining on the Coliseum, and carriage rides through the Borghese gardens.

The deterioration of the standard of living, the shortages of coal, the rationing of spaghetti, olive oil, rice, and milk made life very hard for the women in Rome. Every day they waited in long lines to buy the day's food. Tensions ran high, and inevitably arguments would spring up between those who were able to buy certain foods and those who were not, ending many times in pushing and shoving. There was always a

policeman near the line, watching, and his presence seemed to add to their frustration. I was amazed that my maid, Maria, had no trouble getting food for us.

"Maria, how is it that you can get food for us when everyone else is struggling?" I asked.

"Oh, signorina," she replied, "I just tell them that my signorina is in a *situazione estraordinario*."

"Which means I'm pregnant. Maria, how long have you been telling them that?"

"Oh, ever since I work for you, I tell them that."

"Maria, you've been working for me for over a year. And, besides, I'm a signora. What do they say when you tell them that?"

"They say, *'Bravo.'* They hope it's a boy."

"But, Maria, how long can you keep on telling them this story?"

"Oh, I tell them this till the end of the war."

My main daytime activity, in addition to writing about how women fared in Italy under the austerity, was to climb the flights of creaking stairs to the *Herald Tribune* office. There, over a small radio that Allen had set up for me, I'd listen to foreign radio broadcasts and gather news for him. I'd nearly reached my limit under this restricted routine. But one day, all of my frustration was replaced with enthusiasm, hope, and gratitude, when Allen took me up to the American Embassy and brought me in to see the consul.

"Mr. Cole," he said, "this is Teddy Lynch Getty. She is an accredited newspaper correspondent with the *New York Herald Tribune*, and I would like her passport changed from 'Student' to 'Journalist.'" Immediately, Mr. Cole issued my revised passport.

This was my passport to freedom. Soon, I could go home. To cel-

ebrate, I took Allen to lunch at the Casina Valadier in the Borghese gardens, and to our surprise, we discovered that rationing had found its way even into this elegant restaurant. We could have fish or meat. Not both. Personally, I was so grateful about my new passport, I didn't care whether it was fish *or* meat. I was just plain happy.

CHAPTER 20

KOSTYA

It was at this time that Ethi, the lovely coloratura from Salzburg, was asked to report to the Questura, then a branch of the military police associated with Immigration. Now Mrs. Rodney Jennings, married by proxy to an Englishman, Ethi found herself in a difficult situation. She was an English citizen in enemy country, in dread of being put in a concentration camp for the duration of the war. I offered to drive her to the police station. Signor Arguesci, the head of Rome's police, was very busy that afternoon, and we were detained for hours in the waiting room. Suddenly, we became aware of a very handsome young man sitting in the corner, smiling as he listened to Ethi complain bitterly in English. *"Mein Gott,"* she said, "look what I've done. Now that I am Rodney's wife, I cannot go to him, nor can I sing here, for I am now the enemy."

"May I interrupt, fräulein?" said the young man in perfect German, as he walked over to where we were sitting. Ethi broke into one of her most beguiling smiles and delightedly recounted her whole sad

story in her native tongue to this willing listener. Then she presented me.

"Who are you, and where are you from?" I asked.

"My name is Kostya Berispek. I am a Turkish citizen, and you, you are an American, yes?" He smiled. "Are you studying singing, too?" I nodded.

"Well, when may I have the pleasure of hearing you divas sing?"

"You may come to our maestro's studio this afternoon, if you wish," Ethi cut in. "We'll be there at five thirty." And, at that moment, she was called into Arguesci's office.

"Teddy," he started, "that's a boy's name, no?"

"Yes and no," I began to explain. "It's my nickname."

"Oh, like me—Kostya for Constantine."

"Yes, but Constantine isn't a Turkish name, is it?"

"No," he said, "it's Russian. My father was Russian and my mother Turkish. My real name is Constantine, Constantinovitch Prokofieff. My father died in the Revolution. He was the captain of the czar's guards. My mother brought me up in Turkey and then, when I graduated from university, I went to live in Hungary. I have my own home there, in Budapest. Have you ever been to Budapest?" I shook my head. "No? Well, you will come one day, and you will love it."

"I'm sure," I replied, wondering what made him think that. His eyes twinkled as though they held a secret. They were brown, and so was his hair, which was darker and slicked back, very European. He had a great smile. He was tall, taller than I. I asked him where he had learned to speak English and he answered quite casually, "At school. I speak six languages fluently and understand two others."

"Really?" I figured that was one more than Paul. "And is that helpful in business?"

"Definitely. You see, I am in the export-import business. But, please, Teddy, may I not come to your maestro's home to hear you girls sing this afternoon?"

"Yes. Call us there, and we'll ask him. Here is his number: Roma 582211."

Precisely at that moment, Ethi reappeared, happy that Signor Arguesci was going to allow her to live freely in Rome, as long as she reported to him once a month.

Overjoyed, we said good-bye to Kostya, ran out of the Questura, jumped into my car, and raced off to get lunch. Ethi looked back and said, "*Mein Gott*, Teddy, that Kostya is *so* handsome. And do you know, all the time he and I were talking, he was looking at you."

"That's ridiculous, Ethi," I replied. But it was nice to hear. It had been so long since anyone had looked at me.

We were in the middle of the second act of *La Bohème* when the telephone in the hall rang. The maid poked her head in the door and said, "*Scusi, Maestro, c'è qualcuno chi vuol parlare con la signorina americana.*"

Ethi was in the middle of singing "Musetta's Waltz." When she finished, I went to the phone. It was Kostya. I asked Moreschi to speak with him, and Moreschi invited him over.

He appeared in minutes at the front door. We decided he must have phoned from the corner café. Ethi and I then sang our arias, and he listened, applauded, and complimented us. Moreschi, too. Then Kostya very gallantly invited everyone to dine with him at the Taberna Ulpia, one of the most glamorous restaurants still operating in Rome.

After descending stairs carved out of rock, we found ourselves in the subterranean ruins of ancient Rome, which had been transformed into a

gorgeous dining room. It was a magical evening, and we all sang in the carriage going home.

I didn't plan for Kostya to become such an important part of my life. It just happened. I was heading home after my lesson late the next afternoon. It was getting dark. Kostya had asked me to meet him for a drink at a little bistro near my apartment. Suddenly, the sirens started to wail. Air raid wardens swarmed the streets, forcing people into the shelters. I didn't want to spend time or die in some underground with strangers, so I started running down the center of the corso in an attempt to reach the bistro. I could hear the planes as they roared overhead and saw the bursts of antiaircraft fire, but I kept running through the screaming crowds and clouds of ash till I saw the door of the bistro.

I dashed through it, straight into the arms of Kostya, so scared and so grateful that I just hung on to him. I didn't want to let go. We stood there, his arms around me, for a long, long time. When the sirens stopped and the raid was over, I looked up at him and he kissed me.

It was so good to be held and kissed. I'd almost forgotten what it was like, and I kissed him back. I was so glad to be alive. I could still hear the planes as they roared away, the screaming people, the flashes of antiaircraft fire. All at once, the war became very real for me. The thought that at any second I might just be blown up, that life might end, made the moment I knew I was still living seem so precious, even if it was in the arms of a stranger.

I became aware of those around us, children crying, men swearing, everyone very conscious that for this night, at least, we were the lucky ones. I couldn't stop trembling, so Kostya pulled me over to the bar, where he ordered brandies. I drank mine in a hurry, but it didn't have as

good of an effect as having his arms around me, which felt like being in the arms of a great big bear, but a handsome one with a beautiful mouth. And what an entrancing smile he had. But right now he looked anxious. Was he afraid the planes might return? I knew I was.

We moved to the door. It was dark outside, the streets filled with ash and smoke. People were tripping over each other as they hurried along to their homes. Kostya took my hand and we made our way through the crowd and up the Janiculum Hill to my apartment, climbing the six flights of stairs to my little penthouse. I opened the door, but there was no electricity, so I found some candles. Then, starving, we raided the icebox for whatever Maria had left for my supper: cold chicken, salad, grapes—and a bottle of Frascati that Kostya found hanging off a nail in the kitchen.

We tried calling Moreschi and Ethi, but all the phones were dead. We walked out onto the terrace, where the night sky, devoid of moon or stars, showed from time to time flashes of far away antiaircraft fire, way beyond the mountain range, southward toward Naples.

Below, the city of Rome seemed quiet, except for an occasional whistle or cry of *"luce,"* when someone's lights could be seen. Even in the dark, we could make out the Tiber river, as it wound its way through the city and down to Ostia, Anzio, and the sea.

Candlelight showed faintly through my windows and, not wanting an air raid warden to fine me, we went inside and let down the wooden shutters. It was cold and damp. I went into my bedroom for a blanket. Kostya followed and, like it was the most normal thing to do, we lay down on the bed, pulled the blanket up around us, and held each other for I don't know how long. Still scared the French might come back again, that we might really be hit and die, I shuddered. But when

Kostya kissed me, this time I responded as passionately as he, and found myself wanting to make love with him. To defy death in this terror of war. To belong, no matter what and in that moment, you just need to make love. And we did. I shall never forget the peace it brought me. I was no longer afraid.

And thus began the most passionate relationship I ever had. Absolutely wrong, I know, for I was married to a wonderful man, whom I loved and longed to be with, but hadn't seen for more than a year. A man who believed in me, in my talent, who had given me such a wonderful opportunity to study, who made exquisite love to me . . . but not like this.

I shouldn't have, but I fell under the spell of this young Russian-Turkish boy, who was only a few years older than I, and who, in the next few weeks, absolutely convinced me that we were made for each other, to be together forever. And when I was with him, I believed it, too.

"If Paul loved you, as I do," Kostya would say, pacing up and down, "he'd be here to take you back to America. Divorce him, Teddy. Marry me and come with me to Budapest. Please, I can take care of you."

"Kostya, I can't. I have a job. Anyway, I don't need to be taken care of. I'm a singer. I want to sing."

"Then *I* go to America and see your Paul. He must give you up."

"I think he already has, for the way I've acted, but, no, Kostya, I'm the one who must go back to America and see Paul." I looked at Kostya. "I was hurt by him, but I'm not anymore. Paul's just not like me. We're different, but he's a wonderful man."

"I'm sure he is," interrupted Kostya. "Still, he doesn't love you the way I do. Remember the first day we met?"

"You mean at the police station?"

"Yes. I felt from the first moment that you were the girl meant for me, and now . . . now I know it."

I smiled. "How strange, Kostya."

"What is?"

"I felt the way you looked at me, when you looked into my eyes, like we'd known each other somewhere before. That we were meant to meet again."

"You did?"

I nodded.

"Well," he added, "now that we have, how can you even think of leaving me? We were meant to be together, Teddy. This I know. You may be married to Paul, but you belong to me. It's my heart that speaks."

We were having a *caffè* with Moreschi. I had just finished my lesson, and Kostya had come for me. He was very excited about news he had just received from the head of the Budapest Symphony Hall. They were interested in the concert Moreschi and Somma had offered them, which meant that Ethi and I would be part of a group of artists going to Budapest within a few weeks. I couldn't believe that, in this time of war, there would be an interchange of artists between these two countries, but Ethi and I were overjoyed at the possibility. When she left the studio to tell Moreschi's wife the news, Kostya turned to Moreschi and asked, "Maestro, tell me, is Ethi Jewish, by any chance?"

"No, she is pure Austrian, why?"

"Well, she could be, and that might make a difference in her going to Budapest. I don't think they would accept her. She might even be in danger."

"But she is now an English citizen," I said. "I was there when she gave up her German passport. In fact, I'll never forget the look on that consul's face when she threw it on the floor at his feet."

"Let me go and speak with her," Moreschi said.

When he left, I looked at Kostya. "Do you remember you said to me not so long ago, 'I love you, Teddy. It is my heart that speaks'?" He nodded. "Well, what would your heart say now . . . if it knew that the girl you loved was part Jewish?"

"Are you serious, Teddy?" He looked shocked, dismayed.

"Very serious."

"You never spoke of this before."

"You never asked."

For a moment, he couldn't speak. Then, almost choking, he said, "I would say to this girl, 'I'm leaving.'" He picked up his hat and coat and started for the door. "And, if for some reason I don't come back in time to pick her up for supper, it means—" He broke off. "You see . . ." He looked at me with tears in his eyes. "I was brought up to hate Jews. So this is the worst, the most disturbing problem my heart has ever had to face in its life." And with that, he left.

I stood there beside the piano, not believing that this was happening. I just wanted to die. Why, I asked myself, do people hate each other because of their blood or color of skin? When did this start, and why can't it be stopped? My mother claimed I wasn't a Jew, because she wasn't. She believed this to be true, but then, why did she never allow us to mention the Lytton family? Was it because, if she had, her friends in Greenwich would have thought less of her? Was it that she couldn't have bought the house in Belle Haven, because no Jews were allowed to buy there? I always wondered who these other people were, whose opinions

were so important that they could decide who could or could not live in their community. They weren't better people, or wiser people, or more devoted to God than we. I never was told why I was supposed to hide this side of my family. It made me sad and diminished my self-esteem, because I knew in my heart that I was as much a child of God as everyone else in the world. I thought of Paul's words: *"I'm proud to be marrying the granddaughter of Henry Charles Lytton."* It was Grandfather's qualities Paul admired, not his blood. Many times Paul would say, *"Remember, Teddy, before God we are all equal."*

Maybe Paul thought he was smarter than most people, and he proved it by working harder than most, but he never *ever* made religion or blood a reason for hating people as Hitler did. When I finally returned to America, I was astonished to hear that some people thought Paul was a Nazi sympathizer. He wasn't. How could he be? He married *me*!

Then I thought of what Kostya had said: *"I was brought up to hate Jews."* What a terrible upbringing, to be taught to hate. And that was what was happening all over the world. *You're one of them, Kostya,* I thought to myself, *and you don't even know it.*

I stopped, for Moreschi had come back into the room, shaking his head. "No, Ethi is not Jewish, Teddy, but my asking brought her to tears, for her best friend, Edie von Portheim, in Salzburg, was tortured and murdered . . . *Poveretta*," he muttered.

Then, sitting down at the piano, he started to play the introduction to the aria "Pace, pace, mio Dio" from the opera *La forza del destino.* Turning to me, he said, *"Andiamo alla battaglia con la musica, Cara."*

As the thrilling introduction of the aria began, I took a breath and started to sing. It was almost like a prayer for the world to stop hating, and though I didn't realize it, I no longer thought of just Kostya alone,

but of those who would die in this ghastly war of hate. It was as though Moreschi and I were attempting to dissolve Hate with Love. Suddenly, I became aware that Kostya had come back into the room and was now standing beside me.

As the aria came to a dramatic end, there was a moment of silence. Then the kitchen door burst open and Ethi and the signora rushed in, applauding wildly. Kostya, leaning down, whispered, "Forgive the fool I've been for even recalling words of hate I was taught as a child. I love you, Teddy, now and forever. You are my love, my soul mate." Then he kissed me tenderly, and I realized everyone was staring at us.

Ethi broke the silence with "Bravo, Teddy. See what your voice has done to this young man? Just wait till the world hears you."

And with that they all applauded. I smiled, but I wanted to cry.

CHAPTER 21

THE RIGHT TO GO HOME

Rome in November can be very cold and damp. As the days grew shorter, I'd awaken to find it still very dark outside. Kostya had received word that his mother was ill and he had been called back to Ankara. I had been with him the night he left by train and, though he promised that nothing could keep him from returning to me, I had a premonition that we'd never meet again. It had been eight days since I had stood on the station platform and watched as the train pulled away. With no word from him since, I'd lie in bed alone and wait for the sun to rise beyond the mountains and flood my terrace with its blessed warmth.

One morning very early, the phone rang. It was Allen. He told me that he might be leaving at any minute. He was waiting for orders. Someone would take his place. I was to keep writing and, above all, "Don't be afraid, Teddy," he said. "No matter what happens, you are protected."

I had no sooner hung up than the phone rang again. It was the Maestro. "Something wonderful has happened," he said excitedly. Moreschi

had arranged for me to sing over the shortwave radio to America the following week and, thanks to Allen and the *Herald Tribune*, I was able to get word to my family and Paul, which made me very happy.

The day of the broadcast, I was told to be at the studio at 3:30 A.M. for rehearsal. Moreschi himself would be my accompanist. The show would start at 4 A.M. My excitement couldn't be dampened even by the possibility that this broadcast may have been the Italian government's attempt to lull America's shortwave listeners into complacency. Paul might be listening and, even though I would not be able to speak to him, I could at least reach out to him through song. Hopefully, he might just think I had improved.

As the minute hand moved toward the hour of four, the red light suddenly went on. "Hello, America, this is Rome, Italy," the announcer began. "And tonight we proudly present the lovely singer Miss Teddy Lynch, from the famous Stork Club in New York. She will sing for you the aria 'O mio babbino caro' from Puccini's *Gianni Schicchi*, and 'Pace, pace, mio Dio' from Verdi's *La Forza del Destino*." Then, with great verve, Moreschi thundered into the opening overture, and suddenly I was on. I sang from my heart, and I knew I did my best.

The next morning, Allen called. "You were great," he said. "Come on over to the office, I'm trying to get a call through to Paul in California." I was astonished. I threw on my clothes and ran all the way across Rome to be there if the call really went through.

And it did! Hearing Paul's voice say, "Hello . . . is that you, Teddy? Darling . . . you were marvelous!" made me want to cry.

"Hi," I said, nearly in tears, "I'm so glad."

"Guess who was with me?" He went on . . . "Maria Jeritza, the great Tosca, and her husband, Winnie Sheehan, the Hollywood producer. They'd invited me to dine with them. About a half hour before your

broadcast, we went out to my car and turned on the shortwave band, but there wasn't enough power. So Sheehan said, 'Let's dash over to my studio and get an engineer to turn on the shortwave set there!' We got there just in time to hear the announcer say, 'Hello, America.' I didn't listen to anything else he said, just waited breathlessly until you sang your first tone. It was truly beautiful, darling, I'm so—"

Suddenly, there was a click and the phone went dead. Complete silence. I looked up at Allen. He just smiled and said, "This is war, Teddy."

"I know," I answered, "but he heard me." Years later, I found a recording of that shortwave broadcast.

Hans Hasl, the handsome young Austrian pianist I'd met at Madame Cahier's, often came to my little apartment to accompany me when I needed to rehearse my roles. Exactly one week after the broadcast, while we were working on the opera *Otello*, there was heavy knocking on the door. Maria opened it, and there stood two scowling members of the Gestapo. They pushed past me and walked up to Hans, demanding his passport.

"You have no right here," I said. "This is the home of an American."

"We are Germans," the heavier of the two said. He wore the uniform of an SS officer. "We have jurisdiction everywhere."

"But not over me," I said, placing myself between them and Hans.

The heavyset officer, who was also the oldest, stared at me. I felt his hate and contempt for everything American in his voice as he screamed, "Hans Hasl, get to your feet!" Hans, a musician, was still an able-bodied Austrian male, which meant he was supposed to be in the army of the Third Reich.

I stood between them. "You can't do this. We are in the middle of an aria. This man is a great musician, and I am a singer."

"All right, Miss America. If you are a singer . . . then *sing*!"

I put a hand on Hans's shoulder and he sat down and began, knowing that it would be the last time. I sang with defiance, but with joy at my own freedom—with joy at being an American.

When it was over, the officers were silent. I felt I had never sung better in my whole life, nor had Hans played with greater feeling. Suddenly, the younger officer applauded. The older one demanded that Hans go with them. I started to protest again, but Hans whispered, "Don't interfere, Teddy. You'll get in trouble. This is my problem." They took him away.

Late that same night, after Maria had gone home, I thought I heard a light knocking at the door. Petrified that it might be the two Germans returning, I slipped on my robe and, as silently as I could, made my way to the kitchen. Pulling the blind aside, I could see in the half dark a tall man in the brown robe of a monk standing there. He was carrying a sack of something. Again he knocked. I remained still. Then I watched as he slipped a piece of paper under the door and, turning quietly, went down the stairs, carrying the sack with him.

It was a letter, dated December 1, 1941, and it was from Kostya. I could hardly wait to open it . . . almost tore it in my haste. He wrote that he was sending me sugar and soap and candy. That he had asked this monk to bring it to me. That he loved me, but he couldn't come back to Rome. They had taken away his papers. *What papers?* I didn't understand. He was in Ankara with his mother.

> . . . *but you . . . my love . . . you must leave Italy at once. I fear for your safety. Please, I want you so much to come to me here, but if you can't, you must go home and I shall come to you. Only right now . . . take care.*
>
> *Kostya.*

P.S. If by chance something should happen to me . . . remember
YOU are my LOVE . . . Now and Forever.

Clutching the letter, I ran back to my bedroom, jumped into bed, pulled the covers up, and started to cry. I was scared for Kostya, and I was suddenly very scared for myself.

Early that morning, I quickly dressed and ran down to the office, where I found a rather nervous Allen packing his notes and preparing to leave on his new assignment in Africa. No one was coming to replace him. He confided that he had gotten his exit permit, and he advised me to get mine, also visas for both Portugal and Spain. I went immediately to the immigration office, but was told that all issuances of exit permits for Americans had temporarily ceased.

The next days, waiting for the embargo on American exit visas to be lifted, were terrifying. Rome was chaotic. I went to sleep afraid and awakened with the same fear. I dreaded turning on the radio to listen to the news, but I equally dreaded missing the news if I didn't turn it on.

I awoke early on the morning of Monday, December 8, turned on my shortwave radio, and heard President Franklin Delano Roosevelt speaking these words:

Yesterday, December seventh, 1941—a date which will live in infamy—the United States of America was suddenly and deliberately attacked by naval and air forces of the Empire of Japan . . . With confidence in our armed forces—with the unbounding determination of our People—we will gain the inevitable triumph—so help us God. I ask that the Congress declare that since the unpro-

voked and dastardly attack by Japan on Sunday, December seventh, 1941, a state of War has existed between the United States and the Japanese empire.

I was in shock. America was at war. I was afraid for my country, and afraid for Paul and my family, who were living in California. I visualized the Japanese pouring onto the beach at Santa Monica. I wanted to be there to help, but here I was all alone in an Axis country about to be at war with the United States, and I had to get to the American Embassy at once.

As I approached the grounds of the embassy, I could see it was jammed with excited Americans wanting to know what to do. I could see them inside the entrance. I was stopped by a member of the consulate.

"What do you want?" he said.

"I want to see the consul, please."

"Who are you?"

I wasn't listening. All I could think of was what our president had just said. "I'm an American," I said, showing him my passport.

He looked at it. "What's your name?"

"Teddy Lynch Getty."

"I don't know you," he answered, still barring the way.

"I don't know you, either. That isn't important. I'm an American and I want to speak to the consul *right now*."

I walked past him into the building. He looked after me, shaking his head. The hallways were a chaos of people, who, like me, were in a panic, anxious to be helped. I ran up the steps and literally bolted into Mr. Cole's private office. He looked up quickly, and in a curt voice said, "Yes?"

"I'm Teddy Lynch Getty. Remember me, Mr. Cole? Allen Raymond introduced us."

He looked up again, poised his head at an arrogant angle, and looked down at me with inexcusable haughtiness. "What do you want?"

"I want to go home."

"We told all Americans to go home months ago," he said with contempt.

"That's what I've been trying to do," I replied, "but my exit permits have been denied. Mr. Cole, I'm here today to present my press credentials, and to be sure that my name is on your list of accredited newspaper correspondents. Since my former chief, Allen Raymond, left Italy this past week, I'm the only remaining staff member of the *New York Herald Tribune* in Rome. Please, Mr. Cole, I must know—am I on your list?"

"I don't know," he mused deliberately. "I don't know whether you are or not."

"But I *have* to be on that list." I took out my passport. "Here. Look at it. You issued it to me. It has your name on it. See, it reads 'Correspondent.' To be on the list of American accredited correspondents is my only hope of getting home."

"Well, I'll look into the matter." The finality in his voice indicated he wanted to terminate our meeting.

"But, Mr. Cole, if you don't put me on that list, the Italian Foreign Ministry will consider me suspect. Here is the letter, which Allen Raymond wrote to Ambassador Rocco of the Ministry of Popular Culture. In fact, he wrote it the day you issued my journalistic passport."

"As I said before, Mrs. Getty, I will look into the matter." He turned away, and it was obvious that our interview was over.

I didn't know why Mr. Cole was being so evasive, and acting so un-American in denying me help, or at least hope.

I spent the next two days packing and listening to the radio. On the night of December 10, Berlin broadcast that Hitler would make an important announcement to the Reichstag the next day at three.

The morning of December 11, 1941, I was awakened by the telephone. It was Norman Fiske. "Teddy," he shouted, "get out of Italy."

"I can't," I shouted back.

"Then come here," he said.

A half hour later, I arrived at the Grand Hotel. I went to Norman's apartment, tried his door, it was open. I found myself in his living room.

"Norman, where are you?" I cried.

"I'm here in the bathroom," he shouted. "Taking what may be my last bath." He came out, wrapped in a huge white towel, looking like a Roman emperor in a toga. He walked around nervously, grabbed a cigarette, picked up a revolver from his desk, and checked that it was loaded. Then he stopped and looked at me. "Teddy, what's happening with you?"

"I'm about to be thrown to the wolves by Mr. Cole," I replied. "Please, can you help me?" I was near tears.

"Cole is a bastard," he said. "I'll take care of him."

I was about to go when Norman said, "Do you have any money?"

"No."

He searched the top of his bureau. Stretching out his hand, he gave me twenty thousand lire. "Here, take this. Now go home, and don't worry."

Walking out of the hotel, I saw a mob heading for the Piazza Vene-

zia. One man yelled to me, "Come on, Il Duce is making an important speech." I was swept up by the crowd heading for the square, which was already filled with thousands of students. I stood directly beneath the famous balcony, as the French doors of the Palazzo Venezia suddenly opened and Mussolini stepped out. His short, heavy body was covered by his familiar black tunic. His gray breeches were held in place by a black leather belt, and he had on tall black leather boots. He scowled at the crowd from under his black cap, with its golden eagle emblem of the Roman Empire. Two others moved out next to him. One man wore the navy blue of Hitler's civil service. The other was a Japanese man dressed in a frock coat and silk hat. Mussolini flung his hand into the sky and then spoke into microphones that carried his voice throughout the world: "Italy is now on the side of the heroic Japanese against the United States of America." He continued on about something to do with the united front, but I didn't wait to hear. My only thought was to get back to the American Embassy.

I ran most of the way, and somehow managed to break through the circle of police surrounding the embassy and get inside. Everything was chaotic. There was the smell of smoke, apparently from the burning of documents in various offices. I ran up to Mr. Cole's office. The door was open. He was talking excitedly to his staff. It was obvious that the office was being dismantled. I know he saw me as I stood in the doorway, but he completely ignored me.

I cried out, "Mr. Cole, am I on that list?"

Looking at me as if he had never seen me before, he said, "Not yet."

I hurried out and ran right into Mrs. Wadsworth, wife of our chargé d'affaires, whom I recognized, but who didn't know Paul or me. "Mrs. Wadsworth, I need your help."

———

"Who, may I ask, are you?" she said airily.

"I'm an American, Mrs. Wadsworth. My name is Teddy Lynch Getty. I'm a singer, and I work for the *New York Herald Tribune*."

"What are you doing in Rome?" she managed, as if about to swoon with the nuisance of having to address a mere nobody. But how could I expect her to know me? I had made no effort to join her local social register, even though I was in the one back home.

I ignored her attitude. "Mrs. Wadsworth, Rome is the seat of art and music, where for centuries musicians and artists from all over the world have come to study."

"And do *you* really expect to go home with us?" Her hand swept the room to take in the elite, whom it appeared had her royal blessing.

"I most certainly do," I said.

I tried to sound confident, but inwardly I was heartsick. It was all so un-American. Right here in my own American Embassy, Mr. Cole and now Mrs. Wadsworth acted as if I didn't have the right to go home.

I cry at parades. I stand for our national anthem. My ancestors fought in wars against the French and the British to free our country. I felt one hundred percent American, and I had always been proud that I was. But that day I was ashamed of what a few people who represented my country were doing. *God help all those other poor besieged Americans*, I thought as I hurriedly swept out to fight my own battle.

Paul had read that only accredited journalists would be immediately returned, along with diplomats. In New York, Ware was getting assurance from the powers that be at the *Herald Tribune* that I would be among those listed as their accredited representatives.

I ran up the steps to the office of Herbert Matthews, chief of the *New York Times*. He was alone, sorting out the last of his papers. He seemed

surprised to see me. I told him about my meetings with Mr. Cole, and the experience I'd just had with Mrs. Wadsworth. He was very annoyed with Cole, and excused Mrs. Wadsworth, saying, "Forgive her . . . She's a bloody bore. I'll speak to Mr. Wadsworth. And I'll do everything I can to get your name on the list. Now, go home, and I'll be in touch."

I went to my maestro's studio. I asked him if he could reach someone, anyone he might know in the Swiss legation, so that I could get word to Paul of my insane predicament. He said he would try, then added, "Teddy, you know Monsignor O'Flaherty at the Vatican. Call him."

So I did. "Help me, monsignor, if you can." He promised he would speak with the Wadsworths, with whom he played bridge almost every night.

A few minutes later, Maria called. "Signorina, there are two men waiting here for you." She was in a panic.

"Are they Germans?" I asked.

"Only one."

"Give them some coffee, and tell them I'm coming home now."

"*Va bene,*" she said, and hung up.

CHAPTER 22

LA MANTELLATE

After many kisses and blessings from the Moreschi family, I left. When I reached the street, I was immediately surrounded by the twenty or more little boys and girls who formed my clique. They clung to me and wouldn't let go. I bought them all caramels and hot chocolate at the corner café, then started for my apartment.

Two men dressed in black were waiting for me as I walked into my living room. One was German, the other Italian. I excused myself and went into my bedroom.

"We must take you to the Questura," the Italian called after me.

I closed the door. Maria came in. "If you have anything to hide, give it to me," she whispered.

"Maria, I don't have anything to hide, I love Italy. Where are they taking me?"

"All I can say is, wear your warmest clothes." Her manner told me she didn't think I'd be back soon. She had wormed that much out of them.

I put on a wool dress, threw on my polo coat with its pullover hood, warm socks, and low brogues, grabbed the score of Verdi's *Otello* for something to study, and kissed her good-bye.

Outside, I was ushered into a big black Mercedes. I sat silently between the men as we drove swiftly through the darkened city.

"Where are you taking me?" I finally asked.

"To the police station. We want to question you," the Italian said. "It's routine."

We drove through the dark streets and came to a screeching halt at the entrance of the Rome police station. I was taken inside and ordered to sit down on a bench. The two men disappeared into a room so close by I could hear them talking to a third man.

"What shall we do with her?" one asked.

Two hours later, they came out. "Because of the late hour, we will take you to a nunnery for the night."

In the same Mercedes, we drove wildly through the narrow streets of the city to a huge building bordering the Tiber river. Once inside, I was searched. The guards who worked there took my passport, rings, watch, and anything they said I might use to commit suicide. I was then turned over to some nuns, who led me through a series of dark chambers to the underground beneath the Tiber. One nun walked ahead, the other behind, locking closed each door the first had opened with her huge ring of keys. I counted eight clanking doors. I felt like the Count of Monte Cristo, being put away for life.

Finally, we entered a huge subterranean chamber. Cells lined one side in three tiers. I could hear crying, moaning, and snoring coming from some of the cells. The smell was beyond belief—sweating bodies, foul garbage, refuse, and human excrement. The putrid odors, the

clanging of cell doors, and the rebounding noises closed in around me. When I reached out to steady myself, my hand touched the wall . . . it was wet.

This was not a nunnery, this was Le Mantellate, the women's quarters of the infamous Regina Coeli, an antiquated jail known for its lack of human facilities.

From a dark corner, one of the nuns pulled out a small handful of straw. "You will sleep on this," she said. "We have no more cells."

I was glad to be alone, even if I had to lie on the ground without any semblance of privacy. She walked away, and the other nun, carrying a lamp, followed.

I was suddenly in complete darkness. I felt intense fear. I wanted to scream out "You can't do this to me!" but I knew it would be useless. I pulled the hood of my red polo coat over my head, and lay down on the filthy straw. The cement floor was so cold and damp that it seemed to penetrate my entire body. And although I thanked God that Maria had told me to put on heavy clothing, I was so frozen with fear that I may as well have been wearing a chiffon negligee.

I closed my eyes, trying to blot out the whole scene. I put my hands over my ears, because I couldn't stand the moaning, the snoring, and the intermittent cries of children, not to mention the combined putrid odors. I felt water running down my cheeks and quickly put my hands to my face. They were my tears. "You mustn't cry," I told myself, but I couldn't stop. Then I remembered a promise I'd made to myself, that if faced with great danger, I would turn to God. "Well, Teddy, you're in great danger. It's time to keep your promise."

I began thinking of some of the things I had learned in Sunday school, when I was a little girl. Immediately, I felt better. I knew I was not

alone, not abandoned. I knew there would be an answer. I didn't have to know what it was—I had only to trust God. I guess I must have dozed off, because suddenly I was wide awake. I hadn't really slept, just drifted off . . . but for how long?

I realized that in my dreams I had been rehearsing the words of Italy's last propaganda broadcast before being taken to the police station. It was repeating itself over and over. *"The entire U.S. Pacific Fleet has been sunk. The way is now open for the Japanese to land in Los Angeles, Seattle . . ."*

I turned toward the wall and could feel the damp wet oozing down. I wondered how far below the level of the Tiber we were. Suddenly, the jailers banged on the cell bars. It was 5 A.M., and every cell in every tier was flung open. The inmates began staggering out. None of them looked like people I had ever seen before. They slowly walked toward the open area where I was standing. One young woman stood out among the rest. She was taller, pretty, and wore what I recognized as a Carlin dressing robe.

In perfect English she asked, "What are you doing here?"

"I'm an American," I said. "Italy has declared war on my country."

She was shocked. A nun who saw us speaking came quickly over and herded us to five o'clock Mass. As we walked along, the woman whispered, "I'm the nurse to Princess Pallavicini's children. I'm Irish. Maybe that's why they imprisoned me."

"Shush," the nun said. "Talking is forbidden." She guided us toward the chapel.

After Mass, we were herded into a line and served black bread and a bitter coffee called *orzo* (burnt barley). I was then put in a cell with four other women. One was a Nazi agent, seemingly too unimportant for her government to bother releasing her; another was an Austrian Jewess,

imprisoned for her failure to declare jewelry as she left her country; the third was a young Italian girl, who was serving the eighth month of a life sentence for attempting to steal food during a blackout; and the fourth, an abortionist.

At the end of the week, I asked if I could take a bath. Like the other women, I had been using the hole in the floor at the end of the corridor as a toilet, with other prisoners looking on. I was desperate for some privacy. One of the nuns gained permission for me to go up to the top floor of the prison, to the infirmary, a huge room with an antiquated bathtub standing in the center. The nun handed me a bar of yellow soap (the kind we used for cleaning floors back home) and a large worn towel. "Put your clothes in the outer room," she said. "I'll come back later and meet you there." I bathed, wrapped myself in the towel, and came out to find that someone had stolen my slip.

During the first few days, I hadn't eaten any of what they called food, but gave it to the women who were still nursing their babies. About thirty of them had been packed into a cell right across from mine. At mealtime, the women, all holding their babies in their arms, would push and shove their way close to the bars, frantically trying to elbow one another away from the front. Those who made it would hold their bowls out between the bars and yell out to me, *"D'ai a me."* ("Give it to me.") One day, a poor woman, holding her infant in her arms, yelled out, "Give it to me, Signorina, I need it *more*. I have another baby inside."

Each night in our cell, much to our astonishment, the Nazi prisoner disrobed and washed herself completely in the ice-cold water. She was belligerent to us all, but especially to the Austrian girl, who was very frightened. I became deeply concerned about the girl's situation, as she had been seized by the Gestapo when her plane had stopped at the Rome

airport, en route from Salzburg to Montevideo, Uruguay. "I was thrown in jail because I didn't declare an antique gold ring of my grandmother's," she told me. "It has no monetary value, just sentimental. I am so frightened they will kill me."

On the seventh day of my imprisonment at about twelve noon—just after our usual horrible bowl of soup, which by now I *had* to eat to stay alive—the door to our cell opened and the guards walked in. After looking all of us over, they pointed at me and said, *"Le signorina americana e'libertà."*

"Not before I finish my soup," I cried out, holding on to the bowl as if it were the exquisite soup served at 21. I sat there hunched over, gobbling that soup, thinking it might be my last meal on earth, glancing up occasionally to see if I could determine from the guards' facial expressions what they were going to do to me. Was I really to be freed, or was it a trick to take me out and have me shot?

After I'd embraced my cellmates, they led me away. As I walked down the corridor, the cries of fellow prisoners followed me.

"Teddy, don't forget to tell them about me."

"Call Fernando. He will get me out of here," yelled a voluptuous girl named Giovanna. "He is with the opera."

Another, pounding her breast, cried, "They let you out. While a faithful Italian is left to die."

I was taken to the police station and brought before Cavaliera Aguesci, chief of the Rome police—the same man who had allowed Ethi to stay in the city as an enemy alien, as long as she reported to him on a regular basis. Now that seemed like a lifetime ago. He greeted me with a smile and asked, "How do you like our prison, signorina?"

Frightened at what he might decide to do with me, I boldly answered, "Fine, thank you, Excellence. I'll write about it when I get home."

"Until then," he said, "I'm sending you to be with the other American journalists. How's that?"

"Oh, thank you, sir," I managed to say as I was escorted out of his chambers by two officers.

CHAPTER 23

SIENA

It was getting dark as they drove me through Rome, down the Corso Umberto, to a third-rate boardinghouse, the Pensione Suquet, which I believe had once been a brothel.

After climbing six flights of stairs, I was presented to the detectives, who sat in the hallway, guarding the Americans. Once they got all my papers straightened out, the officers left. The detectives opened the door, and I was pushed inside a huge room filled with smoke. There in the half-light I could barely make out the silhouettes of six men sitting around a table. One of them, Reynolds Packard, quickly got up, came to the door, and stared open-mouthed as I stumbled into his arms. "My God!" he yelled. "It's Teddy Lynch!" And with that they surrounded me, firing questions. "How are you?" "Where've you been for the last week?"

Astounded that I had been imprisoned longer than they had, Packard jokingly conceded that I had a better story than theirs. "Not really," I said, hastily telling them all that had happened to me.

Herbert Matthews and Camille Cianfarra of the *New York Times*; Richard Massock of the Associated Press; and Robert Allen-Tuska, Livingston Pomeroy, and their chief, Reynolds Packard, of Rome's United Press . . . these were my cellmates. God love them. They were wonderful to me.

After giving me food and drink, they showed me to a bedroom guarded by a detective, down the hall but close enough to them so that I could yell if attacked. This made me feel safe for the first time since Pearl Harbor. And for the next five days, I felt secure.

Then on the sixth day, at 6 A.M., the head of the police came to see us. We were herded into the main salon and told to get ready to leave for Siena. Everyone but me, that is. Almost immediately they left, and I was alone.

For the next four days I saw nobody, except for a visit from Monsignor Hugh O'Flaherty. I had a cold and was in bed when he came to see me. He told me not to worry, because he was "in touch with Wadsworth." Pulling his chair up close to my bed, he leaned over and whispered, "Kiss me."

Thinking I should kiss his ring, I took his hand and put it to my lips. But he reached over, pulled me roughly to him, and tried to kiss me on the mouth. I pushed him away, frightened and horrified. Then I looked at him, smiled, and said, "The day I'm free, I'll kiss you, monsignor," and he left.

A week later I was taken to my apartment, where I packed my clothes, then taken to board the night train for Siena with a police guard. When we arrived just before midnight, the town was blacked-out, quiet. We drove to the police station, but the chief was not there. It was December 31, 1941. Finally, after calling all over town, they located the chief in bed with his girlfriend, and asked him to come to the jail.

He arrived within the hour, furious and swearing at everyone. "Rome wants you to put her with the other Americans," the guard said.

The chief picked up a pen from his desk and threw it at the guard, piercing his hand, and screamed, "Rome cannot dictate what I do! This is Siena, idiot. I'll decide what to do with her. Meanwhile, put her in a cell."

This brought me to my feet. I went to the chief. "Please, Excellence," I pleaded through tears I could not control, "please let me go with the other Americans." Seeing my tears, he finally consented. In minutes, Reynolds Packard was called. Under police escort, he took me to the Excelsior Hotel, where I was reunited with the other American war correspondents.

I was given a key to a bedroom on the second floor, next to a large room that we used as a clubroom. We dubbed it the Club Suquet, where we'd start fires in the fireplace, play bridge, read, or sit around and talk about the war, our families, and home. Down the hall were the bedrooms of the other journalists. Everyone chipped in on wine and tortellini, but I bought the chocolates. We ate fairly well.

On the third day we were called before the chief of police and told that we stayed up too late disturbing other guests. I was accused of wearing slacks in the hotel, which was against the law in Italy for women at that time. Two in the group were accused of "smoking pipes in the hotel lobby in an arrogant manner."

Months went by, and the uncertainty of when we would be allowed to leave caused a terrific strain. My situation was the worst, since no one knew whether or not I was to be included on the diplomatic train with my fellow journalists. In February 1942, I wrote Mr. Wadsworth to have someone get in touch with my husband, brother, and the *New York Her-*

ald Tribune to reassure me I was on the list. He never replied. It wasn't till late April that I was told I'd be included.

On May 3, all of us were transferred from Siena to Rome in an already overcrowded train. It only stopped at one station, where a whole brigade of German soldiers rushed aboard. Running madly down the aisles, they smashed everything as they stormed by. I cried as they crushed a cage of birds I'd been keeping, killing them.

Arriving in Rome, we were put up in the Grand Hotel until the morning of May 13, when we left the city with the embassy staff, aboard the last diplomatic train for Portugal. In Portugal we were to be exchanged for Nazi and Fascist diplomats and journalists being returned from America.

As I stepped onto the train, a very tall, attractive Army captain walked up to me and handed me two packets wrapped in blue and pink ribbons. I immediately recognized them as letters from Paul and Kostya, which the police had taken from my apartment six months earlier, the night they put me in jail. Smiling he said, *"Buon viaggio, signorina."* Then, lowering his voice he whispered, "Confidentially, which one do you really love?"

I looked up at him and smiled. "Capitano," I replied. *"You,* an Italian, asking me? Why, I love them both, of course!"

Our diplomatic train traveled through a very dismal, unoccupied France and Spain, finally stopping at Portbou, Spain, where we pulled down our windows and tossed all our bread out to the hungry little children below. When we finally arrived at Estoril, Portugal, by the sea, we were all put up at a hotel. There was a cable waiting for me from Paul at the American Embassy, but I wasn't able to reach him by transatlantic phone. Ware, who was at the *Herald Tribune* office in New York, did call

and, through our laughter and tears, he told me not to speak to anyone, but to write my article for the paper and be ready to leave on the steamship *Drottningholm*, which would arrive in Portugal in a few days. "Give my love to Paul, Mom, and the kids," I screamed, but the phone went dead.

Estoril, a free port, was wild. Every nationality was there—American, French, Greek, German, Italian, Japanese, Russian, Spanish, Swedish, English. The gambling casinos were jammed each night, as were the restaurants. Several nights, when we dined, we were seated right next to the enemy, a table of Nazis or Japanese.

It was strange and scary, and my group wouldn't let me go anywhere alone. During a late supper I excused myself from the table and headed for the ladies' room. Suddenly, I heard a voice behind me saying, "Not so fast, Teddy. Don't worry, I'll wait for you here." It was Bruce, one of the English journalists.

"Thanks, I won't be long," I replied.

At that moment, two very tall nuns in heavy black habits rushed by us and disappeared into the ladies' room. I followed, took a stall, and closed the door. I couldn't help but hear some sort of rustling in the stall next to me. Looking down, I was amazed to see a nun's black robe being pulled up to reveal . . . *boots—army boots!* And they were straddling the toilet. This was no woman, but a man dressed as a nun. What was he doing here? And where was the other one? Was this a trap? Was it me they wanted? Oh my God . . .

Suddenly, a group of young girls burst into the ladies' room, laughing and screaming. This was my chance . . . I had to get out. I made my way through them to the door, and threw myself into the arms of Bruce telling him, "Those nuns aren't nuns! They're soldiers!" As he rushed

me back to our table, I turned and saw that the nuns were now completely surrounded by the girls.

Finally, the *Drottningholm* arrived. We boarded her and headed out to sea, toward America. I slept on deck all the way across the Atlantic because my stateroom was way down in the depths of the ship, and I couldn't breathe there. I wrapped a blanket around myself and lay down on the deck, behind a bulwark and out of the wind. Livingston Pomeroy usually joined me.

The nights were absolutely beautiful. There was a tiny moon and many stars. It was summer. The sea was calm, winds warm. For our protection we were lighted from bow to stern with the words *Diplomatic* and *Red Cross* painted on either side of the ship. Several times during the crossing, a German submarine emerged off our bow at night. Like some gigantic predatory shark, it glided beside us through the dark waters for a few miles, then suddenly disappeared.

Just for fun, I wrote this little ditty to the tune of "Home on the Range," and sang it to everyone in the bar.

> *O please take us home on the old* Drottningholm,
> *Where the unemployed diplomats play.*
> *Where seldom is heard an intelligent word,*
> *And the bar stays wide open all day!*
> *O . . . Say can you see. If you can you're more sober than we.*
> *For we're out on a toot and we don't give a hoot*
> *Till we land in the Land of the Free.*

We arrived in New York like conquering heroes. The harbor was jammed with boats coming to welcome us. As we passed the Statue of

Liberty, my heart skipped a beat. I wondered if Paul would be there to surprise me. Rushing down to my stateroom, I grabbed my handbag and the article I'd written for the *Herald Tribune*. I noticed that my luggage had already been picked up, and I hurried back up on deck, just as the ship made its way into port.

As we drew closer, I could see my brother Ware out on the pier, waving to me. Paul wasn't there. Then a woman officer touched my arm and said, "Come with me, young lady." Obediently, I followed her down several flights to a room with two other women officers. They closed the door and said, "Give us your handbag and take off your clothes. You are to be searched."

As I started to take off my coat, tears came to my eyes. I was in shock. They must think I'm a spy, I told myself. The idea of me being anything but an American who would give her life for her country, and who was now being interrogated as the enemy, broke my heart. I told them this as I undressed. But they just stared at me.

I took off my suit coat and dropped my skirt, still crying. As I started to unbutton my blouse, the door opened and a senior officer walked in. "You can stop now," she said. "Put your things back on. You're free to go."

Turning to the other officers, she said, "We found the girl." Then she walked out.

I put my clothes on and, as I left, I was handed my pocketbook. "Be careful who sees the postcards you have in here, they are very startling," said the first officer with a smile.

"Pompeii?" she questioned.

"No . . . Herculaneum," I said and hurried out.

Down the gangway to the pier, I was photographed by many of the reporters, but finally seeing Ware, I ran to him and threw myself into his

---

arms. We jumped into a waiting limo and drove uptown, straight to the Pierre, where my mom and sisters were waiting for me.

What a reunion! I was beyond happy, even though Paul hadn't come to meet me. He was in Tulsa, as Ware explained, assigned by the War Department to build planes and to train pilots for the navy.

He phoned. It was strange to hear his voice, but it excited me. "Teddy," he said. "I wanted to meet you, but I couldn't leave, you understand?"

"Yes, of course."

"Are you with your mother and the girls?"

"Yes, Paul, and I'm so excited. I still can't believe I'm here."

"Well, you are, thank God. Will you come to Tulsa?"

"Do you want me?"

"You know I do!"

"Then I'll come."

"Soon?"

"As soon as you wish."

"Make it Saturday. That will give you time to be with your mother and sisters. I'll pick you up at the station. Bye, darling . . . Are you sure you're all right, Teddy?"

"Yes, I'm all right. Bye, Paul."

"Bye, Teddy."

As I put the phone down, I thought back to the last time we'd said good-bye to each other, in Rome at the railway station. He'd been leaving on the train for Naples and here we were, two years later, and he was going to meet me at the train station in Tulsa.

To be free in my own country was absolutely overwhelming. To sleep in a nice bed, eat fresh bread and butter, drink fresh orange juice, sip good coffee, munch Hershey bars, and eat peanut butter and jelly sand-

wiches . . . and, best of all, to eat a great lunch ending with a vanilla ice cream sundae covered in chocolate sauce . . . what a treat!

Everyone I saw, even though we were still at war, seemed so free, so hearty, so full of life. It made me so happy to be home again. I couldn't help thinking how lucky we were to live in America, and what a fabulous city New York was.

I had to laugh at the maid doing our rooms at the Pierre. She was astounded at finding bread that I had hidden all over the place. Mom explained to her that it had become automatic for me to put leftover bread in my pockets, fearing I might not get more. The Italian maître d' at the Cotillion Room seemed to understand and, before I left, handed me a loaf wrapped in silver paper. "Signora Getty, don't worry, there's plenty more bread here."

After being interviewed by *Life* magazine, submitting my article to the *Herald Tribune*, and meeting Wild Bill Donovan of the CIA and being questioned by him regarding what I knew about the Italians, I said good-bye to Mom, my sisters, and Ware and left on the train for Tulsa, Oklahoma.

PART II

CHAPTER 24

REUNITED IN TULSA

Paul was there at the station. I saw him before he saw me. He looked the same. He was standing in shirtsleeves, right under the window of my sleeping car. He put out his hand as I stepped off the train, kissed me on the cheek, and said, "Darling, I'm so glad you came." Then he picked up my bag . . . I only had one . . . threw it in the back of the car, and drove me to his home . . . a little stucco house near the Spartan Aircraft Factory and School.

I sat speechless beside him as we drove through the darkened streets, just thinking how strange it was that, after more than two years, we were together again . . . side by side. He kind of prattled on about how he hoped I'd like his house. He told me it was air-conditioned . . . had a beautiful garden . . . I can barely recall a word of what he said. I was in shock.

Then we arrived. He drove up the driveway, got out of the car, took my bag, and opened the front door. I followed him inside. He closed the

door, turned on the light, and looked at me, Then he leaned over, kissed me, and said, "Thank God, Teddy, you're home."

Home. That word sounded so strange.

He lifted my bag and started up the stairs. Halfway up, he stopped and, with a knowing smile, said, "I'll bet you're hungry, darling . . . What can I get you?"

"Just a Coke, Paul, thanks," I answered.

He put my bag down in what I realized was the master bedroom, and went downstairs to get my Coke. I looked around. It was a pretty room with a huge double bed, a fireplace, two comfy chairs on either side, and soft carpeting throughout. There was a bathroom beyond. Across the hall was another bedroom with twin beds. Picking up my bag, I walked into that room, turned on the light, went into the bathroom, where I washed, combed my hair, and came out to find a Coke and some cookies on the night table. I could hear Paul downstairs, talking to someone on the phone about how many planes were being sent out. I sat on the bed, ate a cookie, and drank the Coke. Boy, it was so amazingly good. Then I opened my bag, took out my things, hung them up, turned down the bed, put on my nightie, and crawled in.

I don't remember turning out the light. I only remember waking up. It was early morning. The house was silent. I got up, opened the door, and there on the floor in the hallway was a note. In his familiar scrawl, Paul had written, *Darling . . . I'm at the factory. Call me. Have a good breakfast, love.* So I went downstairs, made a grand tour of the house, had a great breakfast, and phoned the factory to tell him there was a huge black dog growling at me from outside the glass patio door. And, thank God, there *was* a glass door between us.

"That's Hildy," he said on the telephone. "I picked her out at the dog

pound. She was to be killed . . . no one wanted such a monster. I had to save her. They said she was too fierce, but when I walked up to her, held out my hand, and spoke quietly, we bonded immediately. She is a giant briard."

"She certainly is. But where is her food?"

"On the counter. See you later, dear."

I waited until Hildy ran to the other side of the garden. That was my moment. I quickly put her bowl outside the door. And had just enough time to get back inside before she charged. Seeing the food, she stopped, then began eating . . . all the while looking up at me through the black curly hair that covered her eyes. When she finished, she lay down and fell fast asleep. Later, when she awoke, I knew somehow we were going to be friends, and we were, until the day she died.

After breakfast, I carried my tray out into the kitchen. When I returned the butter to the icebox, I discovered its shelves stocked with fresh oranges and grapefruit, jars of yogurt, and the usual bacon, eggs, milk, and bread.

The kitchen cabinets were laden with boxes of dry cereal and natural raw sugar. I remembered these were what Paul usually had for his breakfast, but what I noticed also was that he had washed his breakfast dishes . . . and so . . . I washed mine and Hildy's.

I went upstairs, made my bed, dressed, and stood in the center of the room, wondering what to do next. In fact, I wondered what there was to do.

I thought, *Isn't it wonderful. Here I am in America . . . in a free country. I can just sit or walk or use the car . . . do anything I want, and no one is going to stop me.* I heard birds singing. And downstairs the front door was still open and the morning newspaper lay on the walkway. I couldn't believe it. Things in America were the same as when I had left. It felt like

a time warp, and I wasn't sure what to do. It looked the same, yet I was different.

Paul returned at six, bringing with him two exquisite steaks, which he broiled and served with fresh asparagus and a great big salad. We ate in the dining room. It was still too warm to sit outside. Hildy sat at his feet, and I sat across from them.

After my favorite dessert of vanilla ice cream and chocolate sauce, we had coffee in the living room. He asked me to tell him about the prison, the months in Siena, the men who were interned with me, and the trip back home on the ship. It astounded him that I slept on deck all the way across the Atlantic, and that Nazi submarines surfaced so near to the ship.

Then Paul looked at me. We were sitting opposite each other . . . I, cross-legged on the couch, he in one of the easy chairs beside a table piled high with business papers, books, and mail. Hildy lay at his feet. There was a tall lamp behind him, lighting only our part of the room.

"My God, what an experience. And, you haven't changed a bit. You're still the same determined young lady I last saw in Rome . . . determined to achieve the goal she set for herself. You amaze me."

But I felt changed inside—he didn't see it. "I only did what you and I thought I could do. I tried and I'm still trying. Remember, *you* paid for the lessons . . . I couldn't let you down."

For a moment he stared at me. "But, why didn't you come home when I wrote and asked you to?"

I looked straight back at him. "Why didn't you come back for me as *you* promised? I waited, you know."

"I couldn't leave the country, Teddy. No private citizen could return to Europe once they were here."

194

"But you and Hal went to Mexico . . ."

"That was different . . . also, it was business. Anyway, you were my wife, you should have obeyed me."

"Obeyed you? *I* obeyed my heart, which said, 'Stay and learn as much as you can, because the man you love believes in you and you mustn't let him down.'" I stopped because I was about to cry, thinking what a damn fool I'd been.

"Well, my dear, you were very brave to stay, especially in spite of my only giving you four hundred dollars a month to live on." He looked amused. "I thought you'd give up if you didn't have enough money . . . but, by God, you didn't."

"No, I didn't."

We looked at each other and smiled, remembering, but just then the ringing of the telephone broke the spell. It was a business call from Washington. While Paul took the call, I went into the kitchen, did the dishes, then went up to my room. I could hear him talking—it must have been terribly important, for the call went on for hours.

I undressed, went to bed, and awoke thinking I'd heard a car drive away. I opened my eyes. It was dark outside. I reached for my watch. It was 4 A.M. I put on my robe, and opened the door, but there was no note on the hall carpet, and Paul's bed had not been slept in. He must have worked all night, and that was he who had driven off not more than fifteen minutes ago.

I went downstairs and into the kitchen. He had made a cup of tea and had left a note there for me saying, *Darling, am off to Oklahoma City to meet Captain Balfour. Take care of Hildy. Love, Paul.* But he didn't say when he'd return. I went to bed, but couldn't sleep . . . or did I? Suddenly, I felt a tongue licking my face and, opening my eyes, saw Hildy's

furry black face next to mine. How she'd gotten into the house and into my room, I'll never know, but there she was. Maybe Paul had left her inside to protect me.

It was early morning. I jumped up, washed Hildy's gooey tongue print off my face, brushed my teeth, combed my hair, put on shorts and a shirt, and ran barefoot downstairs and out into the garden with Hildy at my heels.

The air was fresh . . . the grass wet and cool . . . the sun, which would soon force us inside, was just now climbing the sky. Looking around, I was enchanted by the beauty of nature and by the surrounding neighborhood. I could see the houses down the tree-lined street . . . charming Middle America . . . all quiet and peaceful.

I sat for almost an hour out there in the garden, trying to understand what was happening to Paul and me. We seemed like strangers. But in a way, last night I felt we had begun reaching out to each other. Then the telephone rang . . . and he was gone.

I walked back into the house, grateful that he hadn't wanted to make love to me. It wouldn't have been right. I knew I had to tell him about Kostya. I wondered if he sensed there'd been someone else.

Paul had always amazed me by what he did seem to know. Once, he'd said, "Always tell me the truth, Teddy. I can tell if you lie." And I never did lie to him all the years we were married.

I waited for him to call, but he didn't. I wrote letters, phoned my mom, had a light supper, fed Hildy, then lay down on my bed and turned on the radio. There was some sweet music coming from somewhere and I started to think. *When he comes home*, I decided, *I'll tell him everything.* How Kostya and I met at Rome's police station . . . how we both had the feeling we'd known each other in another time. How lost I was without

Paul. How Kostya came to my lessons and how, even though the world was at war, he had arranged, like Paul would have, a concert for me in Budapest, which sadly was canceled. And then, one day, he told me he loved me. I could still see him pacing up and down the room saying, "Paul may be your husband, but you belong to me. We were meant to be together." And I began to believe him, even though I was determined to come home to Paul. And then it happened . . .

I remember running down the Corso that night to get to the bistro, where I was to meet Kostya, when the air raid sirens started. I heard the roar of the French planes as they swooped overhead . . . the antiaircraft firing up at them . . . and everyone in the street trying to hide. The wardens were shouting, the children crying, some women screaming . . . and I just kept running, and finally dashed through the bistro door and into his arms. Terrorized, I held on to him . . . kissed him . . . kept thinking how Paul had forsaken me . . . those were my thoughts . . . and later, when it was safe to go out, we stumbled through the blacked-out streets of Rome, up the Janiculum Hill, to my little apartment. We made love, because that's what you do to defend yourself from the terror of fearing that any minute those planes might return and, this time, you'll die.

Kostya was like a big bear. I felt safe in his arms. I think that was the night I fell in love . . . but I still love you, Paul.

"Do you still love him, Teddy?" a voice asked. Startled, I sat up, opened my eyes, and there was Paul, sitting on the side of my bed, looking straight at me. I put my hand over my mouth. Had I been speaking out loud? Had he heard what I was going to tell him?

"I already knew about Kostya."

"What do you mean?"

"I mean, I've been sitting here listening to you for the past fifteen minutes."

"Then I have been speaking my thoughts out loud?"

"Yes . . . Tell me, Teddy. Do you still love him?"

I looked up. "Yes, I'll always love him, but not like I love you, Paul. I'll never see him again."

"How do you know?"

"I just know . . . I just know."

Paul stood up. "It's very late," he said. "I'm sorry I didn't phone. Now, let's get some sleep." At the door he stopped. "And thanks for telling me. I love you, too." And he left.

The following weeks were unusual. Paul introduced me to Wolferman's, the greatest market in the Southwest, and from then on I was responsible for what we ate. He was gone almost every day from six in the morning until very late at night. I knew he was working with Al Reitherman, his design engineer, to improve Spartan, and had little time for more than a quick "Hi, darling." I spent most days at the house.

Life magazine came out with a very interesting account of my life in Rome's prison with the other American journalists. I was quoted saying that the war had left the women of Italy badly off. When Paul read the story, he asked me if I would be one of the speakers addressing the wives and mothers of the navy personnel, the young pilots that were being prepared to go overseas. Spartan was giving a huge banquet in their honor in the plant auditorium the following Saturday. Although I had never made a speech in public before, I agreed. After telling them how well prepared our air force was to both fight the enemy overseas and to protect us at home, I ended with this:

Knowing they have the very best with which to face the enemy, confident of their ability to stop aggression, protect their loved ones, and end this WAR OF HATE, they will succeed. And you, mothers, sisters, and wives, be strong and brave. Take heart and have faith that your prayers will be answered, because God does guard and guide those who take up the sword on the side of RIGHT. Abraham Lincoln was sure of this. You may recall he said, "Let us have faith that RIGHT makes MIGHT and in that faith let us dare to do our duty as we understand it." Thank you, and God Bless.

Almost immediately the auditorium was transformed into a beautiful banquet hall. A sumptuous buffet dinner was set up at one end, and a dance band at the other. As I stepped down from the stage, Paul came up to me, caught my hand, and whispered, "You were great, darling. They loved you." He looked pleased, and I thanked God he was, for I wanted to please him.

He put his arm around my waist, and we walked through the crowd to our table. I had the feeling this was the first time, since my arrival two weeks before, that this man was laying claim to his wife. For a second I wondered, What was it? Was it me or was it the speech? Several mothers stopped us just to thank me. This was the first time I had met any of the factory employees, executives, and students of the Spartan School of Aeronautics, and I noted the way in which they treated Paul. I saw that he was respected by workers, not for being the boss, but for his diligence, his understanding, and his great sense of humor.

I found this particularly interesting, since Paul was a man over whom society and nobility had fawned, but here he was just another guy, like

the rest of them. They also admired him as a man who could have been given a Navy command or a top desk in Washington, with its attendant gold braid and impressive uniform, but who instead had taken a tough job in Oklahoma to get production rolling.

For a while, I sat intrigued by the wonderful new tunes the orchestra was playing from the Broadway hit show *Oklahoma!* Songs I'd never heard before. So American, they made you feel proud. But later, when the orchestra started playing some of the older tunes, like "Night and Day," Paul took my hand and said, "Let's dance," and we moved out onto the floor of that huge auditorium, as though it were a secret place just meant for us.

He held me close. We moved as one. We didn't speak. We didn't need to. I closed my eyes. I couldn't believe what I was feeling. I let my body follow his. Could it really be happening all over again, like it had those many times years before, when I knew I belonged in this man's arms?

He brushed my cheek with his lips, then smiled down at me. He wanted me as I wanted him, and I knew that he knew I was his. We never spoke. We just left the party and drove home and got in bed.

CHAPTER 25

THE BEACH HOUSE

Paul was a wonderful lover. He was so caring, and now so was I. I wondered, Could it be because of Kostya, or that I was older? But more than the physical act was the love I felt in my heart for Paul. *Webster*'s definition of the word *marriage* is so perfect: "an intimate or close union." Well, that certainly applied to us, and, I believe, to any two people who love each other, whether they've gone through a civil ceremony, or not.

At dawn, we awoke in this little house in Tulsa and, after a hearty breakfast and a salute to the sun, Paul drove away to the factory and I played tag with Hildy in the garden.

After supper, Paul and I sat out on the terrace and I asked him to tell me about Spartan. "Well, darling, I came to Tulsa right after Mama died. That's when they had sent you to Siena. I scarcely expected to spend much time here, but on New Year's Eve I made a resolution in her memory that I'd take over the Spartan factory for the war effort. It was barely functioning when I arrived. Now Spartan has made possible the

flight of some three thousand B-24's, equipped one hundred fifty-five Grumman Wildcats with wings, six hundred fifty Curtiss dive bombers with cowls, eleven hundred Douglas dive bombers with all-control surfaces, and furnished the navy with ninety primary trainers."

"Paul, that's wonderful. How do you remember all those facts?"

"I don't." He pulled out a sheet of paper from his pocket. "It's all here. I just got the report. It took us a year to build an organization, and another six months to attain excellence, but I think we've made a worthwhile contribution to the war effort and without any thought of financial profit." He smiled and then, with a faraway look in his eyes, he said, "But, you know, I really had wanted to get into the navy. I had passed my exams and could have commanded any vessel. I wanted to go to sea . . . Instead . . ."

"Instead, darling"—I leaned over and kissed him—"you're doing a magnificent job for our country. You may not be wearing Navy blues with brass buttons and commanding a ship, but in shirtsleeves, you and your team of factory workers are supplying our air force with the tools to help end this war."

During the weeks that followed, I saw Paul's contribution firsthand. It was obvious that from the moment he had taken over Spartan, not only had the factory been producing, but also the Spartan School of Aeronautics had turned out more than 25,000 Allied and American pilots, among them 1,500 for the Royal Air Force. Three Spartan pilots had received the Distinguished Flying Cross, and three more were with General Doolittle when he made his air raids over Japan. Toward the end of the war, Paul wrote in his diary about how proud he was of his own role and of Spartan's contribution to the war effort.

A few months after I arrived in Tulsa, we moved to a larger house

and lived a life I imagined was routine for an American family of two, one dog, and occasional visitors during wartime. My mother and two sisters, Nancy and Bobby, came to see us. They were now living in Paul's apartment on Sutton Place, and going to the Hewitt School in New York. The girls were adorable and very grown-up. We also entertained men from Washington, who came to inspect or discuss the plant.

In the evenings, it was our habit to eat hearty meals at home and to live a typically suburban life. After all, it was wartime. We'd jump into our Ford sedan (although Paul was in the oil business, we lived by our ration cards, like everyone else) and dash off to see *The Outlaw* or other films playing nearby. And Paul always found time to go to a concert or a new play with me. We finally found a part-time maid, who came to us twice a week. Other days, he tended chores like any husband, sometimes doing dishes with me. He would take out the garbage, rake the lawn, and play with Hildy the dog. Although we lived in a wealthy neighborhood, we didn't live the life wealthy people are expected to live, for it was foreign to both of us. We were too busy—Paul, with his tremendous responsibility at Spartan, and I, now learning to keep house for him and loving it. It seemed to me that we were closer than ever before.

Driving home from the movies one afternoon, I noticed that Paul had gotten very quiet. I was thinking about him, his intellect, his obvious business ability, the love and respect he attracted from his colleagues. It was then that I realized that beyond all this, and even beyond the renewed and exciting love we enjoyed, this man had a certain great quality. I was once again "the stargazer," trying to follow his academic flight through a child's binoculars. I wondered if I could keep up with him—if I could hold his interest.

It was just at that moment that Paul looked over at me and said, "You

know, darling, you made me proud that night you spoke to the mothers of our pilots. You really charmed everyone, and I can't help wondering what they would say now if they could hear you sing. I feel a certain sadness that you have worked so hard and given up so much to prepare for an operatic and concert career, and you're now not singing at all. Just being a housewife for me is not fair, Teddy. Your voice is beautiful, it must be heard. You must start singing again. Let's give a little concert at the house for a group of my friends from the plant."

"But, Paul, I'm really very happy just being your 'housewife.' I love—"

"No, Teddy, tomorrow we'll find you an accompanist . . . and . . . please take time to practice. When you feel ready, we'll do the concert. Okay?" And with that, he looked over at me and smiled.

And so I did what he wanted me to do. Two weeks later, a small group of Paul's friends came to the house and I sang for them . . . The result was inspiring to both Paul and to me. Paul was now even more certain that I should resume my career and, when I received a note from the New Opera Company—a thriving new organization headed by Mrs. Vincent Astor, who had once leased Mother's summer house at Martha's Vineyard—inviting me to audition for them with the possibility of my joining the company for their next season, Paul urged me to go.

I chose Desdemona's aria from *Otello* and, though I was very nervous when I walked out onstage, I lost that fear in attempting to remember my technique. I did my best, which brought from them an invitation to do two Mozart roles in the coming season, on the condition that I stay on in New York for the rest of the summer and work with their coach.

I knew they were right and wanted to do what they said, but Paul

thought I could prepare the roles in Tulsa with Gene Berton and go to New York in the early fall to work with them. The Company didn't agree to this. I don't know why I didn't insist on doing as they wished. I should have. Instead, I went home as he wanted, and never sang with the New Opera Company.

I guessed at the time he really wanted me with him and didn't want us to be separated. I could tell he was happy when I came home. Our days together were becoming maddeningly attractive, for finally I was living a really married life, something I'd never done before. I'd spend the day keeping house, doing the marketing, studying singing, and, when Paul came home in the evenings, I'd listen as he'd tell me about the progress at the factory . . . and the frustrations, too. Sometimes he'd bring Al and Blondie Reitherman home for supper, where Al and Paul would be deeply involved talking about how much more they could do to meet the navy's demands.

Most nights we'd listen to the radio for news of the war, then climb into bed and fall asleep. I thanked God each night for where I was, safe and protected. Lying there close to the man I loved, I realized why Paul was so right not wanting us to be separated at this time, even for three months. For I, too, hadn't wanted to leave him or this novel married life.

Belonging to someone who so perfectly satisfied me sexually and seemed to care that we lived each day together was too wonderful to give up. I decided I was not at all unhappy about not going to New York to sing for the opera company this time.

Sometime that fall, a film company in Hollywood, seeking a wartime story and having read my article in *Life* magazine, asked if I would present a synopsis to them of my experience in Italy. Paul thought it might have value and suggested Gene Berton come out to Tulsa and write it

with me, and also to go through my repertoire of songs to prepare me for a possible audition.

Even though working on the synopsis, which we titled *Music in the Storm*, brought back vivid, horrifying memories of my experiences, it was good for me, because now I was safe in America.

Paul and I spent a wonderful Christmas that first year, just being together. He gave me a beautiful gold-linked watch, and I gave him a pair of pajamas and two Scottie puppies—brother and sister, Penny and Peter. They were only six weeks old. I put them under the tree in a box all wrapped up in silver paper tied with a great big red satin bow, and suitable breathing holes on all sides. It was my hope that the puppies would make up for the death of Paul's little dog Sophie, his pride and joy for ten and a half years, who had died in California the year before. He had talked at length to me about her and, as I presented the box to him, I prayed the new additions would fill the void. And that they did. Paul laughed when he opened the box. They jumped out and Paul raced them upstairs to bed. I followed. He looked at me and said "Why don't you join us?" I did and was kissed to death. The dogs remained as loyal to Paul as he was to them for years to come. Paul was much happier around dogs.

In January, I received a first draft of *Music in the Storm* from Paramount. It was totally unacceptable to me, but Paul insisted that I should go out to California to discuss it with their writers. While there, I could also call on Dr. Lippe, who had been so encouraging when I sang for him and Mr. Behymer three years earlier. I remembered he had asked me to call on him on my return. So Paul handed me the keys to his beach house in Santa Monica, and before I realized it, I was on the train to Los Angeles.

———

Once in town, I headed the car up Wilshire Boulevard, all the way to where it ended in Santa Monica, turned right onto Ocean Avenue, made a quick left at the top of the cliffs, and drove down the ramp to the beach road—then called Ocean Front, now known the world over as Pacific Coast Highway.

What an experience, that first breathtaking view of the ocean—so vast, never-ending till it reached the horizon. For me, coming down the ramp was like gliding down a children's slide into a wonderland. It was wonderful to see again that wide expanse of blue, its waves with their whitecaps following one another onto the shore, and the beach with its row of houses. It hadn't changed at all since I'd driven Paul's mother there in 1939.

Passing Marion Davies's house, I slowed the car and turned in next door at No. 270, a charming two-story, white-shingled, New England–style house with green shutters, sheltered from the street by a high white fence. I parked the car in the garage, walked through the patio, and headed for the house, dragging my two bags and music case with me.

I had scarcely turned the key to the door, when the phone rang and Betzi Beaton, my roommate from our Algonquin days, was welcoming me to California. "Betz," I cried. "How did you know I was coming?"

"Paul told me. He phoned last night," she said, "and Jeannie is here, too. When can we meet?"

"How about lunch at Romanoffs, tomorrow at noon?"

"Great!"

I put the phone back and stood there, lost in thought, wondering how we'd all changed over the years. I was so distracted that I forgot my bags. They were still sitting outside. Dragging them in, I closed the door

and walked through the house, down the hall to the steps leading to the living room. I looked around and loved what I saw.

A thirty-foot-long, high-ceilinged room, windows happily decorated above built-in window seats, bookshelves on one end of the room, simple maple furnishings throughout, and a huge, comfortable-looking couch in front of the fireplace at the other end. Straight ahead was the doorway to the outside porch, which led to the beach and the sea. I opened it at once and stepped out into the blazing sunshine. The sand came right up to the level of the house . . . the sea only forty feet behind. The high white fence, which protected the entire property, ended at the water's edge. I tossed my shoes off and ran out through the sand to the gate leading to the public beach. It was locked, so I just stood there breathing in the fresh sea air, astonished at the tremendous waves curling up almost to the gate, and wondered what would happen if there was a storm, or just a high tide.

Looking up the coast I could see Malibu . . . looking out to sea was Catalina . . . and southward, right next to the beach house, the magnificent home of Marion Davies, which William Randolph Hearst had built for her. Then, beyond, as far as I could make out, were the lovely homes of Anita Loos, Mae West, Mrs. Will Rogers, the Louis B. Mayers, Douglas Fairbanks, and the Jesse Laskys. In the distance, I could make out the Santa Monica Pier with its merry-go-round and restaurants.

There were two master bedrooms in the front of the house, overlooking the sea, each with a bath and a dressing room. I chose the room with the canopy bed and a small marble fireplace with windows looking southward, then I phoned Paul and told him how happy I was to be in his adorable beach house. I also told him how sad I was that he wasn't there with me.

"I'm sorry, too, Teddy," he said, "but happy you like the house."

"I never want to leave, so you must come here," I told him. "It's so like the Vineyard, I love it."

"Isn't the ocean great?" he said, and I could hear in his voice he was missing it. "I wish I could be with you, darling, but I can't leave now. Don't forget to call Dr. Lippe tomorrow. Get an accompanist and sing for him, and let me know what he says . . . and call Paramount for an appointment."

"I will—"

"And by the way," he cut in, "remember to phone me after six. The night rate is cheaper, and we can talk longer. Now good-bye, darling, take care. I love you . . . and say hello to the girls."

Romanoffs was packed. It always was in those days, and Mike, the owner, greeted me with a kiss and a hug. We hadn't seen each other since the Stork Club days. He seemed delighted that I was married to Paul, and escorted me to the table where Betzi and Jeannie were seated. Our reunion was wild. We all talked at once and I was thrilled to learn that Betzi had written a screenplay for Columbia called *The Boy with Green Hair*, and that Jeannie was a successful actor's agent.

I hadn't seen Betzi since our New York days, nor Jeannie, since she and her husband had fled into Switzerland at the beginning of the war. They looked great . . . Betzi, still the blond beauty, and Jeannie with her tousled red hair . . . both tanned, happy, successful, and excited at seeing me.

"How long are you staying?" Jeannie asked.

"I don't know. I've found an accompanist, Marjorie Fahringer, and I'm planning to sing for Dr. Lippe."

"You mean you're going back to work?" Betzi said, wide-eyed.

"Hopefully," I answered.

"So, Teddy," she whispered, "is it true? Are you getting a divorce?"

"Who, me? Divorce? No, I'm not . . . unless Paul's divorcing me. Why? What have you heard?"

"Oh . . . no . . . nothing. It's just that he's there . . . and you're here."

"I know, but it was his idea that I come to California and sing for Dr. Lippe."

"Oh . . ." said Betzi.

"What do you mean, 'Oh'?"

"Oh, nothing. It's great. Welcome to Worksville."

At that, Jeannie cut in. "I have an idea. I want you to meet my best friends, Gladys and Eddie G. Robinson. You know, *Little Caesar.* They love music and art, and maybe they can be of help. May I bring them down to the beach house to meet you?"

"Of course, Jeannie. I'd love to meet them. He is one of my favorite actors."

And so it happened, just like that. They came the very next Sunday, with their son, Manny, laden with baskets of food, just as Marjorie and I finished rehearsing.

Insisting Marjorie stay for lunch, they asked me to sing, which I did. They all applauded, with Jeannie excitedly pacing up and down the living room saying, "I told you so . . . She's great, isn't she? Worked hard . . . went to jail . . . boy . . . I really think she's got it."

"Yes, she has," said Eddie. "You'll go far, Teddy."

"Thank you so much," I said.

At lunch, Gladys, a most attractive woman with great brown eyes and a warm heart, said, "Teddy, your voice is beautiful. You should have your own radio program, and I know just the station that would want you. I'm going to call them right now."

As she left the room, Eddie smiled and said, "That's my Gladys. You know, Teddy, if she thinks you should have your own radio program, you should have it . . . And right now, if she's doing what I think she's doing, you *will* have."

And I did have, and it happened just like that.

Naturally, I had to audition for the executives, who offered me a contract and a time slot. They assigned Neil Reagan, Ronald Reagan's brother, to produce the show, which they titled *Serenade*. It was to start in August.

I was to sing every Thursday evening from 8:15 to 8:30 over station KFWB, from the stage of the Warner Bros. Theatre on Hollywood Boulevard, accompanied by pianist/conductor Leon Leonardi, and the Warner Bros. Orchestra. The format was for me to sing one concert or opera aria and one modern song; the orchestra was to play one number. And I was to have guests, too. Of course, I had Gladys and Eddie to thank for sponsoring me, and Jeannie for introducing us.

Before accepting, I phoned Paul. "Darling, what a great opportunity . . . Sign at once," he said. "And I'll be there. Now, what about your story? Is Paramount still interested? I haven't heard from you in days."

He sounded upset, and later that night I received a letter he'd sent from New York asking, "When will you come back to me?" Of course, now that I had this offer, Paul agreed that I should stay in California.

The very next day, I called on Dr. Lippe and arranged to study the arias I was going to use on my program. I also spoke with the writers assigned to me at Paramount. They were so busy rewriting their last script that we agreed to postpone getting together . . . And so my story was never done.

I worked with Dr. Lippe several times during the summer. I met

with Leon Leonardi to discuss what guests he planned to invite on our show at KFWB, but I was lonely. I really missed Paul, and I think he missed me, too.

On June 16, 1943, Paul sent me a note:

> Tulsa. June 16, 1943
> 7:00 pm
>
> Darling Teddy Boo,
>
> A year ago today I met you at the station — a year lacking three hours. I'm sorry I'm not meeting you tonight.
>
> Work has been hard here but I feel hopeful. Spartan is becoming something to be proud of.
>
> Hilda was clipped yesterday and you wouldn't know her. She looks about as big as Sophie only taller. Must rush back to the shop,
>
> Your sweetheart, Paul

It brought back memories of that meeting, our reunion after so many years of being apart. It also made me cry, because, here we were, doing the same thing all over again.

CHAPTER 26

HEREFORD, TEXAS

One evening, after reading an article titled "The Town Without a Toothache," in the February 1943 issue of *Reader's Digest*, Paul was so impressed, he called me from Tulsa and suggested we meet in Hereford to investigate the story. He planned to drive there and bring Hildy with him. I agreed to hop the train from LA. and meet him there.

On arrival, we located Dr. Heard, the *only* dentist in the entire area. We learned he had found little or no evidence of tooth decay in the people of the county, and believed it was due to the drinking water.

The Hereford city records showed that out of every hundred men in the area, 93 percent were accepted for the armed forces because of good health and almost perfect teeth. It was also noteworthy that in Hereford you couldn't tell the age of a horse, cow, or a dog by its teeth. Hereford is situated on the staked plains of Texas, that wonderful short-grass country, called the Llano Estacado, which fully supplied the nutritional needs of the buffalo, who once roamed this area, and

now supplied the needs of the famous Hereford cows. It just seemed to me that since nature had put such good water in the ground for the citizens and animals of Hereford, surely the same water should be good for the rest of the world.

The slogan "The Town Without a Toothache" kept running through my head. "Paul," I said, "let's take some water back to California and have a chemical analysis made. If it really contains natural fluoride, we've got something no other bottled water has, and we could do this together. I mean, bottle and sell it."

"You're right, Teddy. It may also have potassium and phosphorus, and that would make it even better."

"Oh, Paul . . . can you imagine how it could bless the whole world? Please, let's do it. I'd be thrilled to be doing something like this with you."

"Teddy, dear, it's a marvelous idea and I love your enthusiasm, but to go into business and make it work is a twenty-four-hour-a-day job. Right now my hours are taken up with Spartan. Yours are filled with singing. But let's take a couple of bottles of water with us to California, get the analysis made, and go from there."

Throwing my arms around him, I excitedly said, "Darling, you're wonderful. If this water has what we think it has, we will form the Hereford Texas Water Company and distribute the water all over California and—"

Paul's laughter stopped me, and teasingly he said, "Mrs. Getty, I'm interested in the financial end of this project. How much are you charging per bottle, and what are your delivery days?"

This stopped me. Was he asking me to go into business with him? Was he saying he'd do this with me? I don't believe he had ever asked any

former wife to join him in any business venture. It was exciting to think he might want me.

Well, we filled two bottles with Hereford water, jumped into Paul's 1944 blue Ford sedan and, with Hildy and the water bottles in the backseat, headed for California.

The trip was epic. Starting down the road for Clovis, we were met by thunderous squall conditions with rain, hail, and lightning. One huge black cloud developed into several small whirling funnels, reaching way up into the sky from the fields down the straight road ahead of us, and we had to race the storm half the way to avoid being gobbled up by the whirling dervish wind. It was strange and scary, and, once, Paul just yelled "Hang on" as he drove the car off the main road, across a field, and in another direction to beat that swirling black tornado, which then suddenly changed its course and headed straight for us. Finally, we escaped the storm and reached the little town of Clovis with our water bottles intact and Hildy huddled down silent and still in the backseat.

Leaving the Llano Estacado, those desolate plains of Texas, we took Route 66 to Albuquerque and then Gallup, arriving with the setting sun. The next day, we visited the wonders of the early West—Kit Carson's Cave, the Painted Desert, the Petrified Forest, the Meteor Crater, and then on to Flagstaff. Following the road, we saw the San Francisco Peaks shimmering like golden spheres before us. We drove through beautiful green forests to the Grand Canyon, where Hildy romped and we sat and held hands in the moonlight by the Rim of the Canyon with the rest of the tourists, as a guide recited the legend and history of one of nature's greatest wonders. It was truly inspiring. We hated to leave, but after enjoying that view and drinking in that pure mountain air for

a few days, we headed west through Needles, the desert, and on to our little beach house in Santa Monica, where Peter and Penny greeted us, and rallied around Hildy, Paul, and me for a welcome home and a walk on the beach. At sunset, we made love and fell asleep listening to the sound of the sea.

Early the next morning, we took the bottles of Hereford water to the Truesdail Laboratories in Pasadena, and the next week the analysis of the water proved to be all that we had hoped it would be.

In November, on his way to Tulsa, Paul stopped off in Hereford, looked at some acreage that was for sale, called on the city dentist Dr. Heard, and again discussed with him the value of the water. Paul went to the City Hall of Hereford, talked with Mayor Ireland and Councilman Posey, and arranged to buy our water from the City out of the same wells that had been supplying the citizens of Hereford for the past forty years. To be sure that we would always have the water for our use, Paul also bought a 190-acre farm with a spur connecting it to the railroad track. I still own that acreage today.

About a year later, I could never seem to get more than five hundred customers at $1.25 per bottle . . . Something, may I say, that Paul reminded me of every time my bank account was short and he had to make up the deficit.

One day, in a note to me about the water project, Paul wrote, "Darling, you're too far in the red. You're dropping money down a hole. It's a great idea, but as a business venture—it stinks." Paul had said in the beginning, "To run a business is a twenty-four-hour-a-day job." Since he couldn't possibly give up Spartan for this water project, and—since I was busy appearing professionally as a singer—neither of us could devote our full time to it.

Wouldn't Paul be surprised to know that a gallon of water cost more than a gallon of gas today.

In retrospect, my idea to start the water company may not have been a brilliant decision, but it was by no means a poor investment. Maybe it was just part of the "price Paul paid in the process of my growing up." Nevertheless, it was something special I shared with Paul, and I got a taste of his brilliant mind. Perhaps that is why I continue to hold on to my dream that we may someday bottle that wonderful water again to bless the world. Whenever I think about this water adventure, I give myself an A-plus for effort, and sort of dream that maybe someday I'll put the water in bottles again and—or—well, maybe someone else will . . . and let this wonderful water bless the world.

ONE DAY, OUR dear neighbor Jesse Lasky, the famous producer and an old friend of Paul's, walked up the beach and called over our gate to introduce me to Nino Martini from the Met (New York Metropolitan Opera), who was in California on vacation. Nino had appeared in several of Jesse's movies with Ida Lupino, and possessed a magnificent tenor voice. He was a dynamic and handsome man. He sang for us. Then he asked me to sing, and we sang duets from *Bohème* and *Tosca*, accompanied by Marjorie, with Paul, Bessie and Jesse Lasky, and Eddie and Gladys Robinson as our audience. Nino was so supportive and reassuring about my singing technique. He also helped me arrange my concert and radio programs, and introduced me to an exquisite song—a poem written by Bessie Lasky titled "I Come to You," set to music by Miguel Sandoval. I loved it, learned it, and included it in my concerts and on the KFWB radio program. I shall never forget Nino's interest, his sense of

humor, and his wonderful voice. He was my friend forever, and he helped choose my program for my American debut as a serious concert singer.

On August 22, 1943, I made this debut at the McCormick Gallery of the Santa Barbara Museum of Art. The reviews were kind, not spectacular. I was a bit nervous at first, but they liked the quality of my voice, and especially commented on the fact that I could take my high notes pianissimo (thank you, dear Mme. Marchesi). They found my program interesting, thanks to Nino, who helped choose it. I sang, for the first time in America, "Dos Cantares Populares" by Fernando J. Obradors, and "O Luna Che Fa Lume" by Vincenzo Davica, which I performed in Tuscan dialect. I also sang "La Flute Enchante" from the *Sheherazade Suite* by Ravel, several songs of François Poulenc, and for my aria, I chose Desdemona's lovely "Salce" from act IV from the opera *Otello* by Verdi.

It was exciting to sing a professional concert, but it would have meant so much more had Paul been there. He was in Tulsa and "just couldn't make it," he said. Though I was upset, I reminded myself that we were at war, and Paul had orders for planes and parts of planes to get out for the navy. Fortunately, Nino drove up to Santa Barbara to give me courage, and he saved the day.

Later, Emily Spreckels, who had sponsored the concert, gave a huge party at her mansion in Montecito, where she introduced me to Helen Ainsworth, the West Coast head of the National Concert and Artists Corporation (NCAC), and the head of their New York office, Alfred Morton, who immediately signed me. Naturally, I was thrilled, because among their roster were the Metropolitan opera stars Ezio Pinza and Blanche Thebom, the famous diva Lotte Lehmann, and the renowned pianist Arthur Rubinstein.

But I was still hurt that Paul had not come.

After the concert, Nino insisted I drive back to Los Angeles with him. On the way, we stopped at a roadside inn. Over scrambled eggs and coffee, he proceeded to give me a lecture on how not to be upset when the one you love doesn't show up for your performances.

"Teddy, *cara* . . . first sing because you love to . . . then sing for your audience. Be happy knowing you are giving joy to someone out there . . . and just think what Paul missed." And with that, he pulled me to him and right there in front of everyone in the restaurant, he kissed me . . . a long, hard, passionate kiss. Embarrassed, I got up and ran out to the car.

I needed that kiss, but why did I wish it had been Paul? Nino was such a wildly attractive man, the ever romantic Rodolfo of *Bohème* . . . "You better be careful," I told myself. "With a full moon and the way you feel, you may get into trouble."

Nino appeared, jumped into the car and, leaning over, kissed me. Then he pulled me close, put a robe over my lap, and rolled up the windows, saying, "Night sea air, *molto male per la voce.*" And with that, we roared down the Pacific Coast Highway, arriving at the beach house just as Robert, our houseman, was out on the lawn, raising the flag to the morning sun.

With a *"Ciao, cara . . . a stasera,"* Nino left, and I went into the house and to bed. It had been a great day. I had sung well. People liked me. A top agency had signed me, and a fascinating man (other than Paul) had come to my rescue. He had aroused me, and as I fell into that dreamy state before sleep envelops one, I found myself reliving Nino's kiss and wondering what it would be like making love with him.

The next morning, flowers arrived from Paul, and that evening,

instead of dining alone with Nino, we were joined by Jesse Lasky and Victor Emanuelle. Early the next afternoon, I was called to the Warner Bros. Studio by Neil Reagan, to run through some of the numbers we were going to do for the opening night of *Serenade*, which was to start Thursday night, August 26, 1942, at 8 P.M., over KFWB. Nino came to the rehearsal with me, much to the surprise and joy of Leonardi and the sixteen boys in the orchestra. He sat in the darkened theater all during the rehearsal, and told me later I was the only girl singer he'd ever heard who sang "Marechiare" in Neapolitan dialect, like a real Neapolitan.

He left that night on the train for San Francisco to go on tour. Then he phoned me from other cities to see how I was doing, always reminding me to sing *"for the love of it* . . . not for just one love alone." For as long as I can remember, Nino was my friend, calling from wherever he was in the world, always giving me advice, wishing me well, even telling me to *never* make love before a performance. "Go to a movie," "don't even talk," so you won't use your voice. Then after your performance, and then *only*—make love.

I'll always remember that first night when Paul arrived from Tulsa and came to the broadcast. We ended up at Chasen's. After dinner he turned to me, raised his wineglass, and said, "I'm proud of you, Teddy, you've really done it. Your first professional engagement with your new voice. Marchesi and Moreschi have given you the technique, and now you're on your way." Then, he leaned over, kissed me, handed me my glass, and whispered, "Let's drink to your future, darling. Then let's go home. Waiter. Check please."

By now, Paul seemed able to spend more time in California with me, even though business still compelled him to return to Tulsa and occa-

sionally to New York. Often, such trips were made at a moment's notice, with his saying, "Teddy, dear, I must take the evening train to New York." Frantically, we would scurry about the little beach house, getting him packed and getting his books and papers together. I'd drive him to the train, which left from Pasadena, and, with one minute to spare, he'd kiss me good-bye and dash off.

One evening, while waiting for Paul to come home from the office, I heard the gate close. The bells rang, and when Robert opened the door, I heard him gasp and say, "Oh, Mr. Getty, sir! What happened? Did you have a car accident?"

I rushed downstairs as Paul walked into the house, his face covered with bandages. I looked at him, shocked. "Oh my God! Paul, you're bleeding! Tell me what happened!"

He didn't answer. I reached out to him—he just looked at me, put his hand up, and walked slowly into the living room, then sat down in his favorite chair. I knelt in front of him. He just sat there. "Paul, tell me, please. What happened?"

He looked at me for a moment, then said, "I had a face-lift this afternoon."

"What?! And you drove yourself home . . . How could you? Oh my God, Paul, why?"

"I'm ugly. I don't like these jowls." With that, he put his hand up to his face.

Tears came to my eyes. "Paul, you're not ugly. You're an individual, like Leslie Howard or Leopold Stokowski. When people meet you, they're fascinated. It's something special in that face of yours that makes them realize you have a wealth of knowledge that draws them to you. And besides, you've got a great smile."

He nodded but didn't say anything. And at that moment Robert walked in with a rum and Coke, put it on the table, and quietly left. I picked it up, Paul looked at me, and I followed him when he started upstairs to our bedroom.

One month later, Paul was fine, his face healed, and we never spoke of it again.

Santa Monica was peaceful in those days; no noise on the Pacific Coast Highway, except for the rumble of passing Army trucks. The view from our house was amazing, always luring us onto the beach. The gulls at night slowly heading in flocks toward the mountains, which dipped to the ocean; the view from our bedroom windows of the sun setting; the magnificent air—all made those days seem glorious and fresh. Sometimes alone, and sometimes with our dogs, Penny, Peter, and Hildy, we'd walk along the shoreline on the edge of the ocean and watch the sandpipers scurry ahead of the never-ending waves. And before we knew it, we'd find ourselves at the Santa Monica Pier. At sunset, as we would head for home, there they were . . . those hundreds of seagulls in the sky above, flying northwest in their usual precise formation to their roosting places in the Palisades.

Often, we would dine next door with Marion Davies and Mr. Hearst, just the four of us. Mr. Hearst always looked quite fit for a man in his eighties. It was fascinating to sit at that long table in the dining room, its sideboard laden with the most exquisite silver. After dinner, we'd go into the drawing room, and Mr. Hearst would show early films of Marion, and then preview a new picture before it was shown to the public.

They really seemed to be in love, for they held hands all during the showing of her picture. He never took his eyes off her when she decided to critique a new film. Like a child, she would look up at him as she

spoke, for his approval. I found this very endearing, especially since they'd been together for so many years.

Walking back to the beach house one time, Paul said, "Did you notice how empty the walls looked in the great hall and gallery?" We decided they'd taken the pictures down for safekeeping during the war.

AFTER EMMY SPRECKELS became engaged to Burton Tremaine, we often met them for dinner at La Rue on Sunset Boulevard. Then, when Emmy married Burton and they returned from their honeymoon, we visited them in Santa Barbara and brought them back with us to our beach house. The four of us spent great times together.

One beautiful summer Sunday, while we were all having a leisurely lunch, our houseman, Robert, approached Paul and said, "Mr. Getty, sir, you are wanted on the phone."

Paul excused himself and a few minutes later came to the open door and called, "Teddy, it's for you." Hurriedly, I excused myself and, as I ran into the house, he stopped me and said, "Teddy, there's someone on the phone who is very upset, and you've got to help me."

I asked, "Who is it? What happened?"

Pushing the phone at me he said, "Go ahead, talk."

I whispered, "Talk? To whom? What about?"

Quickly putting his hand over the mouthpiece he begged, "Darling, please . . . Talk."

Completely bewildered, I picked up the phone and said, "Hello?"

In response, a young girl's agitated voice pleaded, "Please, Mrs. Getty, please help me. Please make Paul call Charles for me."

"Well, who are you? And Charles? Charles who?"

"Charles Chaplin," she shouted, "and I'm Joan Barry. Paul knows all about this, and he's got to get Charles to talk to me. I don't know what else to do. Please, please, help me."

"Of course I will. Now stop crying, and I'll talk to Paul about it."

I put the telephone down and Paul said, "Teddy, I'll explain later, when we're alone."

"Explain what?" I replied. "Just tell Charles to call her up. Come on, let's finish our lunch."

As we walked back to Emmy and Burton, Paul put his arm around me and whispered, "Thanks, darling."

When we returned to the table, Robert was serving dessert, but my thoughts were elsewhere, wondering what Paul was going to explain later, and why he had to call Charles Chaplin. What does Joan Barry mean to Paul?

These questions were crowding my thoughts as I waited for him to join me upstairs in our bedroom. I had slipped into a negligee and was in bed, propped up against the pillows on my side. I held a book in my hand and, although I was looking right at the title, I was too upset to see it.

It was an unusually still night . . . so still that from where I lay I could clearly hear the sound of the bell buoy ringing far down the harbor. Through the open French doors, the fragrance of the night-blooming jasmine perfumed the room. As the soft ocean breeze directly, tenderly caressed my face, I dropped my book, leaned back, closed my eyes for a moment, and slowly breathed in the clear, fresh ocean air. I glanced up at the white eyelet-embroidered canopy above me, touched the matching drapes tied back at the side of the bed, and let my hands smooth the silky, pale blue satin coverlet, which covered the summer cashmere blanket beneath. The gleaming white linen sheets were bordered by the same

charming eyelet motif, with my initials, *T.L.G.*, neatly appliquéd in the center. It was all so very clean, fresh, and pretty. To me, it symbolized a sheltered place, a private retreat to share with the man I loved. I wanted everything to just stay as it was. I didn't want anything to change.

But I felt uneasy.

"Hi, darling," Paul said as he entered our bedroom. "You're still awake? You look so pretty . . . Is that a new negligee?" Then, walking toward the bed, as he removed his coat, he continued, "Didn't we have a lovely day? Perfect beach weather and such a delightful lunch. You know, I'm glad Emmy married Burton. He's such a fine, upright man."

Throwing aside the covers, I leaned across the bed. Looking straight up at him, I said, "Paul, why don't you explain what you said you were going to explain . . . Now."

"Some things are hard to explain quickly, darling. It's rather a long story and—"

"Oh. So there *is* something you have to explain?"

"Teddy, dear, we've had a rather long day and I'm very tired."

"Well, Paul, I'm not . . . and we've got all night. So tell me the story."

"Darling, I've never seen you act this way before."

"I've never before had such a reason to act this way. And besides, if you're involved in something, I should know about it."

"But Teddy, I am *not* involved."

"Then why in heaven's name did you ask me to talk to that girl? I don't even know her."

Paul started to laugh and said, "Teddy, Teddy, Teddy . . . what a vibrant, dynamic actress you are. I always told you you'd make a great Carmen."

That did it. I was so furious with him I screamed, "How dare you

make fun of me and the way I feel about us? Go away. I never want to see you again."

And with that, I ran out through the open French doors to the terrace. In a moment, Paul's arms were around me and he pulled me back into the bedroom, pushed me onto the bed and, holding me there tightly, looked directly into my eyes and said, "Now, you listen to me. I am not involved with that girl. I met her in Mexico while you were in Italy. She was very young, attractive, and had aspirations of being a great actress. Many people, including myself, tried to help her. She's not in love with me, nor I with her. She's in love with Charles Chaplin." Suddenly, he stopped talking, looked at me intently and said, "That's the whole story. *Their* story."

Then, without releasing his grip on my arms, he swiftly leaned over and kissed me hungrily, whispering, "Darling, now . . . let's get back to *our* story."

The next morning we had breakfast together out on the terrace, something we rarely did, for Paul almost always combined his breakfast with lunch, and I almost always had breakfast in bed. We didn't talk much. Paul seemed especially deep in thought. Suddenly, he looked at me, reached across the table, took my hand in his, and said, "My lovely, romantic Teddy. Sometimes you are a strange, charming elf, and at other times you can be . . . impossible." Then a big smile flooded his face and he continued, "But I guess that's the price I have to pay for your growing up."

I didn't feel much like a "strange, charming elf" . . . I was a woman in love, wanting desperately to protect the newfound relationship I thought I had with my husband. I was hurt that he didn't take me seriously. My intuition told me I had reason to be concerned that Paul's involvement

with this girl might be the beginning of the breakdown of all I held most dear. I guess I was afraid.

After breakfast I took the dogs for a run on the beach. By the time I returned, Paul had left for his office.

During the next few months, after a heavy schedule of concerts up the West Coast to Oregon and back, NCAC set me up at Paramount Studios for a part in the motion picture *The Lost Weekend*, starring the brilliant actor Ray Milland. I played and sang the operatic role of Violetta in the opera sequence of *La Traviata*. The scene was the stage of the New York Metropolitan Opera House, and, as the sequence opens, I am singing the famous "Drinking Song" from act I, with John Garris. John was an important member of the Metropolitan Opera, and had the most beautiful tenor voice. Singing with him was a joy. Billy Wilder, Paramount's genius, who directed *The Lost Weekend*, had expected it would take all day to film the scene. We ran through a rehearsal, the assistant director called "Quiet . . . Roll it," and we did a take. Mr. Wilder said, "Let's do another." We did. He shouted, "Cut. Print." He was exuberant. We had wrapped up in a few morning hours what could have taken all day.

CHAPTER 27

SONG IN THE AIR

The year 1944 started out with a bang. The bombs weren't just falling on Europe and the Pacific; they were falling on me.

On January 3, 1944, I received a call from Lucille Evans, Paul's secretary. He was in Tulsa. She said Paul phoned her to remind me the telephone bill at the beach house was too high. From now on, if it went over $150 a month, he would take out the phone or deduct it from my allowance. This took me by surprise, for I hadn't thought Paul was in trouble financially. I was so intent on doing well at KFWB, I kind of put it out of my mind and forgave him. Looking back now, I realize it was rude and cruel for Paul to ask her to do this—he should have telephoned me himself.

Around this time I learned that my mother was about to lose Wild Acres for taxes. Apparently, she didn't know how to manage or had not been careful regarding her affairs and suddenly was informed that Mr. Luce at the bank in Vineyard Haven was going to foreclose on her

mortgage. I was afraid the Greenwich house might also be in jeopardy.

I hadn't realized how serious this was, even though three months after I'd returned from Italy, I'd sent the bank the balance Mother owed for her 1941 taxes, at her request, out of my allowance from Paul. (The $400 per month I lived on in Italy hadn't stopped when I was imprisoned, so I had quite a bit accumulated in the bank, by the time I got home.) I was shocked by this news. Then I was told that Aunt Ruth and Uncle Herbert had offered to put up some money, if Paul would, too. But he wouldn't. When I asked him, he simply said, "I can't assume any more Lynch family financial burdens."

I immediately phoned Mother, who admitted she'd run up quite a large bill at the Pierre, intending to pay it off. In fact, although Paul was not informed, Mr. Chocket, the manager, had already agreed that Mother could make monthly installments. Ware, who was employed by the hotel, had run up charges entertaining important visiting clients, which was part of his job. I suppose he ran up personal charges, as well. We found out later that a jealous coworker had sent this information to Paul to cause trouble, and it certainly worked.

Instinctively, I realized it was because Paul was so fearful of being used by everyone—*even his wife, her brother,* and *her mother*—that he just couldn't see any reason now to save Wild Acres. His words broke my heart. It simply revealed how Paul couldn't or didn't trust anyone, not even *me.*

This man, who on one hand was quick to come to the aid of a friend, was also fearful of being taken by one. When he returned to Santa Monica that weekend, I went straight to him. I remember Paul was sitting in his favorite green chair in the living room with all of his business papers scattered around him on the floor. I dropped to my

knees, took off my diamond ring, and said, "Please . . . sell it and save Wild Acres. It really will be worth millions one day." Unable to stop the tears, I started to cry.

For a moment he didn't say a word . . . just looked at me . . . then he reached down, pulled me up onto his lap, and very tenderly said, "Listen to me, Teddy. I know how much this means to you and to your whole family, but it's just not right. Your mother, God love her, is a great lady, but like most women of her generation and upbringing, she has no more sense about money than a child. She has always spent whatever she wanted, has had pretty much what she thought she needed, and now she finds herself in this financial situation. I've already spoken to your aunt Ruth and uncle Herbert and we've agreed to bid at the auction, but if we don't win . . ." He stopped, took out his handkerchief, wiped my tears, and went on, "I'll buy her a house here, darling . . . She can pick it out herself, and she'll be near you. Isn't that more important . . . ?"

I didn't hear him. I wasn't listening. I was visualizing my cute little bedroom at Wild Acres, the parties we had as kids up at the barn, the freedom of galloping a horse over the sand dunes on the beach, the feel of salt spray showering over me as I sailed a Wee Scot close-hauled across the finish line in a Saturday afternoon race at the Vineyard Haven Yacht Club. All this was lost to me forever . . . for my sisters and brothers, too. There was just no place on earth like the Vineyard.

I sighed. "You really never liked it, Paul, did you? You only pretended . . . because of me."

"That's not true, Teddy, I only disliked the mosquitoes. The island is great and your mother's house is magnificent, but not to live in all year round. It's too far out from town, would be dreadful if snowbound,

and it's too much house for a woman alone. Your sisters shouldn't be marooned there, either. Really, darling, they'll be happier out here or in New York . . ." And it turned out that he was absolutely right.

But we lost Wild Acres, and at the time I couldn't believe this man, who claimed he loved me, let it happen, when he could have bought that beautiful house with its fifteen acres of meadow and forest and its own private beach as an investment. It's now worth millions, and those who own it rent it for $35,000 a month in the summer when not in residence. But paying Mom's debts and saving her home was not Paul's business . . . and I should have realized I was acting like a spoiled brat to think he should. I guess for a moment I forgot to be grateful that he offered Mom a house in California near me.

But until it could be arranged, I asked Paul, in a businesslike way, to pay for an apartment in New York for Mother and send my little sisters to a good school for which my allowance was to be reduced to $75 per week until it was all paid back. I felt it only right, as I was now making money with my voice. I reminded him that, years ago, when he originally suggested paying for my singing lessons with Marchesi, I had agreed at the time, but "*only* if I can pay *you* back." It made me feel good now that I could. Not that it was very much . . . but at least I was keeping my word. And from that day on, no matter what I earned, I gave him 10 percent. (I still have the first of my checks to him. And he cashed them.)

On Friday evening, March 24, 1944, I was to appear on Hedda Hopper's coast-to-coast program *Hollywood Showcase*, over the CBS network, and sing "Velia" from the *Merry Widow*, at her request.

The night before, my sister Bobby, who was now living at 325 East 72nd Street, New York, with Mother and Nancy, phoned excitedly to

tell me Paul was named in the Joan Barry–Charles Chaplin case that appeared on the front page of that evening's edition of the New York *Daily News.*

"Is this true Teddy?" she asked, in her little girl voice.

"I don't know, Bobby," I replied, hoping it wasn't. Well, she thought she'd better see what was written and send us the clipping.

When I put the phone down, I just sat there—wondering what to do. Paul was in Tulsa. I was waiting for his nightly call . . . it was getting late. Perhaps that was why he hadn't called. He probably knew.

I was to sing the next evening . . . but if this news broke in the Los Angeles paper by the next morning—could I? Should I sing? Only if no one knows Teddy Lynch is Mrs. Getty. Miss Hopper heard me over KFWB as Teddy Lynch, and that's how I was being presented tomorrow evening. So I told myself to stop worrying . . . and when Paul phoned he said, "The story is absolutely untrue." He told me I must go to bed and get my sleep—that he'd be listening to me over his radio tomorrow night, and that he was coming home to be with me in a week. So I did what he said—jumped into bed and turned out the light. But I hardly slept.

Fortunately, the Los Angeles morning paper didn't carry the story and that evening I appeared on the *Hollywood Showcase* as the guest of Miss Hedda Hopper.

The next morning, nothing appeared in our West Coast papers, and I was thankful for this. I was also grateful Miss Hopper was pleased with me, that Paul heard me over his car radio in Tulsa, that Mom, my sisters, and Ware listened to me in New York, and that Mr. Behymer, having heard the show, booked me on a concert tour that was to start in April.

But on Sunday, April 2, 1944, the *Los Angeles Examiner* carried the story on its front page, with a picture of Paul, Joan, and Chaplin,

and naming Paul "the mystery man of Tulsa," a phrase coined by Jerry Giesler, the famous attorney whom Chaplin had hired.

It seemed Giesler was looking for Paul, so the article stated, "to show that this man, Jean Paul Getty, had more than befriended Joan in 1941" . . . "that they had been lovers" . . . "that he had helped her financially" . . . "that she had been with him in Mexico City" . . . "that she had stayed at the Pierre Hotel in New York, which he owned" . . . "that she had visited him in Tulsa in November of '42" . . . "and he was to be called as a witness in the Chaplin case, which was about to start in Los Angeles."

Giesler didn't really have to look too far. Paul was with me now at the beach house in Santa Monica.

Joan had taken the witness stand at Chaplin's trial on Mann Act charges and testified that it was the actor-producer who had paid her way to New York for immoral purposes. Only, Giesler insisted that it was Paul who figured so importantly in Joan's life, suggesting that was why she had recently gone to see him in Tulsa for help.

It was a real blow to have this published in such a blatant way at a time when I thought I was happily reunited with Paul and trying desperately to establish myself as the singer he wanted me to be.

The morning that the news hit the streets in Los Angeles, I was awakened by a loud ringing. Paul and I were asleep, and, thinking it might be Mother calling from New York at this unreasonable hour, I grabbed the phone. "Hello," I whispered, "is that you, Mom? It's only seven o'clock here . . . Are you okay?" For a moment I heard nothing, then a rather rough-sounding woman's voice, not Mother's, greeted me with a "Hi, Mrs. Getty . . . Is it true you're getting a divorce? That's what it says in the papers."

For a moment I almost dropped the receiver, and then defiantly I yelled, "No, I'm not, whoever you are." And slammed the phone down. At that Paul woke up. "Who in the name of creation is calling at such an ungodly hour?" he asked.

"I don't know, some crazy woman asking if I was getting a divorce."

"Are you, darling?" he questioned.

"Not before breakfast," I yelled back as I jumped out of bed. "Anyway—I want to see the morning papers before deciding."

Throwing on my robe, I ran downstairs to the dining room, where I found the morning paper on the table beside Paul's place setting, which consisted of his usual bowl of shredded wheat, wheat germ, yogurt, raw sugar, milk, toast, and a glass of orange juice.

And there it was . . . in large headlines . . . on the front page of the *Los Angeles Examiner*. "The Mystery Man from Tulsa" by Florabel Muir, with a picture of Paul, Joan, and Chaplin . . . and the story Jerry Giesler hoped would prove that Paul, not Chaplin, was the father of Joan's child.

I stood there, trying not to believe what I was reading, when I became aware that Paul, dressed in robe and slippers, had come downstairs and was standing there beside me.

"It's not true, Teddy," he kept saying. "That bastard Giesler is just using me to defend Chaplin . . . I'd better call Tom." And with that he went into the library to phone Tom Dockweiler, his lawyer. Moments later, the doorbell rang . . . It was someone from the press, and to avoid them, I dashed upstairs, slipped on jeans and a shirt, and escaped to the beach. I had to be alone to figure out what to do.

Next month I was to go on tour . . . Should I? With my husband the "Mystery Man" involved in this scandalous affair with Charles Chap-

lin, beloved by millions, one of the most famous, internationally known
motion picture stars in the world? The press was going to have a ball and
I knew Paul was going to be hurt . . . Somehow, I had to stand by him,
and I would . . . but what should I do about the tour? All these thoughts
ran through my head as I ran down the beach.

I had almost reached the pier when Paul caught up with me . . .
Peter and Penny at his heels. He took my hand and pulled me to him . . .
and we just stood there . . . in the wet sand . . . with the waves curling
up around us . . . not speaking for a long time. I couldn't stop my tears at
the realization that our privacy, the very love we seemed to have found
once again . . . was being taken from us.

"Darling, believe me," he said. "These accusations are not true,
but I have to face them. I don't want this to hurt you more than it has
already, so I'll check in at the Biltmore tonight, where I'll be near the
court. This way the press won't bother you, and, Teddy, you must do
the tour Behymer arranged. It's too great an opportunity to turn down.
Tom thinks it's a good idea, too."

"But, Paul, now you won't be able to come to the last four weeks I'm
singing here over at KFWB."

"I'll be listening. I'm sure the Biltmore Hotel has a radio in every
room." I looked up—he smiled. It was then, at that moment, I knew I
had to trust him, but I was afraid. Taking my hand, Paul said, "Come on,
darling, let's go home and you can help me pack."

That night alone in the house, I burst into tears.

"I love you, Teddy," Paul had said as he left. "If this was my child I
would have told you . . . but it's not. Be a good girl and get on with the
tour." And with those words, he was gone.

The Chaplin-Barry case went on for more than a year, with daily

reports in the newspapers and other men named as having been Joan's lovers . . . but Jerry Giesler seemed adamant that Paul was the father of her child.

To the amazement of the entire court, when Paul finally was called before the judge, he simply stated, "Your Honor, I have, from time to time, helped Joan financially, but I have not seen her for the past three hundred sixty-five days . . . and since no woman has been known in medical history to have carried a child for that long a period . . . *I* cannot be the father."

For a moment there was great silence—then, the entire courtroom burst into applause . . . and the judge excused him.

While this was going on, my brother Ware, who was with the Russell Birdwell Agency, suggested Paul hire them to keep my name out of the papers. Paul took his advice, thus allowing me in April—as Teddy Lynch—to go on tour for the NCAC. It was not without a touch of sorrow in my heart, however, for I knew Paul had had an affair with Joan in Mexico, helping her financially through the years, and I found myself fighting the thought that "out there" might be others intrigued by his wealth and ability as a lover. Paul was the most fascinating man I'd ever known, the provider of a beautiful home, a great lover, and I really loved him. Besides . . . he was kind, my best friend. So I made myself stop thinking bad thoughts and dwelled on how happy we were when we were together. At least . . . so it seemed to me . . . Or is this what a wife feels . . . not really knowing? Anyway, right after the concert tour, on Saturday, April 28, 1945, came the debut of my very own radio show, *Song in the Air*, over the Blue Network (the American Broadcasting Station). I worked with conductor Ernie Gill, his orchestra, and a host of celebrities who helped put on a fun show that was

heard from coast-to-coast each week. I began to feel I was finally making progress.

By now Paul was making many trips back and forth to Tulsa, and no matter where he was, in his office or car, he would catch my program, and phone or send me letters filled with "Bravo's" or critiques of the songs I had chosen to sing.

CHAPTER 28

THE RANCH

During these years, Paul often confided that he longed to have a building large enough to house his growing art collection, which up until then was partly on loan to museums and partly in storage. At one time, he seriously considered building a small museum next to the beach house; even had plans drawn up, but for some reason didn't carry it through.

Then, one afternoon, in the summer of 1945, I had just come in from swimming when Paul phoned from his office. "Get dressed, darling," he said. "I'm coming to pick you up. I want to show you a property." So I quickly slipped into blue jeans and a shirt, draped a towel around my wet hair, and dashed out to meet him. As we took off up the Pacific Coast Highway, toward Malibu, I asked where we were going. He smiled and said, "You'll see, darling." Expecting it might be a one- or two-hour drive, I curled up in the seat and started to towel-dry my hair.

About ten minutes later, just past where Sunset Boulevard meets

the Coast Highway, past that famous restaurant, Chez Roland, where, it was said, Thelma Todd had been murdered years before, Paul suddenly slowed down. He pulled off to the right of the highway and stopped in front of two very large spiked iron gates.

Without explanation, he got out of the car, took a huge key from his pocket, inserted it in a recessed lock, and slowly, the huge gates opened.

We drove through and the gates closed slowly behind us. For a moment we just sat there. It was so quiet . . . like we were in another world. All around were huge trees, big bushes. A winding dirt road lay ahead. I was speechless. We drove slowly past three ponds of clear, fresh water surrounded by lilies and ferns. Paul pointed over to the left and said, "These pools are fed by the only fresh springwater close to the Pacific Coast Highway, between Santa Monica and Santa Barbara. In the early history of Los Angeles, whenever the famous bandit Joachim Murrieta rode up the coast with his men, they always stopped here to water their horses and refill their water bags."

"How fabulous" was all I managed to say, amazed at Paul's knowledge of the history of the place, but before I could ask him to tell me more, we passed a huge sycamore grove—the trees old, bent, and gnarled with time, but still green with foliage. Suddenly, a field of heavily laden avocado trees came into view . . . and a lemon grove across from which nestled a quaint, tiny Spanish adobe house, almost hidden in a sea of flowering bushes. *What fun it would be to live there*, I thought as we sped by. Then finally, rounding a bend in the road, Paul pulled up in front of a magnificent old Spanish hacienda with a tile roof and a tower, which seemed to fit right into the hills behind it, and I heard him turn the motor off.

For the longest moment I just sat there and stared at this rambling

old hacienda, half expecting a Spanish grandee to walk out the front door and greet us . . . but no one appeared.

"Look, Teddy," Paul said, pulling me away and excitedly pointing down toward the sea. "Isn't this view stupendous? See the sailboats and Catalina? What an incredible site." And it was.

Past the sloping luscious green lawn, which ended where it met the lemon and avocado groves below, one could see trees, the blue Pacific and sailboats, with Catalina Island on the horizon, but there was absolutely no sign of the Pacific Coast Highway and no noise from cars speeding by—not like today. It had a sweet acrid scent of sand, clay, underbrush, and fruit, and the cool soft wind coming up the valley from the sea was enchanting.

"Paul," I said, still mesmerized by the beauty surrounding us, "who owns this place . . . and . . . what are we doing here?"

"It's ours, darling," he said. "I just bought it from Claude Parker, who has owned it since the early twenties. He named it the Sentimental Canyon, and bought it from the Marquez family, who were granted the land by the king of Spain when California was under Spanish rule. Just think, Teddy," he went on, "we are the second Americans to own this Spanish grant, which originally ran from Topanga Canyon all the way down to California Street in Santa Monica and back as far as the San Vicente Rancho. Now all that's left of the original Boca di Santa Monica Ranch is forty acres and this great old hacienda." He turned to me. "Do you like it, darling?"

"Do I like it? Oh, Paul," I cried, "it's wonderful! But what about the little house we passed on the way up here? Who lives there?"

"No one, darling. It's a guesthouse . . . and beyond are the stables and homes for the ranch hands . . . but right now, let's go exploring." And

that's just what we did. First, the hacienda itself, with its charming old rooms and, to my delight, a theater with a stage, which I secretly claimed as mine.

Almost immediately Paul began making plans to rebuild the hacienda, to create a courtyard that would lead to the entrance of a museum, large enough to house his growing art collection. Paul had topsoil transported from there to the beach, and arranged for a lawn to be sown and a high fence to be built, and soon we were no longer just a pretty house sitting in sand, by the sea, but a pretty house sitting on the only prettiest green lawn on Santa Monica's seashore.

FOR ME, THE summer of 1945 passed by too swiftly. As I remember it, our marriage seemed to be on the verge of an even higher plane of feeling. We were becoming increasingly sensitive to each other and to the hundred thousand different ways you see and feel and know the one you love and appreciate. There were the good times and the not so good, but above all, I loved and was loved. I felt serenely secure in my marriage, which was all the more exciting because it had successfully bridged the storms of time, war, separation, and other people. Sometimes on a Sunday, Paul's two youngest sons, Paul and Gordon, would come for lunch. They were adorable boys. Well mannered and interested in everything. One Sunday we took them with us to see a matinee performance of *Pagliacci*, with the great tenor Giovanni Martinelli singing the leading role. It was a wonderful afternoon.

On August 6, 1945, President Harry Truman gave the order to drop the atom bomb on Hiroshima, Japan, completely wiping out the city. Five days later a second bomb destroyed Nagasaki, and Japan sued for peace.

On September 1 (Tokyo time), the Japanese Delegation surrendered to General Douglas MacArthur aboard the USS *Missouri* in Tokyo Bay. Paul and I were at the beach house when we heard President Truman and General MacArthur speak, and with tears of gratitude we thanked God that the world was at long last at peace.

The following day, Sunday, September 2, 1945, the world celebrated VJ Day. It was the hottest day at the beach in years; the temperature was 100 degrees. Paul and I spent the morning swimming in the sea and, later, as we relaxed in the large lounge chairs on the cool green grass lawn, we talked about the future of our world at peace.

We recalled that although we had met just prior to the actual outbreak of war, the world had been in an almost constant restless state. We spoke of our love and friendship. How fortunate that, in spite of the chaos of war and the two years of separation, we had found each other again.

I had most certainly grown up a great deal since I'd first met Paul, and like all married couples we had weathered quite a few storms. He wasn't the easiest of husbands. We did, however, try to understand each other, and the trying seemed to be the key. Even though he was a very important businessman and a resourceful one, I felt he needed me, and I knew I needed him.

I was now more mature and capable of understanding the man and the genius inside this man, which drove him to incessantly reach out for greater goals. He was at this time working to make the changeover in Spartan from wartime to postwar production and he worked endlessly and hard to accomplish this.

At the same time, he was in constant contact regarding the plans for the ranch house and the museum. John Byers, who had been the architect for the beach house, was to do the ranch house. Jack Bonar was to do

the interior decorating and the Macco Construction Company to be the builders. This took months of preparation and years to bring to reality, as did the magnificent reconversion of the lawns, orchards, gardens, and courtyard, which landscape artist William Beresford designed. All this, so Paul's precious art objects, tapestries, paintings, furniture, and statuary could be safely and securely displayed in a setting worthy of them.

In the doing, Paul was always leaving for somewhere. To Spartan in Tulsa, to the Pierre in New York, or to Bakersfield to check on a new oil well. I appreciated his desire to spread his wings and fly, but like any woman in love I hated to be left behind when the moment of parting arrived, and I never understood why he didn't want me to go with him.

Rudyard Kipling once wrote: "He travels the fastest who travels alone." Henry Wadsworth Longfellow wrote, "The heights by great men reached and kept / Were not attained by sudden flight, / But they, while their companions slept, / Were toiling upward in the night."

Both of these quotes might have been written to describe Paul—driven as if by some inner force not only to accomplish one job successfully, but, even before its conclusion, to be seeking another. Not solely for monetary gain, but for his own satisfaction and expression. Work was his very own happiness, which he could not share with another. This *was* Paul. He was happy to be married—confident and secure in his marriage—but apparently unable to resist his compulsion to conquer new projects.

Late one afternoon, the telephone rang. It was Livingston Pomeroy. I hadn't seen him since our prison days in Italy.

"Teddy," he said, "I'm on my way to the Orient. Can I stop by for a moment to say hi?"

"Pom—by all means do," I replied. "And stay for dinner."

Immediately, I called Paul at the office to tell him.

"Why don't you two just have dinner together," he said. "After all, I'm sure you have lots to talk about. Besides, I have a full evening of work to do at the office."

Livingston arrived, and it was fun recalling the mad escapades we had gone through in Rome. We had barely finished dinner when Paul walked in. As I introduced them I noticed Paul seemed taken aback by the apparent boyish attractiveness of this young man.

After a few moments, Livingston looked at his watch and said, "Well, if I hope to make my plane I'd better leave." Then, looking directly at Paul he asked, "Mr. Getty, do you mind if I kiss your wife good-bye?"

"Why, uh, no," Paul replied. "Of course not. Go right ahead."

Then he watched as Livingston leaned over, put his arms around me, and kissed me very tenderly on the mouth.

After what seemed more than a moment, Livingston released me, and a bit flustered, excitedly grabbed Paul's hand, pumping it up and down, all the while saying, "Thanks, Mr. Getty. Good-bye, Teddy, *cara*, I love you." And with that, he bounded out the door, through the patio, and down the street to his waiting car.

We stood quietly for a moment as it sped off. Walking back to the patio, Paul grabbed my hand. "I must say, Teddy, that was quite a kiss. Livingston really looked as though he meant it."

I smiled. "Yes . . . I think he did." I always wondered about this kiss, and never saw Pom Pom again.

WHEN HELEN AINSWORTH and Mr. Morton decided to be my agents, after my Santa Barbara concert, I was thrilled because NCAC was world-

renowned and I was very grateful to have that office send me out on concert tours . . . which also resulted in my own radio show over the American Broadcasting System.

Helen, who resembled Kate Smith, was a wonderful human being. Kind and helpful to all her clients, she worked hard to set them on their way, but beneath that infectious laugh of hers was a woman who, in childhood, had been utterly destroyed by her very prominent father, Dr. Schumate.

When she was young, he was embarrassed of her size, and insisted she always walk behind him whenever they were together, thus shattering her self-esteem. Finally, after graduating from Mills College, she married, later divorced, came to Los Angeles, and joined the West Coast offices of National.

One day, I had an interview at Universal Studios, and was promptly sent to sing in the Casbah sequence of the film *Scheherazade*, based on the life of Rimsky-Korsakov and starring Jean-Pierre Aumont and Yvonne De Carlo.

After recording my songs and posing for press release pictures, I sang a concert at Marymount College. Paul was there, and in his diary he recorded, *Teddy's concert a success, I'm proud of her.*

The following afternoon, Paul and I went to hear *La Traviata* at the Shrine, and that evening Paul and Jefty O'Connor attended a reception for Admiral Bull Halsey at Mayor Bowron's house. When Paul arrived home, he was exuberant. He said, "Teddy, tonight I shook hands with a hero."

Late the next afternoon I heard a car swerve into the garage and come to a fast stop. It was Paul. He rushed into the house and called, "Teddy—Robert—hurry, help me pack. I'm leaving on the California

Limited for Tulsa." He had one suitcase full of clothes and four suitcases full of books. I drove him to the railway station in Pasadena and, again, he was off on one of those whirlwind tours of his factory, oil wells, and hotel.

The following week, during the filming of the Casbah sequence at Universal Studios, I suddenly became very ill. It was the first time in my life I had ever been so sick. Harry was on the set and rushed me to a doctor. I don't remember too much about it except that I was able to live through the pain, return to the studio, and film the scene. I went home to bed, and the next morning I awoke feeling fine.

That evening I telephoned Paul in Tulsa and told him all about it. I also told him that NCAC had an offer from an independent producer, who, having seen me on the set of *Scheherazade*, wanted me to play the part of a singer in a movie that was to be shot in January. They suggested I read the script. NCAC did, and thought it would be good for me.

Paul said, "That's great, darling, but it's a long way off. And before you sign a contract, have Tom look it over."

IT WAS SATURDAY, December 15—Paul's birthday. He was in Tulsa. I sent him a huge bouquet of red roses and chrysanthemums. As usual, he was at the factory from nine to six, even though it was a Saturday, supervising the changeover from military vehicle to trailer manufacturing.

I was upset thinking he would not be home for Christmas, but on December 21, he arrived just in time to host a small dinner party I was giving, honoring Vivianne Della Chiesa, who was in Los Angeles on a concert tour.

On Christmas Eve, we stayed at home. Robert was perched atop a

ladder, trimming the Christmas tree, and our house was already welcoming the holiday, with a beautiful Christmas wreath on the front door, a life-size Santa Claus on the lawn, white pots filled with red poinsettias on tables in the patio entrance, and boxes and boxes of ornaments piled high in the living room.

To my knowledge, the only serious fight I ever had with Paul Getty was on this December 24, 1945. I had just finished wrapping the gifts Paul had chosen to give his two youngest sons, Paul and Gordon. Happily, I carried them downstairs to show Paul, who was sitting in his favorite big green chair in the living room, going through a huge pile of business papers, which should have been taboo on Christmas . . . But he looked up, smiled, and said, "Thanks, darling, these wrappings are truly beautiful—I hope the boys also like what's inside."

"Of course they will, Paul," I replied. "Only you better hurry up and deliver them. Christmas is tomorrow, and I'm sure the boys will wake up at dawn to see what Santa has left under their tree."

"Oh, Teddy, why don't you phone and see if they can come and pick them up? I'm sure Mrs. Rork can drive them out this afternoon."

"Paul Getty, are you mad?" I said. "One doesn't ask one's children to come and pick up Christmas gifts from their father's house. The excitement is to surprise them on Christmas morning . . . Also, you can't expect their grandmother to drive. It's Christmas Eve, she's probably extremely busy, and furthermore, the traffic will be horrendous this afternoon. No, you must go now, it won't take you long."

Paul, annoyed, looked up, put down his paper, and said, "Just call, Teddy."

"No, I won't," I snapped back. And with that, I pulled the enormous Christmas wreath off the door, slammed it over his head, and ran as fast

as I could upstairs. I could hear him swearing, "Damn you, Teddy, I'm going to beat you up for this!" So I rushed into the bathroom, grabbed my large hand mirror and scared though I was, faced him as he stormed in. For a moment I thought he was really going to hit me, but I managed to say, "Don't you dare, Paul Getty, or I'll—" and I raised my hand mirror. He stopped, turned, and walked out. I slammed the door shut, locked it, and burst into tears.

Later, I heard a door slam, heard some bells on the front gate jingle, and in minutes saw a sudden burst of exhaust as his car shot out of the garage onto the Pacific Coast Highway. Looking back, I realized that, beyond his being furious at having to give up his precious time, was the worry that maybe the wreath might have ruined his face-lift.

Hours later, he came home and knocked on my door. I opened it, and he stood there for just a moment looking at me; then, taking me in his arms, he whispered, "You were right, darling, forgive me." Unexpectedly, desire for this man swept over me as he kissed my mouth and breasts and passionately pulled me down on our bed. The zipper refusing him, he tore off my negligee and entered me. During those next hours, we were one—the exquisite coming together—the peace of love.

A week later, on New Year's Eve, I hadn't planned a special party or any celebration for us. I just wanted to be with Paul at home.

After dinner I excused myself and went upstairs. I didn't tell Paul, but I wasn't feeling well. I walked out onto the terrace. It was a cold clear night and all the stars were out. I looked over the ocean, watching the waves break into iridescent crests. But as beautiful as it was, it was strange. The instant the waves dashed up to the dark beach below, their brightness was instantly extinguished, as if an unseen hand had turned off a light. It seemed ominous—perhaps because I felt ill. Very ill.

———

Slipping into a gown and robe, I lay down on the bed. I must have gone to sleep immediately.

This was noteworthy. So noteworthy that Paul wrote in his diary that night:

We spent a very quiet New Year's Eve. Home with Teddy.
She was asleep by 10:30. First time in history.
She looked so tired, didn't waken her.
I spent the night in the guest room, so she could sleep soundly.

CHAPTER 29

MY NEW CAREER

Little did Paul know, I walked the floor all night—in pain. By morning I felt better, and Paul had to leave.

"You're full of stones," Dr. Bergman said as he leaned over the foot of my hospital bed, "and I'm slating the operation for tomorrow."

"What do you mean stones?" I asked.

"Gallstones. You're full of them and—"

"Why you're . . ."

"Now wait a minute, Teddy—you're full of stones and besides that, you're pregnant."

"What! I am? How wonderful. Is it true?" I said, not daring to believe.

"Yes, it's true. But if we don't remove the stones immediately, you're going to have a hard time holding your baby."

"Oh—I must tell Paul . . . He's in Tulsa."

"I've already spoken to him, but you should call him. He can't be here, Teddy, but he's sending Dr. Ortman Shumate to consult with me."

Then he handed me the telephone. "Right now, Paul's waiting," and he walked out of the room.

I lifted the receiver immediately, and to my surprise the operator said, "Mrs. Getty, I have a call for you." It was Paul.

"Teddy? Is that you?"

"Hi."

"I told Dr. Bergman to tell you to call me. I've been waiting and waiting."

"Well, he just now told me."

"Teddy—did he tell you about the baby?"

"Yes—are you happy about it?"

"Of course I am! It's wonderful. But, Teddy, he also said that you're full of stones."

"I know. Must be something left over from the war."

"Teddy—stop joking. It's serious."

"I know, Paul, and . . . I'm scared."

"Don't be. Everything's going to be all right. It's got to be, for we're going to have a baby."

I sat up late that night and made out my will on a piece of scratch paper—folded it—and stuffed it into a little receptacle in the post of my hospital bed.

It was six A.M. A nurse opened the door and handed me the phone. I heard Paul say, "Darling, I've been thinking about you all night long. I couldn't sleep. I'm so worried—I don't know what I'd do without you. I don't want you to die. I'd give up Spartan and all I have if you'll only live . . ."

"Paul, dear, you don't have to give up anything. I'll be okay—really. I'm trusting God. You better trust him, too."

"But I should be with you—you're all alone."

"You're with me in your heart, so I'm not alone."

"Teddy, darling, you're such a brave little girl—and I love you."

"I love you, too."

As I hung up the receiver, the nurse came back into the room and gave me a shot. The orderlies lifted me up. I felt I was moving through space. I knew where I was going, but I wasn't afraid. I was just sad that Paul was. A few hours after the operation, Paul phoned but was told I was resting and was not to be disturbed. The next afternoon I was able to talk to him. Later that day he wrote this letter:

Hotel Tulsa
Jan. 27, 1946
Darling,

It was so wonderful to hear your voice this afternoon. But I'm distressed. I feel you are disappointed in me—and I feel I made a mistake in not being with you for the operation. Your love and your well-being mean everything to me.

I was swamped here last week—general disorganization. People quitting, waste and extravagance to be immediately checked, engineering and designer question to be settled that were holding up progress of an important tax meeting to prepare for. I felt I could only leave in case of an emergency. Your operation wasn't an emergency. Ortman, you said, advised you to wait a few days or maybe a week or two. I wanted to be with you and this delay would have permitted me to spend a week at Spartan, prepare for the tax

meeting, and be home the first week in Feb. You then could have the
operation and I would be with you. You wanted it this way,
so did Ortman, so did I.

Foolishly, I advised you to do what neither of us wanted—
have an immediate operation—not even to wait one day, even
though I couldn't arrive in time for the operation. I advised you thus
because I love you and felt your well-being would be best served by
an immediate operation without any delay because a delay would
mean anxious days of waiting would distress and weaken you in
my opinion. I wanted you to clear your mind of any anxiety—to
get this operation behind you at once and not pass days waiting for
it and dreading it. My own personal longing to be with you was
subordinated to plans for an operation the next morning.

Please don't think I've failed you. I didn't mean to—I know now
I should have advised you to wait until I returned.

I love you,

Paul

Two days later, the door of my hospital room opened and there stood Paul with a huge bouquet of red roses. Quietly he said—"Teddy, darling, the doctor tells me you're doing fine and our baby is, too. I'm so thankful." Then he came over and kissed me. For the next week he was with me every day and night. And the day I went home, as they wheeled me from my room, I remembered my will, retrieved it from its hiding place, and tore it up.

More and more Paul was traveling back and forth between California, Oklahoma, and New York. It seemed hard on him but it was even harder for me—having had a major operation and being pregnant

at the same time. I was also concerned because the doctors held little hope that I would have the baby. I was constantly in and out of the hospital for the next four months, and since Paul was away so much, I wrote to my mother that I needed her and asked if she and my sisters would come to the coast and stay with me. Without delay they were on the train, and my friend Churchill Ross met them at the Pasadena station.

After taking their luggage to the beach house, Mother and the girls came to see me at the hospital, where my doctor had sent me due to complications. After talking with Dr. Bradbury, Mother arranged that I be allowed to go home with the promise that I would be kept quiet . . . and not drive for a month, especially not in "that little green Morgan car she runs around in," Bradbury said, feeling I might lose the baby. So I phoned Paul and asked that he rent a heavier car for me. He said, "No, you don't need to drive . . . your mother and sisters are there." I was so taken aback, I started to cry . . . then I phoned his lawyer, Tom Dockweiler, for his advice. "Isn't this baby you are carrying Paul's?" he asked. "Yes," I said. "Well then, pick up the phone, my dear Teddy, rent a car, and charge it to him." And with "I simply can't understand Paul at times," he rang off.

So I did what Tom told me to do. Paul never spoke of it again, and I put the whole episode in the back of my mind . . . along with Paul's strange aversion to paying telephone bills.

It was so good to be home again and to see my lovely "baby sisters," Nancy and Bobby, who were now gorgeous young ladies. Everyone fell in love with them. Our telephone rang like Central Casting, and handsome young men were calling at the house day and night. When the girls were out on dates, sightseeing, or in the pool, Mom and I had

quiet times together, catching up. It was then that she promised that she would stay on in California after my baby arrived. Plans were made for her and the girls to live at the guesthouse on the ranch until we found the house that Paul had promised me he'd buy for her.

Our baby was scheduled to arrive in August. We had already selected names. A girl would be named Louise after Mom (and me), and her second name would be Christina, which means "bearer of Christ." If a boy, his name would be Timothy, because it meant "gift of God." His second name would be Christopher, meaning "bearer of truth," and his third name, Ware, mother's family name.

April 20, 1946

Saturday

Darling Teddy Boo,

Thanks for writing me—the first since March 5. I'm lonely and you don't write me.

It's such slavery here. 13 hours a day trying to get the trailers into production. Meanwhile, the factory is losing money like mad.

I haven't been to a movie or done anything worth writing about.

The little house is still just a basement. My hotel room is cheerless and hot. I want to be with you and Hildy at the beach. Maybe I can settle the factory so I can leave it by the end of the month.

Darling, Ruly Cutten and his bride are in L.A. I think at the Beverly Hills Hotel or the Beverly Wilshire. E. F. Hutton and Company will have the address.

Please call them and show them the ranch.

I love you even if you are mean.

Paul

———

May 9, 1946

Darling,

It was cheering to hear your voice yesterday. You sounded happy and gay. As you know I'm slaving away here trying to manufacture trailers and it is a back breaking job. Once the trailer line is moving I should be able to return home. I am so homesick and anxious to see you.

Now, sweet, I must ask your cooperation in financial matters. I have the following wire from Lloyd Hughes. "Mrs. Getty is requesting reimbursement on numerous clothing bills which she feels we should pay from this office rather than forward the check to you. I have no authority to sign these checks, please advise."

Our understanding is that I pay you a weekly allowance of $100 and this was to pay for your clothes and pin money. I just paid several hundred dollars of your clothing bills and I can't do this and give you an allowance too, for clothes, and now it seems there are additional bills for clothes.

You were sweet and like yourself in your last call, but in the one before you seemed a different girl and not the one that I always loved. You mentioned having something on me or the same effect. Now, dear, you have nothing on me and you never will have. After much cogitation I decided you referred to the Anderson's. Some time ago in a trade with an oil company I took an equity in a house in Castellamara. I considered it a good investment and didn't mention it to you because the housing shortage is so acute that knowing your kind heart, I thought some of your friends would pester you to arrange it or more likely pester me too. Mr. and Mrs. Anderson are not California residents and I did allow them to stay there during

their visit because it was short. I want to see my equity as soon as prices peak, and I don't want troublesome tenants and they are all troublesome now because they have no place to go. It is hard to sell a tenanted place because buyers want immediate and untroubled possession. I don't see that I should be apologetic about this, but if I should be, I apologize.

Now dear, before I left, several times you talked about getting a divorce, setting aside the property settlement we signed, and indicated you were dissatisfied with me, principally I understood, because you felt I didn't give you what I should. If this is your attitude it will be necessary for us to settle this definitely and formally.

I am the head of the household. I am the one that provides the money. I think I provide generously for you. Maybe you don't think so. Maybe you think you can get more money in a court fight. I don't know. I do know, however, that no judge can make me pay the bills for Hereford Water, your singing career and contribute to your mothers support. I don't believe that any judge would give you more than one thousand per month for your support (if there were no agreement) and from this you would pay all your expenditures. As long as I am voluntarily paying your bills and there is no court settlement, you should, in fairness, allow me to determine the amount in advance and not try to take control of the situation. I mean in regard to your personal expenditures.

I hope you don't *misunderstand my frankness. I don't mean to offend you but it was necessary to clear the air.*

I love you and I don't want a divorce and I hope you love me.

Your devoted husband,

Paul

PS: I would particularly like to be with you these months that are so important to us.

I answered Paul's May 9 letter at once.

May 11, 1946
Darling,

Paul, your letter of May 9 arrived this morning and I was happy that you thought enough of me to write what was in your heart. You are mistaken about several things which I feel should be straightened out.

First: I believe you have not stated fully the facts concerning your arrangement with Mrs. Anderson and I am led to believe by certain other facts that I am correct. What I know or think I know is of no importance really except that you have lost your standing in my eyes. I have always looked up to you but I shall no longer unless you are worthy of my faith and trust.

Secondly: Paul, you are very wrong to suggest that I want or desire more than my right as your wife and a woman you love. I have never taken you or your money for granted. I do not expect you to do more than a man in your position can do . . . I have never taken advantage of you . . . and I never will. I do not consider that by being a mother I can suddenly demand and get more materially from you. If, during all the years you have known me, my character has not shown itself to you clearly as one of honesty and faithfulness then it is about time for you to awaken from the dream you have been living in and see me as I really am. I have been most appreciative for all you have done for me—never taking

*it for granted that because of any reason you had to give me what I
wanted, I have deserved all and perhaps more than I've received but
I have never lacked a grateful heart. What seems to slip your mind
is the important fact that prices are from 4 to 6 times higher than in
1939. I do not ask you to pay for my normal wearing apparel but
simply for the clothes I have needed during the months I am carrying
your baby. Dockweiler said "THEY ARE DEDUCTIBLE" SO
HERE AGAIN YOU HAVE LOST NOTHING. As for the
expense of a big car . . . it does seem silly to rent a "[car]" but my
doctor thinks it wiser and God knows after the operation three
months ago and the hard luck of losing a wonderful contract I find
the comfort of riding in a heavy car so important to my life and to
the life of our baby that I can hardly find words to describe it.*

*Thirdly: You refer to paying out so much for my career and
Hereford . . . that no law or judge could force you to pay these bills.
That is perfectly true, but you overlook the simple fact that I, on
my honor have paid you 10 percent of all monies I have received
since my return to this country which makes you my partner, backer
or whatever you care to call yourself. It also shows that I, stand
BY MY WORD, have not used you falsely, that my intentions
have been and are most honorable. I might add that although you
have been so kind in paying for lessons, your own conduct in the
social world we live in has been very hard for me to bear . . . your
association with cheap women . . . plus the notorious and humiliating
Chaplin case has not been conducive to a closer relationship with me.
You know full well that my employing a press agent was an attempt
to hurdle, for both you and me, the unsavory reputation you have
strewn about from this town to New York and back. It is with a*

sad heart I say all this to you for I have loved you dearly and have made every human attempt to abide by your wishes in everything I have done since first we met, trusting completely in your wise knowledge of what was good or bad for me, however I see I have been mistaken, for I now realize that "what is good for Teddy rests solely on whether Paul decides that it will not inconvenience him in any way" first.

To put you at your ease, may I inform you that I have done some research on our problem, which in reality is NO PROBLEM . . . UNLESS you make it so, and have found out a few important points which should make your burden less heavy.

First, all of my clothes, hairdressers, photograph session, publicity and traveling expenses can be definitely deducted from your income taxes . . . as I'm a professional. Also 100% on all lessons. THE Hereford TEXAS WATER CO. is a GODSEND to you for you can write it off completely this year, as you in your bracket need to have some things to write off.

Furthermore and please lets get this straight . . . stop accusing me of spending so much on HEREFORD AS THO IT WERE SOMETHING YOU WERE GENEROUSLY BUILDING FOR ME ALONE. You ALSO OWN A PERCENT OF IT AND ARE BENEFITING FROM IT THRU THIS PERIOD OF LOSS AS WELL AS WHEN WE MAKE IT A PERIOD OF PROFIT.

I have just finished a recording session at A.R.A. and my album will be released in August . . . it might make you some money so be grateful you have such a sweet wife and stop grumbling. THANKS for letting me have mother and the girls out here . . .

Your Teddy

Hotel Tulsa
Saturday
May 18, 1946
Teddy,

   *I must answer your letter but I can't write much because I'm
so tired. I've been on my feet all day, up and down the length
breath of the factory. I suppose the rail or coal strike will shut
us down.*

   *I had no "arrangements" with Mrs. Anderson and there is
nothing untoward or improper about my acquaintance with the
Andersons. I am not guilty of any wrong doing with the others you
mention. RE the Chaplin case she never accused me of anything,
his Lawyers made a great to-do about me and intimated to the press
that once I was on the stand and they could question me and their
client would be exonerated, etc. The first trial resulted in my being
excused by them after two minutes of testimony as follows. Name,
Address, Occupation. Do you know Joan Berry? Did you see her in
1941? Dismissed. The second trial they again broadcast they were
going to tear me wide open etc. And then decided they didn't want
my testimony. Joe Scott did and when I was on the stand asked me
various questions establishing our acquaintance was proper and
the loan was made in good faith and against collateral. Then I was
turned over to his attorney to be torn to pieces on cross examination.
I was asked did you lend Miss Berry money? Answer: "Yes, on
a mortgage." "Did you see her in Tulsa in Nov. 1942?" Answer:
"Yes." "Dismissed." I think this speaks for itself and so did the jury.
I won't go into a money matters now, but I think you should—
among other things—have asked my permission before authorizing*

or ordering an extension to the guest cottage or spending several hundred dollars in renting a big car. I might have preferred to get a chauffeur to drive you in my car. Don't you think you've been rather fresh in these and other money matters recently? It was supposed to be that you spent your allowance as you so inclined, but other proposed expenditures were to be approved by me in advance—not afterwards or not at all.

I'm sorry you used the past time in referring to your love for me. I've tried in my own way I suppose to be a better than average husband to you. However, somethings don't suit you. I'm sorry you didn't have the good fortune to choose a husband that was a success as a husband. Judging from the records millions of other women are similarly not suited. I don't know the solution of something that seems to affect a large percentage of women. It must be the man's fault. Either men are worse now than they were a generation ago or wives are more easily estranged.

I must close now as I'm so tired. There is a smattering of thunder and a storm is approaching after a beautiful day.

Yours,

Paul

As months went on, it seemed almost everyone knew that we were going to have a baby. Danton Walker, the *Daily News* columnist, ran it as an "item," and the Associated Press also sent out the news; so the telephone hummed.

But two months ahead of schedule, on Flag Day, June 14, 1946, Timothy Christopher Ware Getty was born a mere four pounds, fourteen ounces, and was immediately placed in an incubator. He was so

tiny—I cried wondering how such a little being could be or survive, and I prayed so hard for him to live. Paul was at the factory in Tulsa and astonished to hear the news.

He immediately called Dr. Bradbury. "Ray," he said, "I thought that our baby wasn't due until August?"

The very kind doctor laughed and replied, "He wasn't. But babies don't ask. They just arrive. And as for your little redheaded fellow, he evidently wanted to get here ahead of time. He's tiny, but he'll grow."

"But, Ray," Paul went on, "I wanted to be there."

"Well, Teddy was here, and that was all that was necessary, Paul. It was hard on her, having had that operation while carrying a baby, and wasn't easy on us trying to keep her quiet these past months. But both she and your son are fine now, so rejoice, Paul, and we'll see you soon."

Paul didn't make it to the hospital for a week—and by that time "Timmy," as I had begun calling him, was beginning to gain weight, though the doctors had been very concerned. On arrival in Los Angeles, Paul noted in his personal diary:

> *Dashed to the hospital to see my little son Timmy.*
>
> *He is a seven-month baby, weighing six pounds now. Poor little man—he has had a hard time. He must remain at the hospital in an incubator for at least two more weeks.*

One month later, Timmy was released, but we still had to have two nurses around the clock. In fact, the first three months were fearful ones, as his hemoglobin was low, and I had to take him back to the hospital two or three times for transfusions. But finally, the doctors said he was strong enough to "go it on his own," and from then on I was such a

grateful mother, for my child was free, growing, and normal. His presence in our home strengthened my bond with Paul.

Timmy brought me a new career, this time the most important of all—that of a mother. Finally, I had reached the last of the three goals I had explained to Paul. We were at El Morocco. It was crowded, noisy, and we had just returned to our table, when Paul asked me what I wanted to do with my life, and I had said, Be a successful singer . . . marry the man I loved . . . and have his child.

"So, a career comes first, Teddy?" he had said. "How do you think a man would feel about that?"

During our years of married life, I found out how a "man" would feel about it. Paul had encouraged my singing career, I had married the man I loved, and now . . . I was spending almost all my time with him and our little son.

Many times, sleeping with Timmy all night in his nursery, I'd awaken to find Paul leaning over us, after working late at night in his den on business. It was a happiness I had never seen Paul express before. Our completeness was obvious. Paul's personal attorney, David Hecht, once recalled that "With the birth of their child—little Timmy—began the happiest years of their lives."

Like any mother, I spent a great deal of time putting Timmy's baby books in order, and with the aid of one of the nurses (his first), Miss Lindy, dutifully recorded every inch of growth, each spoonful of food, and every present sent to him by his growing circle of admirers. "Lindy" was head of the preemie department at the Santa Monica Hospital, and was on duty the day Timmy was born. I always thanked God for her devotion, love, and care—not only for my little boy, but for the other dear ones in the premature section. Many of these precious little babes

could never have survived past the first few hours and days without "our Lindy." She was an inspiration to the other nurses. At my request, she agreed to come home with Timmy, and she immediately became one of the family. She stayed with us for years.

In addition to being a wonderful nurse, she was a reserve lieutenant in the Army Air Corps, and when she was off duty as a nurse and went out for the evening she would sometimes wear her army uniform with its brass buttons and medals, which fascinated Timmy—and me, too.

Nov 4, 1946

10:30 pm

Darling Teddy Boo,

I just came back from Schrafts—57th Street & Madison. I sat at our little table all alone and thought of you and of the 10 years that have flown by. As best I could I tried to comprehend.

Just 10 years ago, Roosevelt was running for a second term. Fred and I were thinking of forming a political party. I wrote a manifesto and platform. You and Betzi meanwhile were gaily running about. We were all spending an afternoon at their house on E. 11th or 12th. I just left the Plaza and was settled at 1 Sutton Place. I was more an important oil man than I am now. You and I were dating ardently. We were just engaged. I was 10 years younger.

I had recently been up to Wild Acres and loved it—all except the mosquitoes. My darling mama was still alive and well and my eyes still filled with tears sometimes when I thought of Papa, gone 6 years.

You were singing more or less about this time at the Stork and occasionally dating Neil Vanderbilt and Dallas Haynes.

And we used to meet at our little table at Schrafts and dance at the cocktail hour at the Persian Room. I had never heard of Spartan; never dreamed of manufacturing anything. The Beach House was 3 years old and there was no bulk-head, the high tide swept the porch and kept the planks sound, without leaks or splinters. I had a 1931 Duesenberg Roadster and was very proud of it. They never produced a newer model. I loved you then and still do—10 years later.

Paul

CHAPTER 30

SPARTANETTE

O ver the years, wherever Paul was, no matter how busy, if he didn't have time for a letter he never failed to write notes to me like this one from Tulsa.

April 27, 1947

Darling Teddy Boo,

Your lovely hydrangea is still flourishing. I've taken good care of it. I miss you and Timmy—but you most. I'm working seven days a week from 6am to midnight, but results of it are evident. I wired you that Mr. Opperman of Aircraft Products, Santa Monica, will drive my Cad. to Spartan. He's going to bring a smaller trailer to exhibit to us. I wish I was home. Expect to be home next month.

Love & kisses,

Paul

And this one:

May 8, 1947

Darling,

You're a pig. You didn't

tell me we had a coyote

living in the wolf run. Please see

it is well fed and watered. Has

Hildy seen it?

Love,

Paul

May 24, 1947

Darling,

Re Hereford Water. I'm signing $1,426 of checks for Hereford Water but this is positively the last time and if it leads to a break between us, so be it.

I'm sure Hereford Water as a business proposition stinks. Personally, we both believe in it and like it and I wish we had stuck to having Sank Ramey send us filled bottles. I recommend you write a polite note to the customers explaining the situation of delivery costs and set a minimum delivery of 3 bottles. Anyone that won't help that much is not very interested so why pay them to drink Hereford Water. If the business won't break even on the 3 bottles minimum, then send another note asking them if loyal believers in the water (if customers are taking more then 3 bottles more thank them in the note) to order the water direct from

T. Lynch Hereford in 15 gal containers. Mountain Valley does this in many places including L.A. You could then get rid of the white elephant charges in L.A. and anybody that really was loyal to Hereford Water could still get it and you could make some profit instead of using me as a milk cow to feed a white elephant. I'm so tired of being milked to feed the white elephant.

Darling—I won't forget Timmy's birthday. I miss him but I miss you more.

I love you,

Paul

And whenever I sent him a newspaper clipping of a review regarding a professional appearance I had made, he would reply at once to compliment me, and always a note from him if I telephoned him.

I'm so glad you phoned me and told me you loved me!

I feel better now.

I love you.

Paul

Over the next years, during the rebuilding of the ranch, when Paul and I would drive up to see the progress we would take Timmy and Miss Lindy with us, and it was always such fun. Timmy would hide in the bushes, come out and surprise his father, who would immediately turn from a silent and deeply concentrating individual concerned with his huge investments into a playful father—delighted to romp with his young son. Then, Mother and my sisters, who were living in the guesthouse, would invite us in for tea or sometimes for a picnic supper. Timmy

looked forward to these times and as he grew up, enjoyed taking walks, picking flowers, reading, and playing checkers, Parcheesi, or cards with my mother, who he called "Lulu."

I knew little about Paul's business day except when he would do some of his work at home. He'd be on the phone for hours talking to people all over the world. And building Spartan trailers now occupied as much of Paul's time as did the oil business. When he was in California, he tried to find time to be with Timmy and me. One day, before leaving for his office, he stepped into the nursery, where Timmy had built a fort with a huge pile of Lincoln Logs. Indians, soldiers, and cowboys were spread all over the nursery floor. Tim and I were waiting for the battle to begin.

Paul stood at the door for a moment, smiling. Then said, "Hi, everybody, who's fighting who?"

Looking up, Timmy cried, "Come on in, Daddy, you're just in time. I'm the Indians, Mom's the cowboys, and you can be the soldiers and we'll fight you!"

Paul looked wistfully at us and said, "I've got work to do, Timmy, and I'm late now. Maybe later. Thanks for inviting me, son."

Blowing kisses at us, he started down the stairs, then stopped, came back, and said, "Teddy, dear, you know in addition to our line of Royal Mansions and Royal Manors, we're building a smaller trailer. Here's a picture, but it's not named yet. You're usually good at things like this. Have you any ideas?"

I looked at the photograph for a moment, then said, "I might have a name for it, Paul, but if your company uses it, they must pay me."

He smiled. "Darling, that doesn't sound like you to be so demanding."

I laughed. "Well, Paul," I said. "Were you hoping to get it for free?

You were the one who told me to put a value on myself. Remember? Sherman Billingsley and the Stork Club contract?"

Paul smiled again. "Yes, I remember, but— Well, darling, okay, if we take your name we'll pay you three hundred dollars."

"No," I countered. "It's worth five hundred."

For a moment he looked at me, then gave another smile. "Okay, Teddy, what's the name?"

"Spartanette," I said. "Isn't that great? I've got a fabulous idea on how to drum up business. Listen. In every city where you plan to sell Spartanettes, arrange to have a beauty contest. Then, the girl who wins will be named 'Miss Spartanette,' and your new trailer and the lovely girl will be photographed and shown in every newspaper. Isn't that a good idea? It'll sell trailers . . ."

"Uh-huh," he mused. "Yes, it's good. Thanks, dear." He smiled, kissed me, and went on down the stairs.

Well, the new little trailer was christened Spartanette and took to the highways of America, and I got a check for $500 from the Spartan Aircraft Company.

Paul had an unusual way of making a personal evaluation of people. At times when they least expected it, he would pay them a visit. One day, Paul decided to drop in on my brother Ware, now president of the public relations firm of Russell Birdwell and Associates, whose offices were on the fiftieth floor of 30 Rockefeller Plaza. On this particular visit, Paul just dropped in and said, "Hello, Ware. How are you doing?"

"Doing fine, thanks," Ware replied, and proceeded to show Paul the names of some of his accounts among which was Linguaphone, the language school.

"What languages do they teach?" Paul asked.

"More than fifty," Ware replied.

"Do they teach Russian or Arabic?"

"Yes, they do." Ware showed him the price list. "If ever you wish to order, I'm certain they'd be glad to send it to you—at list price."

Getting up from his chair, Paul looked around the office again, admired the magnificent view of Central Park to the north, the New Jersey marshes to the south, and, walking toward the door said, "Ware, will you please order the Russian and Arabic lessons for me? Nice to have seen you again, and give my best to Peggy." Then he walked out, closing the door behind him. Speechless for a moment, Ware mused, *Master of five languages. I wonder why he wishes to study more?*

One day, the billing clerk called my brother.

"Who is this guy, Getty?" he asked.

"My brother-in-law."

"Well, his bill better be paid. I looked him up. He's known as a slow pay."

Ware laughed. "Don't worry, Mr. Getty is good for it."

ON THIS SAME visit to New York, Paul made the Walter Winchell, Eddie Sullivan, and Danton Walker columns:

> "Paul Getty doing the night spots, seen in the company of this and that lovely girl."

> "The mystery man from the West—J. Paul Getty—in town to take a look at his super elegant Pierre Hotel where the maitre d' at the hotel's swank Café Pierre almost fainted when he discov-

ered the man he'd just refused to seat at a ringside
table was none other than the Hotel's owner, J.
Paul Getty, dining 'a deux' with a beautiful socialite."

"Who was the glamorous beauty on the arm of
Paul Getty last night at El Morocco?"

"At the Metropolitan Opera's gala opening of
Othello, oil magnate Paul Getty was seen skip-
ping the second act to sip champagne with his
lovely companion in the Met's fashionable supper
room."

One evening, quite late, Paul called. "Teddy, how are you and how's
my little Timmy?" Rather coolly I answered, "We're both very well,
thank you."

"Darling, guess who I took out to lunch the other day?"

"I haven't the slightest idea."

"Audrey, one of our old friends. We went to Schraffts, and sat at 'our
table.' Remember?"

"Yes, I remember. But who did you sit with at 'our table' at El
Morocco the night before? Remember 'our table,' Paul?"

For a moment there was silence, then, "How did you know I went to
El Morocco, Teddy?"

"Well, I can read. And the columns have been very busy reporting
your nightly activities with all of the socialites in New York."

"That's rubbish. Anyway, it's getting late and I have a very important
meeting in the morning, so I'll just say good night, dear. Call you from
Tulsa. Bye."

And the phone went dead. I felt numb as I hung up. I realized this was the first time Paul had said "good night" without "I love you."

He'd been abrupt, cool, and had made no attempt even to placate me. Couldn't he tell I was upset? But he obviously didn't care to explain. "Being with our dear old friend Audrey" didn't worry me . . . it was those nameless "new ones." And, why was he going out with so many? What was he searching for? *Well, after all*, I thought to myself, *he's been in New York for two weeks, why should I expect him to dine alone every night?* But, why didn't he realize I was lonely and wanted so badly to be there in New York with him, as before when we were dating. Visualizing him with other girls at all the old, familiar places hurt. I started to cry. I so wanted to go out and have fun like a kid again. I hadn't been anywhere with Paul since Timmy was born. I was simply a mother with a child . . . Not so glamorous—or was I just not glamorous to Paul anymore?

Right then, I made a decision. I'd get a job, be seen, and show him. I couldn't let my career end like this. I'd worked so hard to be good, damn it, and I was good. I'd call Mommy Saunders for massages, work with Marjorie, start fencing with Faulkner, ride and swim again—get in shape, fight back.

With that, I jumped out of bed, ran to my dressing room, put on the light, tore off my gown, stood naked before the mirrors, and took a good long look at myself. I was definitely heavier—not really ugly, if one admires Rubens—but there was just too much of me!

A month earlier, Paul had silenced my concern with, "Darling, stop worrying. You're beautiful, and now there's just more of you to love."

Well, tomorrow there's going to be less, I thought, and with that I went to bed.

I decided that if you don't care that your husband is out with other

women, it doesn't matter, but if you do, then don't let him know it, be busy. So I was. I worked out every day. I swam in the pool and took long walks on the beach. I filled my life with as many concerts and guest appearances as I could, sang for the Armed Forces and Air plant workers, continued appearing at the Hollywood Canteen, and by the time Paul returned—although he didn't say a word—I knew by the way he looked at me that I had accomplished the impossible.

But the impossible didn't last very long.

Late one afternoon, driving home from a hair appointment, I was surprised to see Paul's car ahead of me on Wilshire Boulevard in Beverly Hills. Just for fun, I started to follow him in my little Bantam car, thinking to surprise him.

The street was crowded. We had just reached the point where Santa Monica crosses Wilshire when I pulled up right next to him. We were both driving slowly. He was on the inside lane—I could see he was talking to someone and didn't notice me as I came along side. Happily I called out "Hi, Paul" several times. Finally, he turned, looked straight out his window, saw no one, then looked down and saw me, which almost caused him to run off the road. He looked shocked. I could see then that he was talking to a girl, someone I didn't recognize, perhaps someone he didn't want me to know. I ran my little car across the front of his Cadillac, and he abruptly came to a stop. At that, the girl opened her door, quickly got out, and ran past the fountain, across the grassy section of the park, and disappeared behind the trees.

"Damn it, Teddy!" he yelled. "What are you doing?" He looked furious.

"I didn't know you had a date, Paul, sorry! See you later at the beach for dinner. Bye, now." And I drove off.

At dinner, we hardly spoke. Later, when we were alone, he explained that the girl was only someone he was befriending, letting her and her little girl live in an apartment above the garage at the Wilshire House until she found an apartment.

I asked him not to lie to me.

His answer was, "Teddy, I'm much older than you. I've known a lot of girls in my life, and still consider them friends. I also intend to see them when I'm in town. It might be for an occasional lunch, tea, or an early drink at the Beachcombers. Nothing more. It's as simple as that, darling, believe me."

With that, he picked up the keys to his car, saying, "I'll be home early, I'm going to the office," and he walked out the front door.

CHAPTER 31

AND SO TO BED

One evening, Paul returned from work rather early, and as we were about to sit down for dinner, he said, "I have something for you, darling," and handed me a large white handkerchief filled with . . . I didn't know what . . . "things," tied up by a very old ribbon.

Not knowing what to expect, I carefully untied the ribbon and, to my amazement, out fell onto the table the most beautiful collection of diamond bracelets, rings, earrings, and pins. As I stared at each piece he said, "These were my mother's, Teddy, and I want you to have them. But will you promise to give them back if you ever divorce me?"

I looked up at him and smiled. "Of course I will, darling." But I never did.

AND SO TO Bed, a restoration comedy originally starring Edmund Gwenn as Samuel Pepys, had played to good reviews in London, and

was to be produced in Los Angeles at the Stage Theatre. One of the great ladies of the theater, Madame Eugenie Leontovich—the actress, director, and author of the Broadway hit *Dark Eyes*, who had appeared onstage in *Tovarich*, *Grand Hotel*, and *Twentieth Century*—was to direct and play the leading female role, that of Mr. Pepys's wife. The brilliant actor Donald Porter was cast to co-star as Mr. Pepys, Alan Napier was to play Charles II, and I was invited to play the important role of Mistress Knight, the King's mistress.

I was thrilled to be offered the role. It would be wonderful—not only to play the part, but to work with such a great cast. This was really my debut as an actress.

The show opened right after Christmas and was set for a long run. One reviewer stated, "Theodora Lynch sings beautifully and acts well." Another wrote, "Miss Lynch picturesquely blended song with a dazzling presence and competency in her delineation of the smartly deceptive lady who tried to hoodwink a king." A third wrote, "A professional singer makes her first essay of a dramatic role, gorgeously beautiful Theodora Lynch plays with authority and at times even bravura." But the fourth said, "She acted better than she sang." I could've died.

Paul came to the opening, and after the show my most "important critic" embraced me, saying, "Teddy, I've always loved your singing voice, but now I'm enchanted by your speaking voice. Tonight shows you're on your way, although you're not really a great success yet."

"No, I'm not," I answered, "but I'm not a failure either, until I stop trying." His words hurt me, for they showed how much success meant to him. He couldn't stand failures. I'm sure he wanted me to be a success— but, it was taking so long.

And So to Bed and my good reviews attracted the attention of Steve Broidy, president of the motion picture company Allied Artists. After seeing a performance, he offered to test me for a part in the upcoming film *Forgotten Women*. I got the part, and Allied Artists put me under contract.

MONTHS LATER, ON a Sunday evening, when Paul was on his way home from Bakersfield, Timmy, in his sleepers, ready for bed, begged to wait up with me in the living room to say good night to his daddy.

Suddenly, we heard the bell on the patio gate. Paul had arrived. Timmy made a dash up the living room steps to the front door. After scooping his son into his arms and promising we would come up to the nursery to hear his prayers, Paul turned to me and said, "Teddy, come out here for a moment, dear." With that, he led me to the garage and pointed to the low, long, blue Lincoln Continental occupying the place next to his Cadillac. "Darling," he said, "that Lincoln Continental . . . Who does that belong to?"

"It's mine, darling. It belongs to me. Isn't it absolutely gorgeous? I just got it. Don't you love it?"

"But, Teddy, you shouldn't just buy an expensive car. You should have asked me first. If you needed a new car, you know I would have bought one for you. But this . . . I really can't afford it."

"Well, Paul, maybe you can't, but I can. I paid for it with the money I earned. Come on, I've got something to show you." Excitedly, I pulled him into the house and held up my contract from Allied Artists. "Look. Read it. And my salary goes up every six months."

Paul snatched the contract. He scanned it carefully, then, looking at me incredulously, said, "You mean to tell me that they think you're worth that much money?"

"Damn it, Paul!" I shouted. "Yes."

A big smile spread over his face and he burst into laughter, put his arms around me, gave me a kiss, and said, "Teddy, you *are* worth it, and your car is beautiful. When are you going to take me for a ride?"

"I don't know, maybe never," I answered. "Maybe right after dinner." Then taking his hand, we went up to Timmy's bedroom, where he was waiting for us to hear his prayers.

After dinner Paul said, "I've a little surprise for you, too—just a minute—I'll be back." With that, he left the table, went into the hall, then returned and placed a small package in front of me. I took the wrapping off and saw that it was a little navy-colored book titled *Europe in the Eighteenth Century*, and beneath the title, in very small letters, was imprinted *by J. Paul Getty*. I looked at him in amazement.

"It's mine," he said, in a modest unassuming voice. "I wrote it . . . started it in 1941. It was just printed, and I want you to have the first copy."

I opened the book carefully, and there on the first page, in Paul's own boyish handwriting, was *To my Teddy from Paul*. I turned the pages, looking at the exquisite photographs and noting the chapters on history, geography, science, literature, music, art, and daily life. Then I turned to the introduction in which Paul had written:

The eighteenth century, although historically so close to us, is nevertheless separated from the men and women of today by several generations. The last survivors of the uncounted millions who grew

to maturity during the eighteenth century died some sixty years ago. We of the twentieth century have been profoundly influenced by the manners, customs, philosophies, politics and arts of the eighteenth century. I hope that this little handbook may serve to acquaint the reader with the life and accomplishments of that splendid period in the world's history.

Santa Monica, California
July, 1941

I put the book down and looked at him. I was so proud of what he had done, so happy for him, so excited and thrilled by this man's knowledge and, above all, the patience he must have had during these years of research, and I told him so. Paul was so inspired by the love of accomplishment in business but he was just as inspired by the history and beauty of life in centuries gone by. And, like most historians and art collectors, he had finally found his own special period.

ONE AFTERNOON, OVER lunch, Madame Leontovich surprised me by offering me a role in a play she had done years before called *Caviar to the General.* Although nothing had been settled yet, I was absolutely thrilled.

When I reached home, Paul's car was in the garage. I rushed to his room to tell him about it. The door was wide open and the room was in shambles. Books and papers were piled high, several brand-new suits, still on hangers, were laying over a chair, and his ties, shirts, shorts, socks, and pajamas lay in piles on the bed. Robert was folding clothes and placing them in one suitcase while Paul tossed paraphernalia from around the room into another suitcase laying open on the floor.

I stood at the door for a few minutes. Finally, Paul saw me and said, "Hi, Teddy Boo, I'm leaving in an hour. Will you please drive me to the train? I'm really late now, and I still have to stop at the office and sign checks. Oh, by the way, darling, where have you been all afternoon? I tried to phone you but you weren't here."

"I was lunching with Madame Leontovich, discussing a new play." I looked at him, not believing what I was seeing. "Paul, must you leave—just—like that?" I knew my voice sounded childish and overly emotional, but I never was very good at hiding my feelings—and I was sad.

"Yes," he answered. "After all, Teddy, I can't stay on here forever. I've got business to do."

"I know, but I just wish you didn't have business to do and could stay."

He didn't answer. I just stood there helpless and looked around the room. It was then that I saw them—and I knew. There on the dresser, laying next to his Santa Fe railroad ticket, were his passport, travelers checks, and tickets for the Cunard Steamship Line.

When Robert left the room I said, "You're going to Europe, aren't you?"

Paul stopped a moment, looked at me as if he were about to say something, and then, as if changing his mind, he went on packing.

"Paul, please . . . tell me."

"Yes," he said in a very quiet tone. Then enthusiastically he continued, "You know something, dear? I haven't been in Europe for eleven years. That's a long time for me. But first I'm going to Tulsa, and then I'm—"

"Paul, please, take me with you . . . or let me join you later. I want so much to be with you. Just think, it would be the first time we'd been in Europe together since our marriage. We could see Kathleen and Chatin, visit my maestro, and introduce Timmy to them too and—"

"What about this new show you just mentioned?"

"To blazes with it. I want to be with you."

"I'm sorry, Teddy. I can't take you with me this time."

"Why can't you? Darling, it would be such fun being with you in London or Paris—or Rome . . ."

"Teddy, dear, I don't need you in London, Paris, or Rome. Don't you see? I need you here in Santa Monica or Bakersfield. But anyway, when I'm in Europe, darling, this time I expect to be very busy. I'm going to be traveling from country to country, and I have many old friends and business associates I must see. I'd have very little time for you. Furthermore, I certainly don't want Timmy traveling about the continent at his young age. He's far better off here at home. And besides, it would be too expensive."

I was stunned. "Paul, I can't believe what you're saying."

I sat down on the side of the bed, trying to think over what he meant. *He doesn't need me.* That's what he said. Did he mean he didn't want me? To put it succinctly: he was self-sufficient. He was acting as if someone had tied a stone around his neck, and I was that stone. Yes, from what he had just said, it was obvious that if I insisted, I'd be in his way, holding him back from something he wished to accomplish—or could do better—alone.

I drove him to his office, then to the station in Pasadena, and waved good-bye as the train pulled away. I had driven him there many times before to catch the train for Tulsa. Each time I had waved good-bye as his train pulled out, I immediately looked forward to his coming home, but this time was different. I couldn't exactly describe it, for though Paul would return, I felt I had waved good-bye to a period in my life that would never come back to me.

It started to rain just as I drove into the garage. Timmy heard me when I opened the front door and came running downstairs. "Mom," he said, "you're having supper with Lindy and me up in the nursery. Remember, she's leaving in the morning for her vacation."

At supper, Lindy said, "Timmy, you're going to love your new nurse, Lela. She's lots of fun, and don't forget, I'll be back soon. Now, finish up your dessert and let's have our bedtime story."

I kissed Timmy good night and said, "Lindy, dear, when you leave in the morning, send Timmy to me, and have a wonderful vacation. Do drive carefully every mile of the way to Ohio."

Very early the next morning, Timmy tapped on my door and called, "Come on, Mom, it's time for our walk on the beach."

Like all children, Timmy loved to make up scenes and act them out. "Playacting" he called them, and invariably he would "write" a part for me. His favorite play was one we did over and over when we walked up the beach. And each time before we acted it out, he would tell the story as a sort of prologue to remind me of the part I was to play. He'd say: "Now, the story begins with the first time we met. You remember, when I came to you out of the sea? Remember, Mom? You were walking along, alone, and I heard you crying! So I swam real fast right up to you, right out of the sea, and I said, 'Hello! I've come to be your little boy!'" Then, pointing toward the ocean, he continued, "Remember, we met down there where the sea meets the shore, and after that, you weren't lonely anymore."

CHAPTER 32

PERCEPTION

That evening, Lela Clegg, Timmy's new nurse, arrived. A charming, sensible, and happy Mary Poppins–type, she immediately won Timmy's heart. She had been with Bob Hope's children for years. Though she was meant to be temporary, Bob Cummings's family sent an SOS for Lindy to return to California to care for their new infant son, Tony, so Lela stayed on with us.

Exactly two weeks later, I received this letter from Paul on his "first trip to Europe in eleven years" (unencumbered by wife and child).

The Dorchester Hotel
London
June 2, 1949
Dearest Teddy,
   I just wrote Tom approving of the guardians purchase of a Buick for Timmy and maintaining it.

I had a rough trip on the Mauretania.

England is beautiful this time of year. London seems unchanged, no signs of war damage, except around St. Paul's, and there it is for the better. I had dinner with Kathleen and Chatin here last night. They are almost unchanged, and asked a great deal about you and Timmy. It makes me feel old to think it has been 11 years this month since I was here. 11 years!

It seems strange that you are not here studying with Mme. Marchesi.

I think it is a lot nicer in Santa Monica. England has lost some of its charm for me—I expect to see the Shell Co. here and meet George later.

I saw Ware and Henry in New York—they are well.

Wish you were here.

Love,

Paul

On June 14, 1949, I wrote in my diary:

> *Supremely happy day. Timmy's third birthday. A fun party for Timmy and all his little friends, plus a telephone call from his Daddy—"all the way from London"—wishing Timmy a happy birthday and to "watch out for a birthday package and a letter to your Mom, which I have just mailed today."*

A few days later, while lunching out on the lanai with Mother and my lawyer, Ludwig Gerber, the following letter arrived. I begged their indulgence and read avidly.

The Dorchester Hotel
London
June 14, 1949
Teddy Boo!

   Today our darling Timmy is 3 years old! Kathleen and I shopped for a McPherson plaid coat for him, and it should be on its way to you.

   I spent all day talking oil business with the Anglo Arabian and the Kuwait Oil Co's. They are our neighbors in Arabia. It certainly looks like a big depression in the U.S. and business is bad here too. I hate to owe so much money in hard times and expect to spend the rest of my life paying off my debts. Cheerful!

   Thanks for the lovely photos and the sweet inscription.
   Love, Paul

Mother asked, "How is Paul, and where is he, Teddy?"

"Still in London, Mom, but he is so funny. Listen to what he says: 'I hate to owe so much money in hard times and expect to spend the rest of my life paying off my debts.' What a cheerful thought! Honestly, from this letter you'd think he was the only one in the whole wide world who owed any money. Everyone does."

"Well, Teddy," Ludwig remarked, "that's what makes him the stupendous, unique businessman he is, for he's conscientious not only about every single aspect of his business—large or small—but also about his debts."

"Would that others were like him," Mother interjected.

"Ludwig," I said, "isn't my mom the most beautiful mother?"

He smiled and said, "She's very beautiful. And what's more, she

looks young enough to be your sister. You know, Louise, I've always said you and your three daughters are quite special. And as for your husband, Teddy, what he has accomplished this past year is quite unparalleled in the history of the oil business."

Mother asked, "What do you mean, Ludwig?"

"Well, I understand that while the other American oil giant Aminoil were debating whether to make an offer to the Saudi Arabians, and if they did, what amount to offer, Paul just walked right in, fearlessly on his own. With the courage to use only his own capital and the same daring he has always used in the past to challenge the seeming unobtainable, he plunged into this hazardous venture before others dared. And so, he victoriously came out with the prize. In brief, he not only had the ambition, the drive, the courage, and the willingness to gamble his fortune, but he had perception of the ultimate accomplishment."

I shouted, "Ludwig, that's the word! *Perception.* That's exactly what Paul has. Do you know, Ware told me that over a year ago Paul came to see him in New York and asked if he would order a complete language course on records in the Arabic language from one of Ware's clients, the Linguaphone Company. So you see, even then he was planning to learn the language, so that he could speak with the Saudi Arabians in their own tongue—actually speak their language and not be at the mercy of interpreters. And that's why he succeeded. Isn't he terrific? But . . . I still wish we could be together more. It's lonely being married to an 'explorer who now is almost always on safari.' And what hurts me more is that he doesn't need me when he's away—in Paris, London, or Rome. In fact, that's what he said right before he left. And he added he 'needs me here.' So, I'm localized. I'm here, always waiting for him to return. I'm not even a part of this new part of his world. Oh, please understand—I'm

proud and happy for him, and I thoroughly realize that Paul is now in the international arena; but his dreams—his ambitions—are world-projected. And mine? Well, Paul is my world.

"I remember when we first met, I said (and I've said it many times since), 'He is like a comet, and I, like a stargazer, trying to follow his blazing trail across the sky through a child's binoculars.' I guess I should have realized right then that we perhaps were too far apart to begin with. But I loved him and still do, and because I do, I want to protect our marriage. Being separated for so long puts him in a vulnerable position, and I feel so intently the danger of women he will naturally meet, and who themselves are already a part of this new cosmopolitan world of his. Beautiful, elegant, intelligent, worldly, exciting women . . . some who love intrigue and live for it (and by it) . . . some who search out men of status and wealth . . . and some who just like to break up marriages. So, how can I combat this if I'm not there? It scares me, just like it would any woman who loves her husband."

"My gracious, Teddy," Mother said. "I never realized you were so concerned. But, darling, don't anticipate the worst. You know, beautiful, educated, artistic women have always attracted men, and Paul's no exception. Now that he has become more involved in the world of international finance, and his absorbing love of art and his collection, he's bound to be exposed to many women from all walks of life, whether socially prominent or not, who will hold an absolute fascination for him. You know, the right ones."

"Mom, I'm not afraid of those. It's the others."

"Teddy, dear"—and she spoke with great tenderness, just like a mother—"yours is certainly not the 'usual marriage,' for neither of you are 'usual people.' You both have strong, independent natures. Remem-

ber, Teddy, you let Paul come home by himself and you stayed on in Italy. But I'm sure he loves you."

"Yes, I'm sure he does. But he loves his Ardabil carpet too . . ."

"Now, Teddy . . ."

"Now, Mother . . ."

"Girls," Ludwig said, "I don't know about you two, but I need a drink."

On June 22, 1949, Paul called from Anvers. "I've been on the Continent for two days and have a high fever. No other symptoms so far. I don't know what causes it. Teddy, do you know I considered taking the Dover Ostend boat, but took the Dover Calais instead? Yesterday afternoon, as I drove through Dunkerque, the boat I considered taking struck a mine two miles offshore and sank in minutes."

"Oh, Paul, thank God you're safe."

"How are you and Timmy?" he asked.

"We're fine. And I have a surprise for you. Timmy's taking piano lessons."

"Piano lessons? Isn't he a bit young to learn piano?"

"Well, he's no Mozart yet, but he's loving it."

Paul laughed and asked, "How about your show? Is it still running successfully?"

"Yes, darling, we're playing to capacity audiences."

"Teddy, you know it's lonely here, and I dread being sick in a strange land among strangers."

"Well, there are no strangers here, so you better come home. In the meantime, rest, and Timmy and I will pray for you. I wish you were calling me from Santa Monica right now instead of half a world away."

"Darling Teddy, I love you, and I'll call you soon from New York. Bye."

"Bye, Paul. I love you, too."

I started to hang up the phone but I heard, "Oh, Teddy, I forgot to tell you. I lunched with Harold Christie at the Ritz yesterday. Remember him? He remembered you. He said you were such a beautiful girl, and that everyone loved your singing when you were at the British Colonial Supper Room in Nassau years ago."

"Yes. I remember him. Everyone called him 'Mr. Nassau' in those days."

"Well, they still do. Teddy, you certainly must have made an impression on him. Would you believe he had the nerve to ask me for your address and telephone number? I think it came rather as a shock to him when I told him we were married. Strange, isn't it, he didn't know? Well, believe me, he knows it now. I stopped him cold."

A few days later, Timmy and I were having breakfast when the telephone rang. It was Paul. He was calling from Paris to say hello and to reassure himself that we were well. "What room are you sitting in?" he asked. "Is Timmy with you? What are you two doing exactly?" Did it in some way reassure him he could call "home" and find us right where he'd left us?

Timmy excitedly begged to talk to his dad, and after a few breathless moments, during which he told his daddy how well he could swim across the pool, he relinquished the phone to me and dashed off to nursery school with Lela.

I sat there for a long time, just wondering why he'd want to know what we were doing. It was quiet in the house, only the sound of the sea, and only Robert calling to Hildy and the puppies for their breakfast broke the silence. What was it? What possible reason could it be that Paul didn't want us with him this time in Europe? And as for not being able

to afford us, or our being in the way of any business deal he wanted to make, that was absurd . . . Or was it?

Then suddenly it came to me, and I knew . . . and the knowing broke my heart.

My presence in Europe, being Paul's wife and half Jewish, might very well have ruined any deal Paul was about to make with the Saudi Arabians. How I wish he had told me this, for it must have been the reason, and he must have been extremely upset, not wanting to hurt me . . . But more important, he didn't want to lose the deal.

CHAPTER 33

NEW YEAR'S EVE, 1949

Paul was delayed in Paris by business and didn't return to New York until late November. Then he went on to Tulsa.

After hurriedly finishing his work at the factory, accompanied by his eldest son, George, and Pop Morey, one of his most able assistants, the three drove to Kansas City. On arrival Paul telephoned to say, "Darling, we're having dinner at the Muehlebach Hotel, then on to the Ice Follies, then I'm going to catch the Super Chief, which goes through here about midnight, heading for California—and you, my love. I can't wait to see you, Teddy."

"I can't wait to see you, and Timmy keeps saying, 'If Daddy doesn't hurry up, he's going to miss Christmas.' Wait till you see him. He's grown so much." It had been eight months since Paul had seen Timmy.

"I'll bet he has. Give him a kiss for me. I've missed him, too, but Teddy, dear, I've missed you more."

Two days later, very early in the morning, I drove over to Pasadena in

my Continental to meet Paul. He looked wonderful. And when he kissed me, I knew how much I'd missed him.

We drove hurriedly to the beach house. Paul was anxious to see our little redhead, who, as planned, was waiting with a warm "Welcome home, Daddy." Then Timmy dragged his daddy to the living room, where he played his "first piece" on the piano for him.

Paul was visibly affected by Timmy's concentrated effort, and applauded him. Then, it was his turn to surprise Timmy, and he sat down at the piano and played a Rachmaninoff prelude for us. Timmy watched his father, intently fascinated. When Paul finished, Timmy walked over to the piano, took one of Paul's hands in his tiny little hands, and said, "Oh—thank you, Daddy, for such an excellent concert."

After we three lunched on the terrace, Timmy went upstairs to take his nap, Paul left to look at his new office in Santa Monica, and I dashed off to shop for "something special" for dinner. With the car loaded with groceries, I picked Paul up at his office and we started for the house.

Having come home at this time was of particular importance to Timmy. He was not quite three when his daddy went to Europe, and for the next eight months his waking hours had been spent in the company of his mom, his beloved "Lulu," his aunts and cousins. While he always expressed deep affection for each one of us, it was apparent that this little man relished his relationship with Paul. Although he didn't try to emulate his daddy, his attitude was one of a self-appointed assistant as he listened to Paul giving orders to the ranch foreman, Pat Fleming, regarding the care of all the animals and the pruning of the lemons and avocado groves. And although Timmy remained silent, he watched the developments at the ranch with tremendous interest and seemed to

assume a certain responsibility as more statuary, furniture, art objects, and tapestries arrived and were brought into Paul's museum.

One of our most enjoyable activities at the ranch was the exciting excursion up the steel spiral stairway from the second floor to the top of the watchtower, and if we were lucky, it was the day of the races.

We usually went to the tower in the afternoon because that's when the water—"white-capped" by the prevailing northwest winds—made the "beat to windward" a wet one for the fleet of tiny sailboats racing offshore. This excitement took place right in front of us—as if we could reach out and touch them as they made the turn. At that point, Paul would say, "Watch, Timmy, they're going around the last buoy. See? They're setting their spinnakers for an exciting homeward run 'before the wind.'" Fascinated, we'd watch them from our tower post and, as each sailboat "came about" and headed south, throwing sheets of water across their bows, we were always glad they were on their last lap, bound for the finish line off Santa Monica Pier. We never left the tower until the boats—"wee tiny specks on a whole lot of blue" (as Timmy called them)—were safe in the harbor.

We never left the tower without a last farewell look at two tall, slender, white-barked lemon eucalyptus trees, which stood like sentinels on the far side of the lawn. When the wind blew and the boughs would bend and sway, a third tree could be seen growing beside the smaller one. Timmy would ask, "Daddy, tell me the story again about the three trees."

Whereupon Paul, with studied seriousness, would say, "Well, son, you see, when I bought the ranch, you, well, you weren't quite born yet, and—"

Timmy would interrupt, "Well, where was I, Daddy?"

"Well, you were . . . well, you were . . . on the way. And when you arrived, I had these three trees brought in, and I personally helped to plant them. To me, they represent the three of us. Your mommy, you, and me."

Timmy never seemed to tire hearing "the story." In fact, he always seemed as impressed as if he were hearing it for the very first time. And, he believed "the story" was true. I always loved to hear it, and I wanted to believe it, too.

Paul was now more than ever consumed with business. He was at his office every day, constantly on the phone. Most evenings when I'd come home from a late reading, I'd find him in the living room, sitting in his favorite big green chair, a rum and Coca-Cola on the table by his side, surrounded by piles of papers, maps, and reports he had brought home from his office to study. After a quick "Hi, darling," I'd run upstairs to kiss Timmy good night and then join Paul for dinner, after which he'd go back for a while to his papers and I'd go out to the lanai to read.

We'd end most evenings walking across the lawn as far as the gate, to look out at the sea. If it was stormy, we'd watch the thunderous waves sweep up the beach almost to where we were standing, then, in an instant, watch them be sucked back down into the sea by the fierce undertow. How wild to think that, two steps beyond that gate at high tide, we might well be fighting for our lives. How exciting to know we were safe in that little beach house Paul had built so many years ago. No matter how high the tide, or dangerous the winds, that house, built on pilings, could withstand any storm, even earthquakes. And with Paul's arms around me, I knew there was no safer place on earth for me.

Months flew by. The weather beautiful, Indian summer in late

November. Before we knew it, it was Paul's birthday, then Christmas Day, when Mother, my sisters, their husbands and children, and Paul's dear cousin, Hal, joined us for the all-day celebration. We spent hours exchanging and opening presents. Timmy was thrilled at the surprises Santa had left for him. Then, after a delicious turkey dinner, we all went for a long walk down the beach, and in the late afternoon had a Christmas swim in the ocean. Later, a very tired but grateful family said their good-nights. After everyone drove away and Timmy went up to the nursery, Paul and I fell into bed.

Timmy was up early the next day. He just couldn't wait to play with his new toys. Paul rose rather early, too, and was busy for hours talking business on the phone. At noon I was relaxing out on the terrace, enjoying the summer sun, when Mother stopped by with some strawberries. Paul joined us and greeted Mother warmly. Later, after waving bye to her as she pulled out of the garage, he turned to me and said, "Teddy, you're so lucky to have your mom." Then, in a sad voice he continued, "You know, I'm an orphan." Without another word he got in his car and was off to spend the day at his office.

What did he mean that he was an orphan? It wasn't until much later in the day that I suddenly remembered that his mother and father had passed away many years before. No matter how important or accomplished this man was, for a moment, he was just a little boy again, who felt alone and lost without his parents.

It was New Year's Eve, December 31, 1949. Paul and I were giving our first dinner party at the ranch house. We had invited fifty guests to dine, and fifty more would arrive just before midnight to help usher in the New Year.

The ranch house was ablaze with lights and filled with flowers. We had a strolling combo for dinner, and an orchestra to play from ten P.M. on, for dancing in the theater ballroom.

The caterers had been busy since five. The kitchen was humming with last-minute preparations of trays, and trays of hors d'oeuvres were placed in the butler's pantry, and bottles of champagne chilled for serving.

By 7:45, everything was in readiness . . . except Paul hadn't come home yet.

Promptly at 8:00 I met Timmy (who was wearing his Merry-Mite white suit) at the top of the grand staircase, and together we came down to wait at the entrance to receive the first guests, who would arrive at 8:15.

The intercom buzzed. We knew the guard had opened the lower gate and someone was arriving. Five minutes later Mother's car drove up and she, looking especially beautiful in a powder blue velvet gown, rushed in and said, "Teddy, the fountain isn't turned on in the courtyard. And the lights are off in front of the guesthouse. You look so pretty in your new red gown, Teddy. Where's Paul?"

"He's not home yet, Mom."

"Not home yet?"

"Mother, why don't you and Timmy go in the theater room and look at the bright decorations."

The Edward G. Robinsons were just arriving when I was called to the telephone. It was Paul. He said, "Hi, darling. I just picked Mitch Samuels up at the Beverly Hills Hotel. We're at the beach house on our way to the ranch as soon as I change. Mitch is anxious to see you again. By the way, is Timmy with you?"

"Of course he's here. But, Paul—what happened? Why are you so

late? Your friends—the Parkfords—are walking in right now. And David
and Virginia Mdivani."

"Well, take care of them, darling," he cut in, "and I'll be there shortly."

"But, Paul, what kept you?"

"Dear, if you must know, I stopped off to see an old friend at the
Beachcombers."

"Oh, are they coming here tonight?"

"Teddy, if you keep me talking, I'm never going to get there."

"Okay. Okay." I left the telephone to find that Mother, who was in
the drawing room, had taken charge and was entertaining Sir Charles
and Lady Mendl, the Jesse Laskys, Eddie and Gladys Robinson, the
E. A. Parkfords, and my acting coach Eda Edson, whose husband, Ross
DiMaggio, was talking to Atwater Kent about the great advance that had
taken place in electronics, since the early days of radio.

I was standing in the entrance hall, where I could hear the laughter
from the lanai and the animated conversations coming from the drawing room. The music of the strolling players attracted my attention as
they approached me. With great gusto they were playing one of Mexico's
most well-known songs, "La Cucaracha." As each musician passed by, he
smiled, bowed, and then marched on. I was enchanted.

But suddenly I was amazed, for there, bringing up the rear, was
Timmy, singing and slapping a tambourine in tempo with the music.
When he passed in front of me, he stopped, smiled, bowed, and said,
"Hi, Mom," and then continued on with the rest of the men, singing,
"La cucaracha, la cucaracha, ya no puede caminar." I don't mind telling
you, as I watched my little redhead march out of sight, my eyes filled
with tears.

At that moment I felt an arm go around me. Paul whispered, "Dar-

ling, I'm here." He turned me to him, and seeing the tears in my eyes, said, "Don't cry. I'm here."

I said, "I'm not crying."

"Well, Teddy, then what are you doing?"

"Paul, you would never guess in a million years."

"You look so beautiful in that gorgeous red gown. Are you really the same girl with the fierce voice I talked to only half an hour ago? You sounded so annoyed, you almost frightened me away."

I just smiled. Then, becoming aware of Mitchell Samuels standing at the door, I called out, "Mitch. Welcome." I walked over to him, extended my hand, and said, "Come on, I want you to meet some of our guests before Paul shows us the museum." I took his arm, Paul took my hand, and the three of us went into the drawing room, where by now all the guests had assembled. Everyone was enchanted when Paul gave a preview of his new museum. The great collection, even in those days, was unique. The jewellike setting of each gallery displayed to perfection the magnificence of each piece of furniture, tapestry, painting, carpet, and sculpture.

Later at dinner, Mitch asked, "Paul, do you have any pictures in color of the ranch house, the museum, and the most important pieces of your collection?"

"Yes, Mitch, we have a few."

"That's not good enough," Gladys Robinson said. "Paul, you should have your entire collection photographed in color. And what's more, you should have it done in motion pictures. Then you could send copies of it all over the world to schools, colleges, universities, clubs, and then—"

"Paul," Jesse Lasky broke in, "Gladys is absolutely right. Do it even

if you don't send it out. Have it done for yourself. You could always have a copy with you wherever you go, and then as you add new works of art to your collection, you can run the film and decide exactly where each new piece should be placed."

"What a good idea," Mitch added. "It would be a help to me, too. In fact, to any collector."

Paul listened, thought for a moment, and then, looking directly at Eda Edson, said, "Well, Eda, how about it? When can you film it? I loved the film you did of Teddy, you know, that test?"

Eda smiled and said, "I'll be happy to do it, but only on the condition that you appear in it, too." They decided to film it sometime in April.

By eleven o'clock, dinner was over, the orchestra was playing in the theater room, and the friends invited for supper dancing had all arrived. After being allowed to stay up to hear the "big music," and telling me he had decided to become an orchestra leader, Timmy went happily off to bed.

I watched as the lights lowered, leaving only tiny spotlights twirling overhead. Then the orchestra broke into an exciting bolero, sending everyone onto the dance floor. Almost immediately, the theater room took on the look of a nightclub. I closed my eyes, and suddenly I was back at the Club New Yorker. The girl and the song was mine, and Paul was saying, "Darling, shall we dance?" He took me out onto the floor and held me close. It felt so right, I wanted it never to stop. But it did. "Sorry, Paul," David Mdivani said as he cut in, "I must dance with my lovely hostess." And the moment was lost; I was in another man's arms.

As the old year slowly neared its last moments, I made my way through the dancers, from room to room, checking to be sure there was champagne on every table. Then I slipped through the French doors

and out onto the terrace, where I stood alone for a moment, looking out over the huge lawn surrounded by the wall of towering trees. Hidden illumination, assisted by the light of a very bright moon, made the whole area a fairyland setting.

Suddenly, the orchestra broke into the familiar strains of "Auld Lang Syne." With the sounds of bursting balloons, screams of laughter, champagne corks popping, the old year was coming to an end. Then the music stopped, and shouts of "Happy New Year" floated out from every room.

I looked up into the night sky and said, "Happy New Year to you, World."

"Happy New Year to you, darling!" Paul said as he came toward me, carrying two glasses of champagne. I took one and we stood there looking at each other for a long moment. Finally, he raised his glass and said, "Well, darling, here's to the beginning of the second half of the twentieth century. I wonder just what it holds for us."

"I wonder, too," I said.

CHAPTER 34

I CAN'T LIVE
WITHOUT YOU, TEDDY

One evening Mother invited us to dine at her new home in Brentwood, the one Paul had given her. He was very complimentary on the way she arranged her lovely furniture, her choice of color schemes, and her excellent dinner. Driving home he said, "Your mother is a remarkable woman, and so attractive. People half her age would be thrilled to have her youthful figure."

On arriving home I looked through the day's mail. Then I rushed to Paul's room, carrying a letter from Hans Hasl, my accompanist in Rome. Hurriedly, I tore the envelope open and we read:

Augsburg, 18 January 1950
Bavaria, Germany
My dear Teddy:
    When I received your Christmas card I could hardly believe my

eyes! You wrote: "I hope you remember me." Teddy, how could I forget you? About two years ago I read about your making a success with your voice, but surprised you were also in the water business. I kept the article in my "top secret" box.

Today, in the Paris Herald *I read the following: "Wife of American oil man J. Paul Getty—Theodora Lynch, accompanied by Forrest Tucker and Carmen Cavallero and his orchestra, today planed from Hollywood to Hereford, Texas and in ceremonies at the Jim Hill Hotel, Miss Lynch was made Honorary Mayor of Hereford for her outstanding efforts to promote the City through her Hereford Water Company. Later, as honored guest of the City she rode with the Mayor and other officials in the parade honoring—"Hereford Texas—Town Without a Toothache!"*

To bring you up to date about me. First—I shall never forget the last time I saw you—that day when those SS Agents came to arrest me at your apartment and they ordered you to—"sing—if you're a singer!" I was so proud of you—you gave them a magnificent performance of Otello. I will never forget either, how fearful I was that they would put me to death. I was afraid for you too, but I was helpless. They "escorted" me to the German border, where the Gestapo picked me up. I was under house arrest.

In 1944, I met Lorranianes "a gang of resistance." I was with them helping and awaiting the arrival of the Americans.

The SS used bloodhounds to catch us. Some of my friends were caught and executed. I was lucky. I had that day gone to the Church and hid in the loft.

When the Allied Forces arrived, I offered my services to them.

Happy days at the beach house
with Paul. (I was getting fat.)

A PR shot done at our
home in Malibu, the
Getty Ranch (now called
the Getty Villa).

At the Getty Ranch,
which was being
remodeled, 1947.

St. Louis Globe-Democrat,
June 23, 1948.

t. Louis Globe-Democr

ST. LOUIS, WEDNESDAY MORNING, JUNE 23, 1948

Her Husband Has $80,000,000,
but She'd Rather Work

By SHEILAH GRAHAM

*Written for the Globe-Democrat
and North American News-
paper Alliance*

HOLLYWOOD, CAL., June 22.—Meet the richest girl in pictures—Theodora Lynch. "Every day people call me up and say, 'Your husband has $40,000,000,'" declares Theodora — Teddy to her friends—waving a well-manicured hand on which nestles a huge solitaire diamond ring.

Miss Lynch is married to Oilman Paul Getty, who does not have $40,000,000 — he has $80,000,000. His wife, described by Producer Steve Broidy as "a new Theda Bara with a great voice," does not actually have to work (one of my understatements!). Last week, however, she signed a seven-year contract with Allied Artists for two pictures a year. So I have tea and cinnamon toast with her at her beach "cottage" to find out why she wants to be a little working girl.

★　★　★

"I GUESS it's because I don't want to make a career of my marriage and because I was used to working before I married Paul," says Miss Lynch, a striking brunette with very flashy black eyes. "I started as a singer in the Stork Club. When I came back from Italy in 1942, Sherman Billingsley sent me a whole case of liquor and said 'Any time you want to come back, your job is waiting.'"

★　★　★

WITH HER black orbs gazing longingly on the Metropolitan Opera House, Theodora sailed for Italy in 1938 to get her voice trained. She married Getty in Rome in 1939. During one of his visits back to this country, Pearl Harbor catapulted America into the war with Germany and Italy. "I was just about to sail for the United

THEODORA LYNCH

ago to crash the movies. "I played the opera singer in The

I asked her. "Rotten," she replies. Her press agent winces

"He travels a lot himself, you know—he's now in Mexico on

A very glamorous me!
(PR shot by Wally Seawell)

Under the beautiful François Boucher
Beauvais tapestry at Getty House.

Above left: With my pet lion at the ranch. The cage is still there.

Above right: My sisters, my mom, and me at the beach house. *(Photo by Harold Davis)*

I knew he was not a saint!

Tulsa, Oklahoma
September 3, 1943

Teddy darling,

I have just received the telephone bill for 4-2216 for the period from July 11th to August 10th in the amount of $103.89, of which $99.76 are toll charges.

You will simply have to stop this extravagance or else I will be forced to have the telephone disconnected. You must think that money grows on trees. Furthermore, this is war time and it is your patriotic duty to eliminate all unnecessary telephoning and long distance especially. I have spoken to you many times about your extravagant habit of telephoning right and left all over the country upon any excuse or no excuse at all.

I am sorry to be cross in this letter, but your big telephone bills would wear out the patience of a Saint and I am not one.

Love,

Paul

Standing with Allied Artists president Steve Broidy *(right)*,
right after we'd signed a contract.

With Liberace at the Brown Derby.

From Scheherazade.

Soprano Teddy Lynch as an Oriental songstress and
Jean Pierre Aumont as the young Rimsky-Korsakoff
await action on the set of Universal's forthcoming
production "Shahrazad."

From a screen and test shot
by Wally Seawell.

WATER TO HOLLYWOOD

SELLING water to Holly-wood, according to some cynical observers of the film-land scene, is like trying to sell iceboxes to the Eskimos.

But heiress-singer Theodora Lynch is using H²O to build herself a new career and for-tune in the land of the movie stars. Miss Lynch, who is the granddaughter of Chicago de-partment store owner Henry C. Lytton and the wife of Texas oilman J. Paul Getty, doesn't have to worry about where her next diamond is coming from.

Yet as an importer of water from Texas to Hollywood, she is up to the top of her pretty neck in a business promotion that promises to make her in-dependent, on her own hook, for life.

It all started a couple of years ago when Teddy, then on a coast-to-coast concert tour, read a magazine article about the town of Hereford, down in Deaf Smith County, Texas. Known as the town without a toothache because the heavy fluorine, phosphate and potassium content of the local water supply prevents tooth decay, Hereford's citi-zens are so healthy that dur-ing World War II, 96% of the inductees from the town were accepted for military service.

This was double the average for the nation. All of this, Teddy found out, was due to the unique Hereford water supply.

The advertising and sales possibilities of this health-giving water were innumer-able. Teddy decided to do something about them. She bought two 5,000-gallon storage tanks in Hereford, arranged for a supply of the water, leased a 10,000-gallon glass-lined tankcar and set up a distributing firm in Holly-wood. It costs her $1,000 to haul 10,000 gallons of the water from Texas to the Coast and she sells it for $1.25 a gallon, which is good busi-ness, however you look at it.

Top names of filmdom flocked to subscribe to her service. Such stars as Bing Crosby, Bob Hope, Joan Craw-ford, Ginger Rogers, Arlene Dahl and Gloria Swanson, among many others, are all regular customers. Now that the bottled water part of her business is organized, Teddy plans to expand, using the Hereford water as a basis for toothpaste and cosmetics.

Teddy, who has already been successful as a nightclub and concert singer, now seems set for life in the business world.—T. A.

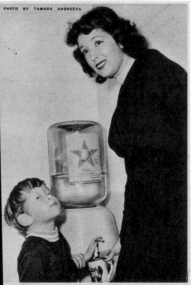

PHOTO BY TAMARA ANDREEVA

Theodora Lynch's son Timmy (with her) is one of the best ads for her Hereford water, a health drink because of chemical content.

The Heiress Who's Making a New Fortune Selling

Above left: With Bette Davis and Robert Stack at the beach house.

Above right: Still from the movie *The Lost Weekend*, the *New York Journal American*, January 7, 1945.

A write-up about Hereford Water Company, which I started with Paul.

My grandfather Lytton
and me in Chicago.

Playing the piano
at Getty Ranch.

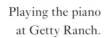

Paul at Spartan Aircraft Company in Tulsa during the war.

Paul dining in Saudi Arabia, trying to complete the Kuwait deal.

With Timmy at the
Getty Ranch.

Timmy at four, playing the
piano at the beach house.

With Timmy at Getty Ranch. *(Photo by Wally Seawell)*

Paul showing Timmy how to open a secret drawer in an
eighteenth-century desk at the Getty Ranch.

With Timmy at the beach house. *(Photo by Wally Seawell)*

Timmy with Candice Bergen and Liza Minnelli at his birthday party.

Timmy's last visit with his father in Paris.

Son Of J. Paul Getty, Richest Man, Succumbs

Continued From Page 1

17985 W. Pacific Coast Hwy., Malibu. One of the wings, attached to the ranch house is the famed J. Paul Getty Museum, housing millions of dollars worth of art treasures.

Who's Who lists the Malibu home as Getty's official residence, although Getty has not visited it in seven years.

Ever since Timothy was stricken with a brain tumor five years ago he had always talked to his dad by phone whenever Getty was away on one of his many trips. He would call him several times a week.

Last October, the boy had un-dergone two operations. He seemed to be coming along well. But last Thursday he went back to the hospital, this time for scar-removing plastic surgery and his condition suddenly became worse.

Four days later, as authorities frantically attempted to reach his father, Timothy died.

The services, which will be private will be conducted at Forest Lawn, no date has been set yet, nor is it known whether the boy's father will attend.

With the boy was his mother, Louise Dudley Lynch Getty, who sang professionally under the name Teddy Lynch. She is divorced from the boy's father, and was Getty's fifth wife.

Getty Delaying Plans to Attend Son's Rites

J. Paul Getty, regarded as the richest man in America, yesterday said he had not yet made plane reservations to attend the funeral of his 12-year-old son here today.

Getty said in Lugano, Switzerland, he still was awaiting a telephone call from his former wife in New York and his plans depended on the call.

Services Today

Private services for Timothy, who died Sunday in New York when his heart failed while he was recovering from minor facial surgery, will be conducted today at Forest Lawn Memorial-Park.

The child, whose last request had been to talk with his father by telephone so he could ask for a personal visit, will be buried near Getty's parents at Forest Lawn.

The oilman was not reached in time to fulfill little Timmy's wish and he said in Switzerland yesterday he did not return to the United States during the operation because he had been assured "it was no more serious than pulling a tooth."

He added quietly, "The fact that I was not there with him has caused me very particular grief."

Getty and the boy's mother, Mrs. Louise Dudley Lynch Getty, are divorced. Timothy was the youngest of his five sons.

Five Soviet Subs Off British Coast

LONDON, Aug. 20 — Five Soviet submarines passed from the North Sea into the English Channel today and continued on the surface toward the Atlantic Ocean.

Los Angeles Times

Vol. LXXVII, Thurs., Aug. 21, 1958

Every Morning in the Year
Daily Founded Dec. 4, 1881
The Times Building
202 W 1st St.
Los Angeles (53), California
Phone MAdison 5-2345
Classified Advertising MAdison 9
AT NEWSSTANDS—Single Copies
Daily, 10 cents; Sunday, 20 cents
Entered as second-class matter Dec.
1881, at the post office at Los Angeles,
Cal., under the Act of March 3.

BY CARRIER
Daily and Sunday .... $2.25 per
Daily only .... 1.80 per
Sunday only .... .20 per
Beyond 75-mile zone .... .25 per

MAIL RATES PAYABLE IN ADVANCE
CALIFORNIA ONLY
Daily and Sunday, one month ......
Daily only, one month ....
Sunday only, one month by mail ...
OTHER STATES
Daily and Sunday, one month .....
Daily only, one month ....
Sunday only, one month ....
FOREIGN COUNTRIES
Daily and Sunday, one month ......
Daily only, one month ....
Sunday only, per copy ....

Poor Little Rich Boy Dies With Song of Faith in Heart

LOS ANGELES (P)—The poor little rich boy provided his own requiem — a simple poem of faith.

The lad was Timothy Getty, 12-year-old son of oil multimillionaire J. Paul Getty, said by some to be America's richest man.

Timothy's poem was read at his funeral yesterday. Somehow it brightened the little Church of the Flowers in a way adult speakers couldn't.

Getty himself did not attend. His former wife, Mrs. Louise Dudley Lynch Getty, the boy's mother, was present.

Timothy was a friendly, outgoing boy, a bit on the philosophical side, perhaps because of illness. He underwent several operations for a brain tumor.

While recuperating in New York he met Roy Campanella, Los Angeles Dodgers catcher who suffered a broken neck in an auto accident. Campy gave the boy a baseball.

"Why didn't you sign it," asked Timothy.

"I have a little trouble writing," said Campanella.

The boy paused. "I'll pray for you," he said.

Facing his last operation — a minor one to remove scars of previous surgery — he wrote a poem about God and winning each fight. But he lost his own fight last Sunday when his heart failed after the operation.

His mother was at his side. Getty was in Europe. He said the fact he could not attend the boy's funeral caused him "particular grief."

The highlight of the Christian Science rites was the reading of Timothy's poem:

"God protects me through the night.

"God will help me each fight.

"Because His love is oh, so dear,

"I know in God I cannot fear.

"God will show me, day by day,

"If I follow in His way."

Timothy was entombed in a mausoleum near Red Skelton's son, Richard, a schoolmate who recently died of leukemia.

The press accompanying Timmy's death: "Poor Little Rich Boy Dies," the *New York Herald Tribune*; "Getty Delaying Plans to Attend Son's Rites," the *Los Angeles Times*, 1958; "Son of Oilman J. P. Getty Dies," *Mirror News*; "World Wide Hunt For J. Paul Getty," *Herald Express*, August 20, 1958.

Richest Man's Son Dies Suddenly

World Wide Hunt For J. Paul Getty

J. Paul Getty, America's richest man, was the object of a world-wide search today. Its object—to inform the billionaire oilman that his youngest son, Timothy, 12, is dead.

Timmy's last wish was that he be able to see his dad.

The youngster's body will be flown here tonight for burial at Forest Lawn. Services will be private and are thus far tentative.

WAITED SURGERY

Timmy died Sunday in a New York hospital where he was to undergo surgery to erase the scars of a brain tumor operation he survived last year.

Getty, whose oil interests girdle the globe, is presently traveling and could not be contacted immediately. One of his homes is here.

Timmy's mother, the former Louise Dudley Lynch Getty (known in filmland circles as Theodora Lynch) was at her son's side when he died.

EN ROUTE HERE

She is en route here to complete funeral arrangements.

Timothy, who always had a fondness for music, asked his mother to sing several of his favorite hymns as he lay on what doctors did not realize was his death bed. The physicians said he died of a heart ailment.

Ever since Timmy was stricken five years ago, he and Getty have maintained almost constant telephonic contact. Recently, his mother, Getty's fifth wife, took the boy to Paris to visit the fantastically wealthy Getty.

Mirror News - Aug 20/8

Son of Oilman J. P. Getty Dies

Relatives were attempting today to find J. Paul Getty, reputedly the richest man in America, to inform him that his son Timothy, 12, died Sunday in New York after undergoing surgery.

Getty, whose fortune is estimated between $700,000,-000 and one billion dollars, has been living abroad since 1951. He has homes here, in London, Paris and Saudi Arabia.

Divorced in 1956

He was divorced here in 1956 by Mrs. Louise Lynch Getty, former actress, mother of Timmy, on her plea that he went to Europe in 1951 and never returned.

Mrs. Getty was known professionally as Theodora Lynch when she married the oilman in Rome in 1939.

Timmy's last request was to talk with his father by telephone and ask him to come to his bedside, relatives said.

Timmy Stricken

Timmy, stricken five years ago with brain tumors, had often received several calls a week from his father.

The boy underwent two operations last October. He was back in the hospital last Thursday for plastic surgery to remove scars. His condition worsened, and he died Sunday night without hearing from his father.

The boy's body is being flown here for private funeral services under the direction of Forest Lawn Memorial-Park.

Candidate Attacked

SANTIAGO, Chile, Aug. 19 (P)—An unknown assailant threw acid last night at Presidential Candidate Jorge Alessandri but the politician escaped injury.

Warner's **EXCUSEZ MOI**

my letter to Dr Kupperman

September 11, 1958

Dr. Herbert S. Kupperman
350 First Avenue
New York 10, New York

Dear Dr. Kupperman:

I cannot thank you for your letter of condolence. To me it is as insincere as your care of my son from the day we returned to University Hospital on August 13 to the day he died on August 17.

I can only think of you as I last saw you...the day of Tim's operation when you came to the hospital at about 2:00 P.M. and asked me in the hall, "When are you going to California?" and I replied, "I hardly think this is the time to ask such a question Doctor, Tim is in the operating room." Then I asked you if you were going down there, if you would please take him his "Teddy Bear", and you said, "What will they think of me...carrying a Teddy Bear?" I replied, "They who see you will think you are being kind."

Let's face the facts, Dr. Kupperman...You, the consulting doctor on Tim's case, did not visit him the day after the operation...you did not come when you were called on Saturday morning when he went into SHOCK AT EIGHT O'CLOCK.... You were not available until 4:00 or 5:00 that afternoon...and the reason given for your absence was that you had an attack of asthma.

When you found you couldn't come, WHY didn't you call someone else in? You gave orders over the phone, but you were dealing with steroids and you should have been with your patient to see their effect. The fact that you DID NOT RETURN THE FOLLOWING DAY AT ALL simply means that you did not want to ruin your summer Sunday by driving into the city from Jersey.

I personally know that you were called. I personally tried to get you. I personally asked Dr. Hoen to get you, even as late as 5:00 P.M. Sunday. I WAS THERE. I know, even though I never went through medical school nor attended one of your courses that there is a code of ethics in the medical profession which you have broken. You live by these man-made laws. You have broken them. You are a disgrace to Medicine and to your fellow man.

You failed a little boy who trusted you to care for him. You failed yourself.... and I shall pray to forgive and forget you.

Timmy's mother,

My letter to Dr. Kupperman about the death of my son.

On my yearly visit to Paul and Timmy's gravesite, July 2013.
(Photo by Jerry Zucker)

Just last year I gave three concerts in Stuttgart and one in Ausburg.
I am now conducting.

    Tons of love from your old friend,
    Hans

P.S. Please write to me.

"It's incredible," Paul exclaimed.

"Yes," I said. "Reading this makes me remember everything I want to forget."

"Well, Teddy, you're a long way now from that Roman prison and the frantic days of insecurity."

I ran to him. "Hold me. Make me feel secure, Paul."

"You are secure, darling."

"No, I'm not. You see, I feel that your life—your interests—have grown so much bigger now, as they should. I don't blame you for this, but your time is so taken up by business, also by what you call 'old girlfriends'—like the one you were with New Year's Eve at the Beach-combers. Please"—I pushed him away—"Don't stop me. I know all about her. It's, well, it's just . . . we simply can't. We can never be as close as we once were because by leaving me for months at a time, you are forcing me to accept a situation I abhor. And when I'm alone, I just feel lost . . . so insecure that I could cry. Be honest—you and I both know that when you leave for Europe again, you won't be taking Timmy and me."

He didn't answer. I turned, started to cry. "Oh, how I wish I were such an important human being you just couldn't live without me."

"I can't live without you, Teddy. I love you. There's no other woman. It's just that I'm involved in the most important deal I've ever attempted to work out, which leaves me no time for you and Timmy right now. And really, Timmy is too young to travel. He's much safer here . . . also I really can't afford—"

"Please, Paul. Don't say you can't afford it. Remember, last year you said that, too. No, the real reason is, you must feel free . . . And I understand—well, I mean, I'm trying to understand."

I started to walk out of his room, but he shut the door. I stopped and looked at him. He walked over to me and tenderly wiped the tears from my face, kissed me, and said, "I love you."

When Paul left for Europe the next spring, I refused to be sad. On June 14, 1950, my son became a very grown-up little boy of four, and at his birthday party, he showed how grown up he was by putting his arm around Liza Minnelli and kissing her soundly on the cheek, much to the horror of Alexis Sharff sitting on the other side of him.

During that summer, I spent long hours getting to know Timmy better. Each day we swam, played in the sand, walked by the seaside, and sometimes we'd go shopping, and that summer he had his first haircut. (I saved his hair.)

He rode his tricycle—I rode my bike.

He had his friends in—so did I.

He practiced his piano—I studied my singing scores.

We drove to Santa Barbara with the top down, and as we spun along the wonderful winding coast road, listening to the wind, the sound of the waves, and the magical music blaring out at us from the car radio all at the same time, Tim laughed and chatted away like a magpie. We sang every chorus we knew at the top of our lungs. We fished off the pier, sailed in

a sailboat, and when we returned home, we planted a garden and played croquet on the lawn. With my mother and my sisters and their children, we visited museums, the zoo, Del Mar, and studied the stars through the telescope at the Observatory. And each night, just before bed, Timmy and I said our prayers. I couldn't believe how fast summer went by.

In the fall, Paul returned to New York, then went on to Tulsa and after that to California. I was to meet him at the Pasadena Station, but I arrived five minutes late. The train had come and gone. Paul was nowhere in sight. I phoned his office. There was a message that he had taken a taxi and I was to meet him for dinner at the Rendezvous Room of the Biltmore Hotel at eight.

I arrived exactly at 7:59 P.M. He was waiting for me. I rushed into his arms; he kissed me and held me tightly. Then, as we were being shown to our table, he said, "Darling, I should have waited for you at the station. But when I didn't see you, or the car, I just took a taxi. I should have phoned you, but I had a proxy meeting downtown."

"Well, Paul, I'm just glad you're home." After dinner we went to the Philharmonic to hear Tagliavini's concert, then drove to the beach house. Along the way, I asked many questions about Europe and our friends. Paul's description of his life was so fascinating that I had to tell myself not to be jealous.

Arriving home, we were greeted by Hildy and Jocko, the French poodle who'd been a present from Betzi. Wild with joy at seeing Paul, they were all over him, almost knocking him down. Paul rushed up to the nursery to take a look at his sleeping son, then joined me on the terrace, while Robert carried his bags up to our rooms.

"It's so good to be home, Teddy, dear," he said. "I've missed you and Timmy and our sweet little house." He sighed.

"And the sea . . . and the waves pounding up on the shore," I added. "Can you hear them, Paul?"

"Yes, darling, it's the Welcoming Home Committee!" We both laughed as he reached for my hand and led me upstairs to our bedroom, where he took me in his arms and kissed me passionately. Then, unzipping my dress, he pushed me down on the bed, where we made love.

CHAPTER 35

INNER VOWS OF THE HEART

It was December 15, 1950, an important day. Paul's fifty-eighth birth-day. Precisely at nine A.M., Timmy, Paul, and I had breakfast out on the lanai, after which we presented him with a tray of useful little gifts, including a pocket-size binocular and initialed gold cuff links. Then we three went for a walk up the beach with Hildy and Jocko.

Hildy, somewhat fatter and older, was not as fast a runner as she had been, but what a great big black furry loving giantess she was! Still obeying Paul's every command, she'd dash out into the huge oncom-ing breakers to retrieve a piece of driftwood he had thrown out for her. Jocko spent his youthful energy just dashing madly up the wet sand, trying to catch a sandpiper. More often, I found myself wonder-ing, now that Paul's gigantic business successes dictated that his social activities parallel these achievements—meeting exciting, important people—would the simplicity of our home life be boring, uninteresting to him?

Later, we sat poolside to watch Timmy swim across the pool underwater, do a fairly good racing dive, and swim down the length of the pool without stopping! "He's absolutely fearless," Paul said. "Such a strong swimmer."

We three spent the entire day together, catching up on the past months. But since Paul had been gone for so long, I wondered if we could reach across that barrier of time and pick up as we were before he went away.

And what about the beautiful women in Europe, who had become a natural part of Paul's life? Could I compete with their glamour and allure?

Was all this just my imagination, or was it really happening? Being careful not to show it, I tried to reason it out with myself. Even though he had gone away so many times without me, I wanted to believe him when he'd say, "Teddy, I love you. There's no one else."

We had known each other so long and had gone through so much together that I felt we belonged together. But more than that, we had made a marriage vow! Not the vows spoken at the marriage ceremony, but the inner vows of the heart, which, unspoken, hold two people closer than any matrimonial law or writ of court.

We dined alone that next evening at our beach house. I was wearing my prettiest gown. Paul's look of admiration assured me that I looked very attractive. He seemed to be studying me. I felt he liked what he saw—his wife, in his home—something to be proud to come back to. Or could it be a look of pride of possession—that it was his, to leave behind whenever he wished to be alone?

Or . . . Let's face it! Was he perhaps comparing me with another woman thousands of miles away?

I couldn't tell what he was thinking as he looked at me, but I'll bet he never dreamed that I, the woman looking at him with such a sincere look of love for him on her face and an even deeper love for him in her heart, might at the same time be considering cutting herself off from him . . . rather than let our love die a slow death.

Dinner had gone on longer than usual, and we weren't aware of the hour until, suddenly, from the top of the stairs, we heard Timmy's eager, long-suffering little voice calling, "Mom, please! Isn't it time yet? Lela says I have to go to bed!"

Bless his heart. He had been waiting all evening to help blow out the candles on his daddy's birthday cake. "Come on down, Timmy," was all I needed to say. There he was in minutes, standing in his "night-nights," looking like a little cherub.

"Happy birthday all over again, Daddy," he said, leaning up to kiss Paul. Then, sliding onto the chair between us, his eyes fastened expectantly on the door to the butler's pantry.

Paul was in great spirits, pleased when we toasted him with ginger ale, and sang "Happy Birthday," as Robert appeared carrying the cake. With Timmy's help, Paul blew out the candles and cut the cake, which we had with ice cream. Then Timmy gave both of us a great big kiss and ran upstairs to bed.

Christmas morning, 1950, started at sunrise, with Timmy checking to see if the peanut butter and jelly sandwich he'd left on the table for Santa Claus had been eaten. The weather was so perfect that everyone who came to the house just naturally ended up at the beach. As we walked along, we all were very happy, until the conversation drifted to the war in Korea and how badly we felt for those boys who were in the midst of it. I couldn't seem to stop thinking about them. Later, when everyone had

gone and the house was very still, I wrote down my thoughts in this little poem:

Christmas used to mean to me, children's joy around the tree.
Lights, laughter . . . a day of fun, with loving gifts . . . for everyone.
A time for remembering those so dear, who came to our house every year.
And from those dear ones far away, a card or call on Christmas Day.
But this Christmas it seems to me, the day is filled with solemnity.
Tho childish laughter I still hear, yet many a mother sheds a tear.
For all the children are not at home, some still in far-off places roam.
Some still must fight so we be free, to worship this day of Nativity.
Dear Father–Mother of everyone . . . Help us, that the soldier lay down
  his gun.

As for me, personally, Christmas had been such a glorious day I wished I could stop the clock and defy the twenty-sixth of December to show up! But I well knew that days move on without ceasing, in strictest rhythm down the measured corridors of time. And before I could even protest, it was already the day after Christmas, and events as usual were quick to take over.

Paul's eighteen-year-old son, Paul Jr., drove down from San Francisco to visit his dad, and stayed for several days in the guesthouse at the ranch. He had dinner with us the first night. He liked Robert's cooking so much that I didn't have to do much persuading to get him to come to dinner every night while he was in Los Angeles.

"He is such a fine boy," Paul remarked, "but not quite as well informed about things as I was at his age."

"How could he be, Paul? He's not you!" I said.

We had no plans for New Year's Eve, since I wanted just the two of us to celebrate quietly. Paul had gone to the ranch early that afternoon to look over some plans for a possible addition to the museum. Timmy and I made several calls to his little friends, stopped by Mother's to wish her a Happy New Year, then scooted on home.

When I reached my room, there was a written message on my desk from Robert:

> Mr. Getty telephoned and said he could not be home for
> dinner.

My heart almost stopped. I could hardly breathe. *Not home for dinner? But it's New Year's Eve. Where is he, and who is he with—this time? Oh my God, how could he . . . ?*

Lela had already gone to a New Year's party, so Timmy had dinner with me. I watched television with him until eight, and then after reading a story, he was off to bed.

With a fire in the fireplace, a tray of freshly baked cakes, and a bottle of Dom Pérignon on ice, I waited for Paul. The clock struck midnight, the telephone rang. I grabbed it—my kid sisters were on the other end, screaming, "Happy New Year!"

I hung up and burst into tears. Finally, I wrote this note:

> Paul, I waited for you. It's now 12:30, I'm going to bed. I don't
> know where you've been all evening, nor whom you've been with.
> Don't wake me. We'll talk tomorrow.

313

Here's Donald Duck! You gave him to me as a symbol of your love. Now, I'm giving him back to you.

Teddy

I put Donald and my note on the pillow of his side of the bed, drank the last of the champagne, turned over, and cried myself to sleep.

CHAPTER 36

TRIAL SEPARATION

January 1, 1951, was to be a memorable day in the life of one Teddy Lynch Getty.

It was 5 A.M. I reached for Donald, he was gone. It was still dark outside. Was the sun late in rising? No, I had awakened early, even earlier than the birds. There wasn't a sound, except the incessant pounding of my thoughts . . . Sad thoughts that had finally resolved themselves into this final decision: *I must step out of this uncertain, obscure role as Paul's wife and step into a role I can play.*

I could no longer even imagine sharing this man, Paul, with others, and pretending I didn't care. Because I cared terribly—so terribly that I preferred to end our relationship rather than watch it disintegrate. I would no longer enact a part foreign to my nature. I lived with myself and had to be true to that self or the very structure of my being would fall apart, and I wouldn't have any reason for being. I had a right to be me, not a phony me.

With this decision came a feeling of peace, a feeling of security. I was my own self again! Suddenly, I felt buoyant. Joyful. Like a kid. I jumped out of bed, slipped into blue jeans and a shirt, walked barefoot down the stairs, through the house, and went outside. I stepped onto the lawn. The grass was wet and icy-cold on my feet. The air was bracingly fresh. I closed my eyes for a second and inhaled deeply. I felt so alive! I looked up just in time to see the sun coming up behind the Palisades. How wonderful! The beginning of a new year! A new day! My new life!

I was just putting the finishing touches to a bowl of cut flowers on the huge round coffee table in the lanai when Paul walked in. He came over, kissed me, and said, "Happy New Year's, darling. I want to talk to you . . ."

I put my hand up and pushed him away. "I want to talk with you, too, Paul, but it'll have to be later, because our guests will be arriving any minute."

Just then the outer-gate bell rang. And our friends arrived.

After a delightful luncheon, we watched the Rose Bowl game. Unhappily, UC Berkeley lost to Michigan, and after much discussion, we left the sports world, and said good-bye to our friends. Finally, we were alone. It had been obvious all day that Paul was anxious to talk with me, and now was the moment.

"Darling," he began. "You arranged such a lovely day." I could tell by his voice he was upset. I didn't answer. He went on, "That was a fabulous luncheon. Everyone enjoyed themselves, didn't they?"

"Yes, but I want to talk with you—about us—our future, and the way I feel." My heart was pounding. My mouth was so dry, I could hardly speak.

"Teddy, I'm sorry about last night. It—"

"Let's forget last night and talk about tomorrow, Paul. I want a divorce."

"Teddy, no, you don't mean it."

"Yes, I do."

"You mean because of last night?"

"It was New Year's Eve and you didn't come home! You drank champagne with her—whoever she is—not me. It's cruel. Don't you think that hurt?" I looked straight at him. "This isn't the way married or unmarried people who love each other should live. And I just can't live this way, not anymore. It's killing me. Either I'm the woman in your life, or I'm not. And the way it looks, I'm not."

"Teddy, that's not true. I don't want you to divorce me. You're being irrational."

"*Irrational?!* Are you crazy, Paul Getty?"

"Teddy, please. I love you. I don't love anyone else. And you . . . you love me, too, don't you?"

"I do, but I don't want to be unhappy anymore." I started to cry. "Don't you understand? I'm unhappy."

"Darling, last night was wrong, and I'm sorry. I've made mistakes. But we've been together for so long, please forgive me. We'll work it out."

"What do you mean, 'Work it out'?"

"We could have a trial separation. You've heard of people doing that, haven't you?"

I sighed. "Yes . . . I mean, what do we do?"

"You talk it over with Ludwig, and then tell me what he says."

"But, I'm not married to Ludwig Gerber, I'm married to you, Paul Getty. *You* tell me."

———

Just then the phone rang. It was for Paul, and I ran out to the beach . . .

In May, Paul left again for Europe, and I drove him to the station. I was very sad and quiet as we drove along. Several times, especially whenever a street signal stopped us, he would reach over and hold my hand, telling me that I must "not act like a child and sulk, but be an adult and try to understand."

"Paul, I'm not sulking. I'm just sad, and I feel lost. In fact, I'm terribly lonely, and you haven't even gone yet."

"Lonely? Why, Teddy? You have Timmy, your mother and sisters, and . . . Why, you have everything you need."

"Yes, Paul, I have Timmy, my mother, my sisters, and everything I need, except a husband. And I'm the kind of woman who needs a husband."

"But, Teddy, you *do* have a husband. It's just that I can't always be home."

I was silent. I was trying not to cry. Not just because of this lonely moment of separating, but because I could see the long lonely months ahead without him again.

As I swung the car into the railroad station and came to a stop, Paul turned and looked at me for a moment. Then, putting his arms around me, he pulled me close to him and said, "Darling, you simply refuse to grow up. You know, you make me feel like I'm deserting you, when all I'm doing is what I must do if I'm to stay in business. Don't you realize that there are thousands of people depending on me? Don't you understand that it's important during this period for me to be at the helm, when I'm needed?"

"Yes, Paul, I understand. I really do understand."

"That's good, Teddy. Now, what about you? Are you going on with your voice?"

"Yes, of course I am. Only just for a split second in time, I sort of wished that we might have had a few months this summer to be together as we once were, without any thought of career or business. But I see this is an impossible wish, and I shan't ever mention it again."

"Well, dear, if I had your talent, I'd get back to work. You've already spent too much time and money on your career, and you're still far from your goal. Here you are, a beautiful woman, your singing voice is right now, your film test shows you can act . . . You can do concerts, musical films, or opera, yet here you sit, putting your personal life ahead of your work."

"That's not true, Paul. I only put *you* ahead of my work."

We weren't aware of it, but the train had pulled in. I could see the porters, flagmen, conductors, and the passengers hurrying to board. Paul held me, kissed me, then we both got out of the car. I stood by his side as the porters loaded his suitcases and boxes of books onto their carts and into the Pullman car. Suddenly there was the familiar shout of *"Alllll Abooooooard!"*

As Paul started for the train, he pressed my outstretched hand, and said, "Stay right here, darling, and I'll wave to you from the platform of the rear car," which I believe he did until the train pulled out of sight . . .

But I had left. I don't know why I drove so fast from Pasadena to the beach. I don't know why I drove directly onto the Santa Monica Pier. I don't know why I stopped at the merry-go-round with its flying horses. I don't know why I chose a big black horse to get on, or how I managed to get him . . . There was such a crowd clamoring for a big black horse.

But I do know that when the merry-go-round slowly started to move, and the music of the organ started to grind out the familiar "Skater's Waltz," and all the other people on their horses were laughing and grabbing for the brass ring, I just threw my arms around my horse's neck and burst into tears. When the merry-go-round stopped, I got off and went home.

CHAPTER 37

FAITH WITH REAL COURAGE

In January 1952, Paul was still overseas. Timmy, now five, went back to the Brentwood Town and Country School, and on Saturday afternoon, April 12 of that same year, I gave a party for children at the ranch in Malibu, inviting them and their parents to come dressed as pirates and hunt for buried treasure.

History books say that, in 1616, the explorer Juan de Iturbe was attacked by Dutch pirates and lost a ship in the waters near this ranch. The treasure was reportedly brought ashore and buried "in the Sycamore Grove near Castle Rock." Smugglers, including Joaquin Murrieta, had often used this area as a hideout in the centuries since then.

Believing that this 160-acre Boca de Santa Monica coast ranch was filled with buried treasures, I decided it would be fun to have a Treasure Hunt party. I invited children in the community and also children of some of the stars we knew, namely Betty Hutton, her husband, Charles O'Curran, and her two daughters, Lindsey and Candy; Joan Bennett

(Mrs. Walter Wagner) and her daughters, Stephanie and Shelley; Dorothy Lamour, her husband, William Ross Howard, and their two sons, Ridgley and Tommy; Mr. and Mrs. Don DeFore and their offspring, Penny, Dawn, David, and Ronald; Judy Garland and her daughter, Liza Minnelli; the Edgar Bergens and their daughter, Candy; and the John Farrows (Maureen O'Hara and their brood of six moppets, including Mia).

We asked Art Linkletter, the famous television producer, to supervise excavation operations by handing out maps and shovels. The children happily searched and dug on all parts of the ranch grounds to find small pirate chests filled with toys, chocolates, and coins. Others rode ponies, took carriage rides around the ranch, listened to the Mexican band, played games all afternoon, and feasted on hamburgers and hot dogs. It was a great day, and everyone had fun—even though the chests of gold were never found.

Instead of a party at home on Timmy's sixth birthday, we drove to Palm Springs. Early each morning before sunrise, a cowboy would bring horses to our bungalow, and we'd ride out across the desert, ending up at a real covered wagon, where we were given breakfast, Western-style, and serenaded by the ranch hands and cowboys singing old cowboy songs. It was like a history lesson for Timmy about the early days of California.

In the afternoons we'd always go swimming in the hotel pool, and some nights we'd have supper at a funny little restaurant right near the movie house on Main Street, where, to the delight of every child in town, they often showed Western movies.

The night before we were to go home, Timmy said he felt ill and that his head hurt. His eyes were red, rather bloodshot. Thinking it was from too much sun, I had us stay indoors the following day. But when he still

complained, we immediately went home. I took him to an optometrist in Santa Monica, who sent us to an ophthalmologist in Westwood. During the examination, this doctor took many X-rays. Waiting in the outer office for his report, Timmy grew impatient "just sitting there," so Lela took him out to our car, where they could turn on the radio and listen to music.

Finally, the doctor came out and said, "Mrs. Getty, will you please come into the X-ray room?" He then showed me the X-ray prints and said, "See the dark spots?" and he pointed them out. "Mrs. Getty, I'm so sorry to have to tell you this, but Timmy has a tumor on the optic nerve. He will lose his sight, perhaps even his life, if you don't have him operated on immediately. The first thing you must do is to talk this over with your husband, and if you want the name of a neurosurgeon, I can help."

I stared at him, not sure if I'd heard what I thought he said. Then I thanked him and walked out of the office, frozen with fear, but inwardly screaming to myself, "No! *No!!* *No!!!* It's not true! This is just a story about a little boy who doesn't even exist. It's not about Timmy . . ."

Yet I knew it was true. I had to get control of myself. I mustn't look upset or Timmy would see it on my face. I stood in the corridor for several minutes, and from the open door of the building, I could see my little redhead in the front seat of the car. He was having an animated conversation with Lela, laughing and acting out what he was saying. Tears came to my eyes, and I prayed. I ran to the car, opened the door, and enthusiastically slipped into the seat beside him.

Fortunately for me, he spoke first: "Mom, what did the doctor say? When will I get my glasses? I can't wait to show them to the kids at school. When will I get them, Mom?"

"Real soon, darling. Real soon!" Then, with my beloved little magpie chattering away, we drove home.

As soon as Timmy and Lela went up to the nursery, I went directly to my room, closed and locked the door, threw myself on the bed, and burst into tears. All I could think of was how I could prepare him for the testing times we were going to have to face. How could I tell this little child, who had just turned six, about the agony he might suffer from an operation? An angel, my own dear little boy. Oh God, please, God . . . Why? What was this horror? Where did it come from? And why so suddenly? I thought back over the past year, trying to recall if he had ever complained of this trouble before. He hadn't, or I would have done something sooner. No, it was as if some evil thing had enveloped us without warning.

It must have been hours before I finally got up. I washed my face in cool water and then placed a call to Paul in London, but I couldn't get through to him. I couldn't even find him. I knew there were hours of delay on all transatlantic calls.

Out of desperation I called my lawyer, Ludwig Gerber. I was relating to him the appalling verdict of the X-rays, when Timmy phoned me on the intercom to come and join him for an early supper.

At midnight Ludwig called and said, "I got in touch with Paul's attorney, David Hecht, who finally located Paul by phone in Naples and told him about Timmy. Paul sent this message:

Tell Teddy to take Timmy to New York at once to be examined by Dr. Lawrence Poole. He is one of the finest neurosurgeons in the world.

The message also said:

Tell Teddy Paul will meet them in New York. Tell her not to be afraid, and not to let Timmy know anything about it.

After I hung up the receiver, and after making sure Timmy was fast asleep, I told Lela. She was shocked. Being a faithful nurse, she assured me she would in no way show fear in front of Timmy, and immediately helped me to prepare for our trip.

The next day I told Timmy we had to go to New York for some tests, that we were going on the Super Chief, and that in Albuquerque he would meet some real Indians. I told him that in New York, we'd visit the Statue of Liberty, the Museum of Natural History—where he'd see the dinosaurs—and we'd even get to ride to the top floor of the Empire State Building! It was so hard to pretend it was to be a fun time, but I *couldn't*, just *wouldn't* let him see my fear.

Next I called Mother, and, sobbing like a child, told her all about it. Thank goodness she was strong in her faith that God would direct us all the way. This helped me keep up. I realized there was only one thing I must do: be strong for Timmy's sake. So I prayed to be strong, and I listened for guidance.

Two weeks later, Timmy, Lela, and I boarded the Super Chief. It was June 26, 1952. How could I ever forget? On the way to the train, I stopped at Santa Monica Hospital to see my sweet little sister Nancy, who had just given birth to her firstborn, a fine son, Kit. She looked so beautiful and happy that I worked hard not to break down and tell her about my own son. I could hardly hold back the tears when I realized

that, only six years ago, I had been in that same hospital, giving birth to Timmy . . . and now I was taking him on a long, frightening trip to another hospital in a faraway city. But I couldn't upset her. I embraced her and said, "Paul called. He is coming to New York, and wants us to join him there. Isn't it wonderful?" Then I dashed down the stairs to join Timmy and Lela, who were waiting in a taxi, and we sped on to the railroad station in Pasadena.

No sooner had we settled in our Super Chief drawing room, than I felt reassured. Nothing could happen to Timmy. His daddy would be with us. Soon.

The trip across country tested my self-control. It was hard for me not to let Timmy know that I was looking for symptoms: headaches or red eyes. But with the exception of feeling a little bit tired at times, he was his usual adorable little-boy self. Just a very happy fellow. We spent many hours in the Dome Car, watching the sunset and looking up later into the starlit sky.

At Albuquerque, an Indian chief came aboard and rode for about an hour, during which time he told some mighty tall tales to Timmy, an avid listener. Then from the chief's collection of Indian jewelry, I bought Timmy a silver ring and a bracelet, which resembled a gauntlet. Timmy cherished the gauntlet and I still have it on my dresser.

Later that evening, Timmy, Lela, and I dined in the Turquoise Room, then climbed up to the Dome Car. There, under a beautiful starry night sky, we talked about how big our country was, and how brave the early pioneers, who crossed it in their covered wagons, had been.

"How could they do it, Mom? Weren't they afraid?"

"No, Tim, they weren't afraid because they had their eyes on the

goal always, and they weren't about to let scary things frighten them away. And so they kept right on and made it.

"Mama, why does everything always seem so much more scary in the dark?"

"It really isn't, Tim, it just seems so. It's just our fear that makes us afraid."

"Like our president said, Mom, there's nothing to fear—but fear."

"That's right, Tim. Where did you learn that?"

"At school! The teacher said President Roosevelt said it. Did he, Mom?"

"Yes, he did . . . and we must never forget it, either."

"Mommy, tell the dream story about fear and the bear, will you?"

"Well, once upon a time, in *Midsummer Night's Dream*, there was someone named Theseus, who said that *in the night, imagining some fear, how easy is a bush supposed a bear?*"

Timmy laughed heartily, as he always did when I told the story about the "bear and the dream." Then we said so long to the night, the stars, and the Milky Way, and headed for bed.

As we started down the narrow stairs to the car below, I put out my hand and said, "Careful, son. Let me go first. The train is going very fast now."

He stepped back and said, "Why, Mom—of course. Ladies first, always."

We laughed at each other as we climbed down the circular stairs and made our way through the club car to our drawing room in the next car, where Lela was waiting to put Timmy to bed.

After Timmy went to sleep, I slipped into my negligee and settled

down to read my Bible. I leafed through the pages, and then read the ninety-first Psalm. Then I read it again. With the comforting thought that no matter what battles we might face in the days ahead, God is truly our refuge, I closed my eyes, grateful to feel a certain peace.

We arrived in New York at eleven in the morning. There to greet us was my brother Ware, who drove us to the Hotel Pierre, with the luxurious suite that Paul had arranged for us.

Timmy was a bit tired and, after a quiet lunch, took a short nap. I seized this opportunity to call Dr. Poole's office and make our appointment for the next day. The phone rang constantly. Mother called from Brentwood to encourage me, as did my brother Henry from Washington. There was no call from Paul.

The next morning, Monday, at ten o'clock, Dr. Poole began examining Timmy. At eleven o'clock, I was told that Timmy would have to be operated on a week from that day. At twelve noon over transcontinental phone, Paul's attorney David Hecht told Paul the awful news. He sent word for me to be brave, to keep Timmy's spirits up. He said he was coming home on the *Queen Mary*, sailing that very day. His New York office would make arrangements for us to board one of their tugboats to meet the ship when it arrived in New York.

Five days later, Timmy, Lela, and I—along with my brother Ware, his wife, Peggy, and their children, Terry and Sharon—were thrilled and excited as our tugboat drew near the big liner. But as we inched closer, our captain received a ship-to-shore message from David Hecht that *"Paul is not on board!"*

Our trip had been in vain. I was deeply hurt for Timmy's sake, as were the others. But quickly, we all tried to make light of it, even making up a story that the boat was so crowded that there was no more

room, even for Daddy. Fortunately, the leviathan's decks overflowed with returning vacationers, so our story seemed logical.

Sensing Timmy's disappointment, the captain asked that he join him on the bridge to "help him steer," and to speak to the commander of the *Queen Mary* on the ship's radiophone, which Timmy proudly did as we scooted closer and passed under her bow.

When we returned to the hotel, Timmy was very tired, and I could see his eyes were bothering him. My heart ached for my little son, but I called out gaily, "Beat you to bed, Timmy!" And with that, he showed us he could do it. When he fell asleep, I went to my room and tried to quiet my fears. If only Tim would sleep and awaken rested. But the fact that he appeared to be getting worse, and in such a short time, was appalling. Oh, if only I could see or even talk with Paul. I felt such a need for him to reassure me that we were doing all we could for our son.

Timmy slept peacefully all night. In the morning I told him I was sure Daddy would be on the very next boat, that Dr. Poole wanted to do a series of tests, and that he would be going back to the hospital on the following Monday.

But in the meantime, we were going to have the most fantastic Fourth of July weekend with his cousins Sharon and Terry at their home in Lawrence, Long Island. Although Timmy appeared lethargic at times, he swam in the ocean and in the pool at the Lawrence Beach Club, went for a ride on the neighbor's antique fire engine, and, with the other children at the club, he watched as the rockets and flares lighted the night sky.

When we returned to the Pierre on Sunday evening, this note from Paul was waiting for Timmy:

Naples

June 29, 1952

Darling son Timmy,

    You are the best boy in the whole world and I love you.

I hope to see you soon.

    Father

Timmy was thrilled with "his very own letter" from his daddy. He folded it and put it in his little wallet. I was grateful he understood that his daddy wanted to come, but I was furious that Paul didn't say, "I'm trying to get there as soon as possible."

Early Monday morning, Ware called for Timmy, Lela, and me in a limousine, and we drove through Central Park and up Riverside Drive to the Presbyterian Hospital, where Dr. Poole was waiting. Greeting us warmly, he said, "Tim, I want to make some tests on your eyes tomorrow, so I'd like you to spend the night here. I've arranged that your mama and Lela can stay here tonight, too. Won't that be great? So now, let's get busy, shall we?"

Timmy was completely relaxed about the entire procedure, except when they took his blood count. But soon even that was forgotten, and we spent the balance of the day playing checkers and the guessing games "animal, vegetable, or mineral" (which Timmy always won). Then Ware and I took turns reading stories to him, and later in the afternoon, when Lela took over, we went for a walk, bringing back ice cream for Timmy.

After he went to sleep, we drove to the hotel for dinner, where David Hecht found us in the Cafe Pierre. He sat down and said, "Teddy, Paul just called and apparently is so deeply broken-up—he even cried over

the phone—that he isn't able to come to New York. He told me that you should tell Dr. Poole 'to go ahead with his brave little boy.'"

In other words, he wasn't coming.

At 5:30 the following morning, the door opened and a nurse came in. Timmy was still asleep. In a brisk voice she said she had come to shave his head. I asked her to follow me and we went out into the corridor. I said, "Dear, I just can't allow you to do such a thing. It would frighten him too terribly. I'm sure Dr. Poole can order it done after he has been anesthetized."

She was very cross and kept insisting, but I stood in front of the door barring her way. Just then Dr. Poole arrived. When I explained that I couldn't possibly allow Tim to be frightened by such a scary procedure, he agreed it could be done later. I was very grateful, but sorry the nurse was so arrogant as she walked away.

Forty-five minutes later, Tim awoke and was given a pill. Soon he became very drowsy and was wheeled out of the room and taken up in the elevator to the operating room, where Dr. Poole and his team began the operation to remove the tumor. I remained in my room, and prayed. At 8:30 A.M., Ware and Lela came in, and we waited together.

Six hours later, Timmy was brought down to his room. His head was bandaged. He was coming out of anesthesia and waving his little hand to me. Any mother knows the feeling in such a moment as this, which can never be expressed in words. In deep humility and gratitude I kissed his dear hand, then left him in the care of the two special nurses and followed Dr. Poole into the next room, where he told us he was satisfied with the operation. He said that although there was still more to be removed, it was not malignant.

Ware had gone directly to the phone to relay the news to Paul via

David Hecht, when suddenly the door burst open. One of the nurses ran in and spoke to Dr. Poole, who hurriedly followed her out.

Lela and I, not understanding what was happening, just stood. Then we heard the orders being given and saw ice being rushed into Tim's room. In seconds Dr. Poole returned and said, "His temperature is going up, and we can't seem to stop it." Turning to Lela he said, "I need you to help," and they rushed out.

I was alone. I stood still a moment, then fell to my knees, closed my eyes, and prayed. How long? I don't know, but when I opened my eyes Dr. Poole was standing beside me.

"It's stopped," he said. "The temperature is going down. Thank you for your prayers. He's going to be all right. You can go in and see him now."

I ran in, and there—in a blanket of ice—was "Paul's brave little boy." Alert, and with a little half smile he said, "Mama, they sure tested me. Look! I'm on ice!"

I laughed right out loud, but inwardly said, *Thank you, dear, dear God.*

A few days later, my brother Henry came up from Washington to see Timmy. He, Ware, Lela, and I did our best to fill each day with interesting things to talk about, and plans for interesting things to do when Timmy would be released from the hospital. Paul called us daily and was pleased and grateful for Tim's improvement. Dr. Poole was more than astonished and delighted at his patient's progress. Finally, the great day came! Timmy was discharged from the hospital with instructions that we return to the Hotel Pierre, where Tim should rest for a few weeks before returning to California.

About an hour after arriving at the hotel, Paul phoned from France. The connection was a bit weak at first, but in seconds there was perfect communication. I was so happy, I fairly shouted, "Oh, Paul, you should

have been here this morning. Just before Timmy left the hospital, Dr. Poole asked that he appear in front of the entire hospital staff in the hospital amphitheater, which we gladly agreed he should do."

"But, Teddy, why did he want him to do that?"

"I don't know. I guess he wanted them to see how well he is. Anyway, Tim was wearing a little astronaut's uniform we bought for him at Schwartz . . . also a helmet."

"A helmet? Teddy, how could he take it off?"

"Wait till I tell you. I was worried about that, too, but as they wheeled him into the amphitheater—this huge place, with the doctors and nurses seated in a half circle—a most attractive lady doctor, who had been among those taking care of Tim, walked up to him and said, 'Good morning, Timmy . . .'

"At which point, Tim told his orderly to stop, stood up, and, taking off his helmet, he bowed and said, 'Good morning, Doctor Bright Eyes, how are you?'"

"Teddy, I can't believe it."

"Well, Paul, it's true. And what is so wonderful is that all who were there saw his little shaved head and Dr. Poole's very fine work—a beautiful result—without having a word said to remind him of the experience he had just gone through. Oh, Paul, it was a beautiful morning! And now he has been released in my care, and we just arrived at the hotel."

"Yes, I know, darling. I tried to get you earlier."

Although we kept receiving letters and phone calls from Paul, it was apparent to me that he was not coming to New York. I had managed to live through these ghastly days and fear-filled nights on his promise that he would be with us any minute. I had hoped he would

personally check things out with Dr. Poole, observe the situation, and follow through as he did with his important business deals. Even closer to my heart was the hope that this terrible ordeal Timmy had so bravely fought through would bring Paul out of his worldly world *des affaires* into the simplified glorious world of his *famille* . . . but that obviously had only been my hope.

We stayed at the Pierre a few weeks longer. Then one early morning, Dr. Poole phoned and said he felt that Timmy could return to California. At his request, I immediately went to his office to have a final conversation about Timmy. I was filled with fear when I left the office, and through David Hecht, I at once relayed Dr. Poole's report to Paul:

Some of the tumor is still there. It will grow again. Timmy must undergo another operation in about five years. In the meantime, he must take a series of cobalt treatments. Hopefully he can return to school in the fall.

It was early August when we returned to our beloved beach house. Timmy was so happy to be home, he ran out on the lawn and knelt down on the grass. "Oh, Mom, we're home!" he kept saying. But the cobalt treatments he was to take and the prediction that one day he would again face another operation left little for me to be joyous about.

At first the treatments made Tim ill, but he was obedient to his doctors. He was patient with the problem of not seeing as well as he should, but happy when he was fitted with reading glasses, so he could again do his school homework.

One day I found him looking at himself in the mirror.

"Mom, I look like a college professor—don't I?"

"Yes, you do, Tim, you really do. But before I can call you Mr. Professor, I think you need to learn a little more."

"Like what, Mom?"

"Well, you've lived by the side of the sea all your life, but have never been to sea. Right, Tim?"

He nodded.

"So, how would you like to spend an adventurous week sailing up and down the coast?"

"When do we go, Mom?"

"Tomorrow!"

Early the next morning, Timmy and I boarded the big ship *Celeste*, owned by my friends, Mr. and Mrs. Myron Shane. We spent several days cruising, then headed for Catalina Island, where we dropped anchor in the picturesque old harbor among the many other boats already moored there. We fished and visited the quaint town of Avalon, where we met Frenchie Small, who drove the great team of horses and carriage that met the daily steamer from Wilmington. Frenchie was also in charge of the stable for the Wrigley family, and he taught Timmy to ride, slowly and carefully. Timmy took lessons with him every day, and it was a joy to see him so happy. Finally, Tim became so enchanted with horses, and so sure of himself as he "helped" Frenchie around the barn, that Frenchie showed him how to drive his big team.

That did it. We ended up buying two horses and a pony from Frenchie—in Timmy's words, "One for Daddy, one for Mom, and a pony for me"—and we had them sent back to our ranch. Once we were home, Timmy and I rode every day that we could, after school and most weekends.

Just as I had hoped it would, all this happy activity blotted out the

unhappy memories of Tim's time in the hospital. He again was the happy, inspired little boy he had always been. And what's more, having become a seven-year-old in June, he decided it was time to start a savings account at a bank—where another happy event took place. He received a plaque as a member of the Hopalong Cassidy Savings Club.

In September, Timmy returned to school and joined his former classmates in second grade. On October 15, Lela left on vacation, and a Mrs. Bollinger took over for her. That same day, Timmy proudly joined the school's baseball team. But when he couldn't see well enough to catch the ball, a boy yelled, "What's the matter with you, Timmy? Can't you see?"

He just answered, "Sorry," and walked off the field.

We didn't talk very much about it at supper, but after he went to sleep I wrote this note and left it on his desk.

Oct 15, 1952

Timmy Dear—

If you take all the water from all the 7 seas and put it all together . . . it still can't sink a ship, unless it gets inside the ship. The same with someone else's evil or wicked thoughts. They can't hurt you unless you accept them—unless those thoughts get inside your thinking . . .

So watch what kind of thoughts you let in!

Love you,

Mommy

P.S. Take care of Mrs. Bollinger and make her feel at home.

Although Tim didn't get to play baseball, three months later he made the swimming team, and in less than two years he could jump his pony and joined me at my fencing lessons with Maestro Faulkner.

Meanwhile, the letters from Paul kept coming. Often they were a jumble of love for Timmy and me, mixed with concern about finances.

Hotel du Rhone, Geneve
Oct 12, '52

. . . As to the horses. You will have to pay for them. You don't seem to understand that I can't afford to pay a nickel to you on top of the fantastic sum you are getting. The joint privilege, due to change in rates, is now worth less than $15,000 a year. Anybody else would ask you to cut the monthly sum in half. I haven't done so as yet but please don't expect anything over . . .

. . . I miss Timmy very much. I envy you being so near to him. He is a very good boy . . .

Bye now.

Paul

Hotel Ritz, Place Vendome, Paris
Dec. 4, '52
Dear T.

Your sweet letter of Nov. 26 just arrived. It was forwarded to Dusseldorf, just missed me and re-forwarded here. I feel very sad and lonely at not being home for Xmas. I feel so far away, so far away in distance and in time. I often think of the little beach house and our darling son. It is a privation to be away from him. I expect to be here

during holidays, but I'm not looking forward to them. I won't even have a tiny tree. Hope you and Timmy have a nice big one.

I am very pleased that you have paid and will pay for your calls and horses. I only want what's fair for the horses' upkeep, probably Beresford and Williams could establish the fair amount. As long as you pay your bills with reasonable promptitude, I will tell Fero not to deduct it from your check.

As to the bills for the trip and medical expenses, I'm glad that you realize they are enormous. I think that the doctors, with the possible exception of Dr. Poole, grossly overcharged you. You should always, if there is time, and there was in this case, have an agreement in advance as to what the charges will be. Some doctors like to charge a rich person 20 times more than their regular fee. As to Dr. Jaffe's bill of $1,000, I would like to know the details, and if the charges are his regular office charges to the public, or special charges for the rich Mrs. Getty. X-ray treatments in Dusseldorf cost $2.50 each, yes, two dollars and 50 cents by the best specialist. You must insist that you pay of what others pay and keep away from the high bidders, they're poor doctors anyway . . .

I don't think you take enough pains, in advance, to determine the charges. Frankly I never liked the Cedars of Lebanon Hospital. It may be a movie type joint. I will investigate these charges and get the reasonable portion of them paid. I hope Timmy can keep away from doctors, except for a $10 visit. I don't think doctors can do much for him now, except for a check-up, and that shouldn't be more than $25 unless the doctors charge on the ability to pay and not on a tariff and I avoid such doctors.

I've asked Hecht to study the hotel bill, and that I or the trust

will pay for the necessary and proper charges. You are to pay for any charges personal to you, i.e. your personal phone calls, excepting to me. Your cash advances, theatre tickets, entertaining, C.O.D.'s, etc.

If you would make a budget in advance and keep current on it, there would be a good saving of money and fuss. Know in advance just what you are going to obligate yourself for.

It is wonderful that Timmy is so tall and weighs 67½ lbs and that his eyes are better. Poor darling! . . .

I've spoken so much about bills and money. These are important factors in peace of mind and love and friendship . . . As I recall, we never had much discussion of bills or money until the last 7 or 8 years. The first 7 or 8 years we got along fine, and you seemed to manage very well and get a dollar's worth for a dollar spent. Must close now and go to dinner.

Bye now.

Paul

Did Timmy get my letter?

I wish I could describe the surprise, joy, and wonderment that Timmy expressed when he came into the lanai early Christmas morning that December 25, 1952, where on two huge tables I had set up my gift to him. On one table was a Silver Super Chief electric train, with its orange decorated engine and the familiar Dome Car—the observation car at the end of the train. And on the other table was a freight train hauling tank cars, cattle cars, and even a red caboose! Both trains were perfect replicas. When we turned on the electric switch, he shouted and laughed—and was so fascinated, he hardly looked at his other gifts.

And he was not the only one. My family and close friends (especially

the men) who came to spend Christmas Day with us played with the trains all day. That evening, after our guests had gone home, Timmy, dragging a great big teddy bear, started up the stairs to bed. Then he stopped for a moment on the landing, turned to me, and said, "Mama, I'm sorry Daddy couldn't make it home for Christmas. He must be lonely so far away from home. Do you think he got our gifts? And the little tree we sent . . . Do you think he got that in time for Christmas Eve?"

"I'm sure he did, Tim. You'll see—we'll hear from him soon."

"I hope so, Mom. I hope he's as happy as I am. This was the most wonderful Christmas I've ever had. I hope you had a happy day, too, Mom. I hope you liked what I gave you."

Little did he know that just being at home, seeing him becoming stronger and stronger, was the *only* gift his mother wished to receive.

"Timmy, today was the happiest ever. And your gift was the most lovely present I have ever received."

Hotel Ritz. Place Vendome, Paris
Jan 7, 1953
Darling Timmy and Teddy,
    I am so thankful to you both for the Xmas you gave me. My little
hotel room was brightened and given a Xmas look by the little tree
and its nine candles, and the pretty Xmas packages under the tree. I
thought of you and the beach house and of other Xmas days.
    Love,
    Paul

When this letter from Paul arrived, we knew that our effort to stretch our love of Christmas across the sea to include him had succeeded.

CHAPTER 38

A SENSE OF SECURITY

During the early part of 1953, days turned into months filled with hope, then fear, for we were back in a hospital again. The anxieties I had lived with ever since that horrifying moment at the ophthalmologist—the grave hours during his operation in New York and Paul never showing up—paraded through my memory like pictures on a carousel slide projector. I wanted to forget and forbid any new terrors from appearing.

I was grateful Paul paid for Timmy's doctors and hospital, but furious when his lawyer told me Paul was now complaining about the enormity of the bills. When Paul called me from London and started to complain, I yelled, "Damn it, Paul! If you could hear your son screaming in pain while being treated in the next room, you wouldn't dare speak about bills. You'd be praying. For God's sake, what kind of a father are you?" I burst into tears and hung up the phone.

Timmy needed his father. I needed him, too. I had asked him so

many times in the past, but he never came. And here I was, one year later, still alone and afraid.

I suddenly remembered another picture. It was the moment in the hospital when Dr. Poole rushed into my room after the first operation, saying he feared for Timmy's life. I'd fallen to my knees and prayed. I then felt a great peace. Oh, if only I could feel that again.

Slowly, softly, this verse from the Bible filled my thoughts: *"Acquaint now thyself with Him, and be at peace: thereby good shall come unto thee."* That's what I must do—pray—and I did. I became stronger, and never gave up hope for Tim's recovery.

Months passed and we were back at the beach house in Santa Monica. It was Mother's Day, May 10, 1953. I wrote this little poem to Timmy.

Because of you, I'm a mother
Because you are my son
And Mother's Day means this to me
It's every day—not one!
My wish for you: That you will walk
Thru life—expressing good
Reflecting only His perfection
This is my motherhood!
Love, Mommie

On May 25 we received this letter from Paul:

May 25, 1953
Dearest Teddy and Timmy,
Here's an item which may be of interest to you . . . I'm on route to

Paris and then am invited to the Coronation by Lord David Beatty
and Lady Beatty, Jefty's Niece. I'm so tired of constant travel and
of carrying an office around with me in my luggage.
    Miss you, Love,
    Father

I answered immediately:

Dear Paul,
    Nice to hear you're going to the Coronation. Best to Jefty's Niece.
    Too bad you still have to carry your office around in your
luggage, but you've always done this—and it's worked. Rejoice!
You're a successful businessman—but you're a hopeless father.
    Love,
    Teddy

On Tim's seventh birthday, June 14, 1953, Paul phoned to wish him
a Happy Day, just as lunch was being served. Tim shouted, "Hi, Daddy!
You ought to be here. We're sitting out by the pool having hamburgers,
hot dogs, and lemonade. Daddy, I wish you were here to meet my birthday
guests—five boys! Tommy and Pat Burke, Dickie Fedderman, Johnny Jan-
necke, and Tony Ballentyne. They're all great guys—real good friends."

"Girls?"

"No, Dad. For once, no girls. Just us guys."

Before Tim went to bed that night, I gave him this poem I'd written.

For Timmy on Flag Day, June 14ᵗʰ, 1953
We Salute our Country's Flag Today, brave banner of the Free

---

and we know that wherever it may wave, waves the symbol of Liberty.
Our Stars and Stripes—our Colors true, have long withstood the test,
have proven 'gainst the strongest foe, our way of life is best.
But man's worst enemy still is man. So be it—till man shall resolve
to turn from the Bondage of human fears and Spiritually Evolve.
So bless this day for the Flag we love and bless its sweet memory
for this is the day that God designed to give you, my son—to me.
Happy Birthday Darling!
Love and Kisses, Mamma

The summer months flew by. Paul was still deeply involved with his ever-growing empire in Europe, living mostly in the south of France, occasionally visiting friends in Switzerland and England, always phoning us or dropping short notes to keep in touch.

He wrote as though it saddened him to have to say he couldn't make the trip home "just yet." I felt he was almost embarrassed, but he needn't have been. No one was more understanding than Timmy of another's problems. It was enough that Daddy was busy working, that he missed Timmy, and that he was trying to finish and come home. That he hadn't succeeded yet, Timmy understood. I had just stopped caring.

After almost two years of expecting Paul to act as a father, I had lost my respect for him. Paul should have come home, or should have asked me to bring Timmy to him as soon as he was well enough to travel, and he hadn't done either.

Aug 5, '53
Hope the moths are not in my clothes!
Dearest Teddy,

I haven't heard from you for a long time. Just reread your letter of last June. You write so well, and from the heart. I liked your poem. Remember when one of your poems was published by Winchell?

I think so often of our darling little boy. It is a real sorrow not to be with him every day. I hope his health is improving. I admire both of you for your courage.

Timmy, your father loves and misses you.

As ever, Paul

IN EARLY AUGUST I got a call from Paul's friend Bill Gaston, who was staying with the Dudley Murphys in Malibu. He said Paul had told him all about Timmy, and could we meet for dinner one night.

Strangely, I had reservations for dinner that very evening with Mother and Timmy at Dudley's famous restaurant, the Holiday House. Though Bill had a business dinner planned, he said he'd stop by our table to say hello.

I thought it would be exciting to see him again. We had first met in New York in 1936, when Roosevelt was running for a second term. It was then that Bill, Paul, and Bill Lawrence of the *New York Times* (also known as "Atomic Bill") were thinking of forming a political party.

Mother, Timmy, and I were already having dinner when I looked up and saw Bill Gaston striding through the crowded room, coming straight toward us. It was as if John Wayne had suddenly ridden in on his horse the way every woman's eyes turned to look at him. And I felt at that very moment this man was going to be the next important man in my life.

After saying hello to Mother and Timmy, he looked at me and

smiled. "Teddy, it's good to see you again. You're looking as beautiful as ever. May I call you tomorrow?"

"Yes, please do," I replied, and he left to rejoin his business dinner. All the way home I couldn't stop thinking of Bill, and wondering why Paul would have sent him to see me. Bill had driven Paul up to Mother's house in Greenwich for our engagement party, and he was still one of the most attractive men in the world I lived in.

He came from a prominent Boston family. His father was first the mayor of Boston, then the governor of Massachusetts, and a founding member of the Shawmut Bank of Boston. Bill was on the Harvard football team, and after graduating from Harvard Law School, joined the Air Force as an aviator during World War I, received the Navy Cross for valor, was shot down over the English Channel, and was miraculously rescued by a fisherman within six hours. Years later, he joined the New York world of Wall Street and married Kay Frances. When that didn't work, he married Rosamond Pinchot, with whom he had two sons, Bill Jr. and Jimmy. Then he married a girl from Texas, Lucille Hutchings, and they had a son named Tommy. Bill spent most of his winters in Connecticut or traveling the world and summers on his island in Maine with his boys and friends. While staying on the island one summer, Clare Boothe Luce wrote her famous stage play *The Women*.

Bill phoned at ten the next morning and asked if I would dine with him that night. Instead, I suggested he come to the beach house for lunch. It was a beautiful California day, sunny and warm, and we spent the afternoon catching up on the years.

Finally, he asked me how Tim was doing. Just then, Timmy and Lela came in from the beach, and he excitedly asked Bill to come up to his

living room, where he had set up his trains. When Bill returned, he said, "Teddy, you have a great son. I've invited him to come to my island in Maine next summer, if you can arrange it. I think he'd have a good time. My youngest, Tommy, will be there."

"Sounds exciting, Bill. We'll try and make it," I replied.

He then asked that I have dinner with him the next evening at Ciro's, as he was leaving in two days for Santa Barbara. His good friend Katherine Dunham was performing there, and he wanted me to meet her, so I happily accepted.

Ciro's on the Sunset Strip was quite the place in those days, and meeting Katherine Dunham and watching her performance was inspiring. She danced like a princess of the ancient world of Haiti—wildly, proudly—singing her songs accompanied mostly by woodwinds and drums.

Bill asked me to dance. He held me close, and as we danced I closed my eyes, and, for a moment, I forgot all of the agony of the past four years. Was it the music, or this man? I loved being held by him, for he made me feel young again, wanted again, happy and carefree. I felt alive.

We left Ciro's at 2:30 in the morning, headed for the beach. As we drove up the Sunset Strip past other clubs like the Players and Macambo, I was amazed there were so few cars on the road. Then, when we arrived at the area where the Strip opens up and becomes Sunset Boulevard, Bill suddenly stopped the car right in the middle of the road, turned, pulled me to him, and kissed me passionately!

At that very moment, sirens blew, and spotlights were turned on the car. In minutes, we were surrounded, I thought, by the entire Beverly Hills Police Department. One officer walked up, stuck his head in

the window, and said, "Hey, Connecticut, can't you do this at home?" I almost fainted. But amazingly Bill talked himself out of a ticket.

After they left, we had a good laugh. Bill put his arm around me, smiled, and said, "Now I better get you home, Teddy." At the gate to the beach house, I thanked him. He kissed me good-bye and said, "I'll call you from Santa Barbara." Then he drove off up the Pacific Coast Highway, and I went inside the house, feeling like a schoolgirl.

Timmy and I continued to get regular letters from Paul, telling us about his work and his travels, always regretting not being with us, promising to return home "as soon as business permits."

Paul wrote me this from Interlaken, Switzerland:

Sept 9, '53

Teddy Boo dear,

Your sweet letter just came. It is nice to hear from you and darling Timmy. Yes, I enjoyed Harry Lipton's candy very much. Thank you and Timmy again. I thought I thanked you weeks ago.

. . . I'm pleased Timmy swims so well. But, I don't want him to go into the water alone. I've been working so hard. As you know, PW has half its assets in the Eastern Hemisphere and I'm the only PW man over here except a 31 year old geologist in Sicily and he, though a good man, has his hands full. Also, he doesn't have my experience. I'm anxious to get home.

This place is very near to Grindelwald. Remember September 1939?—14 years ago!

I wish we could be together on your birthday. All my best to you on September 13 and always.

Love, Paul

On December 13, 1953, Paul wrote from Paris:

Dearest Teddy—Soon I'll be 61. Wish I were home. Sometimes it seems as though it were last week! We are rushing toward our destination! I'm very sad not to be home for Xmas. It isn't a real Xmas when one is away from home, sitting in a hotel room. Last year your little tree and candles made my room seem more cheerful and gave it a look of Xmas. We are due to ship our first tanker load of oil from the Neutral Zone on Jan. 13 and although I've tried hard, I still don't have a boat for that date. I'm returning home as soon as business permits.

Merry Xmas and Happy New Year to you and Timmy.

Love, Father

On January 5, 1954, he wrote:

Dearest Teddy and Timmy,

Thanks again for the lovely cheerful Christmas presents and the tree. Alas, due to the strike they arrived Dec. 31st. But that made up for a rather bare and dreary Xmas . . . I long to be home again . . .

Love to you both,

Father

After receiving Paul's January 5 letter, I dashed off a quick note, asking that Timmy and I come over to see him, that it would do his little son so much good to see his daddy, and I needed his advice on many things regarding Tim.

This was his reply:

Jan 18, '54

Dearest Teddy,

I think it is very nice that you and Timmy want to visit me in Feb. I wrote you that it was impracticable but apparently you didn't get my letter.

I am expecting to leave on short notice for Arabia, my plans are uncertain. I hope to be back in Calif in April. So, a visit now is inadvisable. The ocean is very rough, Timmy might fall and hurt his head—and he has enough trouble already.

I advise you after this when somebody wants to give you a wounded deer, to tell them to give it to the Humane Society. I don't want the deer at the ranch, since it is illegal to keep them. I also, of course won't pay any bills for it since I didn't authorize them.

I have a vast amount of work here. The correspondence I have is unbelievable. I could keep an office busy and I have no help. They're more bother than they're worth.

Am anxious to see Timmy—but in California.

Love to you both, Paul

The night I received Paul's letter, I responded at once.

Dear Paul,

The DEER you objected to in your Jan 18th letter was not a gift from one of my friends. It was a sweet DOE with her little FAWN who was attacked by a Mountain Lion early one morning as they gambled (sp) across the lawn in front of the Ranch House. The Doe tried to save her baby, who died horribly. Darrell Link shot the

Mountain Lion and I called a Vet, but later the mother died too.
That's the whole story, and I paid the bill!
   Love, Teddy

PS: Instead, could we meet you in Cannes or Venice en route to
Arabia? Please advise.

Paul refused my request, suggesting the trip would be "needlessly extravagant." I felt Paul's saying *too expensive* was not the reason he didn't want us to come. I realized his trip to Saudi Arabia was the most important business venture of his life, and it was definitely the wrong timing for us, so I waited.

And waited.

In the meantime, we got more letters.

Then on June 23, 1954, I received a note from Paul, saying he had returned to Paris after an extraordinary successful trip to Saudi Arabia. He enclosed a letter from his attorney David Hecht, who had relayed a message from Dr. Poole stating, *There was little hope for Timmy's future.*

June 23, '54
Dearest Teddy,
   I enclose letter from Dr. Poole. I suggest you consider treating
Timmy with the new machine at Boston, built I believe, by MIT.
It has several million volts of capacity and can reach deep inside
the body without harm to healthy tissue. This of course, only, if
necessary. I believe ordinary old fashion x-ray is not much use.

———

I am longing to see Timmy and I understand how lonely you feel sometimes when you have to make decisions.

My work here has kept me very busy. I plan to return home late this summer. Dr. Valentine was here and said you were very nice and helpful in opening the museum.

As always,

Paul

I was shocked by this news, and wrote to Paul at once.

July 1, 1954

Dear Paul,

Your letter with David Hecht's enclosed in which he relayed Dr. Poole's shocking report that "there is little hope for Timmy's future" is enough to strike fear into the most courageous of hearts. And yours Paul, is so matter of fact. It contains no warmth of understanding—no outstretched hand—no word or sign of hope from you for this mother and her little son.

I have begged and implored you for more than two years to allow me to bring Timmy to you, that we wouldn't bother you, that we would only stay a few weeks, but you have always said, "No." Since you have never come home even for one week to see him, and believing the worst—that time is of the essence—what on earth holds you back from wanting to see him quickly?

If you believe these horrifying reports of Tim's doctor, how can you not say—"Come here at once with Timmy—we will employ the

very best doctors we can find—God will help us and we will stand together." But you haven't.

Paul, don't you realize that Timmy has needed his father—that he has needed you to tell him he is wanted and loved? Don't you realize that he might feel you have deserted him for your work—or whatever? I guess the fact that Tim has gone so bravely on—thru the "Valley of the Shadow" clinging so constantly to God—and too, the fact that I have needed to see you, to count on your wisdom and knowledge to know what is right to do for Tim—has made your indifference cut more deeply into my heart.

Since, during the past two years, you haven't come home as you had so often promised you would, and you won't agree to allow me to bring Timmy to you—let's not pretend anymore, Paul. I know now that you aren't coming home to us, because I know you don't want to, and so I have finally come to the tragic realization that you have no real concern for either Tim or me. Your actions have made this clear for so long that I have had to wake up—face the facts—that our "separation agreement" hasn't worked and have come to the conclusion that it's best we get a divorce.

Please remember I loved you and hopefully waited for you even tho my heart and courage broke when you didn't come back and stand with me thru Tim's awful operation, and your actions have been the greatest disappointment of my whole life. But Paul, I don't condemn you—I feel sorry for you and pray that you will wake up and learn true values. God bless you dear—goodbye and thanks for the good parts of the past 15 years.

Teddy.

July 4, 1954

Dearest Teddy,

 Your letter just came. I am deeply distressed. I've tried to do my best as a father but apparently I've failed. I love Timmy and think of him every day. I long to see him and be with him. I plan to be home in late August or early September. The doctors in Europe are not as good as in the U.S.A. And, I hope our Timmy doesn't need any more doctors. I worry about him.

 It has been a great strain on you, I know. And you have been alone, without me to help you with Timmy. You have more money than anybody else and you can do as you wish, travel to Europe or stay home. Of course, you wouldn't expect me to pay for the trip when you get more than any bank president. Sometimes, I've thought I'd like to borrow money from you, but I won't try. I'm very tired of Europe, very tired of hotels—I long to be home.

 Love to you and Timmy,
 Paul

PS: I expect reserve steamship passage to N.Y. very soon.

Paul's letter showed me I'd finally gotten through to him. He had woken up to the facts—the sad facts regarding Timmy that he quite naturally tried to avoid facing—facts I had had to face alone. I really hadn't thought about who was going to pay for our trip to Europe when I'd asked him to let us come. I honestly didn't care, I'd willingly pay. I just wanted him to see Timmy, wanted to bring his youngest son to him, since he couldn't seem to come home.

On July 18, Paul wrote again. At last it looked like he was coming home on the *Queen Mary*, sailing September 16.

Paris
July 18, 1954
Dearest Teddy and Timmy,
    I finally got a cabin on the Queen Mary *sailing Sept. 16 for New York—I haven't a place for my car on board yet—so it may have to go on another boat. I hope you like the 2nd canary. Doesn't it sing and does it like the 1st canary? I'm longing to see you.*
    Fondest love, Paul

The two canaries he spoke of were his birthday present to Timmy on June 14, just what he had asked his daddy to give him, and they did sing, and filled the beach house with their happy little voices. Tim was very happy, too. He now had one pony, two dogs, one cat, one hamster, and two canaries to love.

On August 3, 1954, Paul wrote Timmy, mentioning his plan to return to New York. In anticipation of meeting Paul in September, we left immediately for New York on the fastest plane. Seven and a half hours—it was thrilling. We stayed for a few days at the Pierre Hotel. Then one day, as it was nearing Paul's arrival in New York, the telephone rang. It was Paul. He had to again postpone his trip.

I was both infuriated and saddened, for Paul had once again let us down. I decided that, since Timmy had never been to my family's summer home, we'd motor up to the Cape, take the steamer over to Martha's Vineyard, and visit my aunt Ruth Shorey in Vineyard Haven. She was delighted to have us and we stayed with her for a week.

On our last night there we stopped at Menemsha, the old fishing village with its quaint charm, to watch the fishermen as they came in to the harbor at dusk with their daily catch. Then we took Lambert's Cove Road off the main highway onto the one-way sandy road through the woods. We reached the open field, where a quarter of a mile ahead was our old summer home, Wild Acres, standing silhouetted against the evening sky and the sea beyond. It tugged at my heart.

The next day we said our grateful good-byes to Aunt Ruth. Since Timmy had never seen the snow, I decided we'd stay on in the East. I called Ware and rented a small house down the street from the Silvermine Tavern, just outside Norwalk, Connecticut. I enrolled Tim at the Daycroft School in Stamford, where he progressed slowly but happily in his studies. He now wore glasses, which helped him see better. He took up the drums, and each day practiced faithfully. Fortunately, our house was out in a rural area, so the drums didn't bother our neighbors—the squirrels and birds, and the fish in the Silvermine River.

Very early one morning, the phone rang. It was Bill. He'd found us through Ware, and he wanted to take me to lunch. Promptly at noon, the bell rang. I opened the door, and there stood a suntanned Bill Gaston, looking extremely attractive and healthy. He leaned down, kissed me, then took my hand. We walked over to the tavern, where we lunched and spent the entire afternoon catching up. It was exciting to see Bill again. When I spoke of my fears for Timmy, he was tender and kind, which gave me the sense of security I needed, but on September 12· we were back at the hospital, seeing Dr. Hoen to face more tests.

By October, Timmy was released and we were out in the country again. I felt he was okay, so back to school he went.

On Thanksgiving, we dined with Ware and Peggy at the famous Sil-

vermine Tavern. That weekend Tim and I went to New York to visit the dinosaur hall at the Museum of Natural History. One special afternoon we even sat in the very front row of a matinee performance of the musical *Kismet*, starring Alfred Drake and Joan Diener. The music by Alexander Borodin was so beguiling that Timmy memorized the entire score, and would happily sing "Baubles, Bangles and Beads" for anyone!

We spent our very first white Christmas at home in the coziness of our little rented New England house, which looked like the picture post-card of an old saltbox, set right in the middle of a snow-covered lawn. The trees glistened with icicles, and you could just picture Santa Claus coming up the driveway on his sleigh.

Mary Barns, a loving neighbor from down the road, came to help and care for Timmy. Her husband, Ed, made life happier by keeping us warm with a supply of logs for our fireplace, and would take us out in his sleigh, even some nights through the snow-white countryside, when the moon was full and the air crisp—our favorite time. This was most healing for Timmy, though we still dreaded the pending spring checkup with Dr. Hoen.

When that time came, we drove into town and stayed at the Pierre, so we could make our early-morning appointment with the doctor. The night before, on our way to dinner, an attractive elderly couple joined us in the hotel elevator. The gentleman looked down at Timmy, smiled, and said, "Young man, where did you get that beautiful red hair?"

Looking up, Timmy answered, "God gave me mine, sir—and Eliza-beth Arden gave Mom hers." That brought a big smile to all of us, just as we reached the main lobby.

The following morning we met Dr. Hoen, and that, too, brought a smile to both of us, for he seemed pleased again with Timmy's progress.

———

CHAPTER 39

A DIFFERENT LIFE

Ritz Hotel

London, W.1.

April 6, 1955

Darling Teddy,

Emmy was here to tea yesterday. She and Burton and Burton's pretty daughter. They have had a pleasant stay in Europe and expect to be home next month.

I was profoundly shocked and depressed to learn from Emmy how darling Timmy's sight is. I had no idea his sight was nearly gone and that he had to be led by the hand. Oh, our poor boy! And he is such a brave boy. I know how much you must suffer. My thoughts are with you both. You are a devoted and wonderful mother. I hope and pray that his sight will be restored to some degree.

I plan to be in New York next month. We can have a good talk
then. I am so anxious to see you both.
Love, Paul

When Easter arrived a few days later, Paul phoned and spoke with Timmy for quite a while. Then he asked me if I thought Tim was well enough to travel, and if so, "Will you and Timmy join me in Paris?"

I couldn't believe him, but we were thrilled and deliriously happy over the prospect. I immediately arranged for passports and purchased our tickets (Paul paid for them). Believing we might stay on in Europe, I sent our personal things to be stored at the Pierre. On June 4, 1955, when our lease ended on our little furnished house and school closed for the summer, Tim and I excitedly boarded a night flight over the Atlantic for Paris.

The trip was inspiring; we had two wonderful seats in first class, and almost immediately after takeoff we had a delightful dinner served by Maxim's of Paris, with all the charm of home—bone china, linen tablecloths and napkins, silver, and beautiful little bouquets of flowers on each tray.

At sunset we went upstairs to the club lounge and, passing over Martha's Vineyard, we looked out through the huge observation windows and saw the *Nantucket Lightship* holding its lonely vigil. We sat up at the bar with the other passengers, and after a little snack and a glass of milk, we went below, settled ourselves in seats that had now become roomy relaxing berths, thanks to the flight attendants, until—the sun woke us up and we landed in Ireland. It was there that Timmy asked the captain's permission to go out to meet an Irish policeman. Fortunately, there were

two at the gate, and Timmy walked up to them and said, "I'm Timmy Getty from California, and *I'm* Irish, too."

They laughed and said, "Pleased to meet you, Timmy," shook his hand, then escorted him back onto the plane. In no time we would be in Paris, and we'd see Paul.

We were both so excited. Questions were racing through my mind. *What was he like? Had fame changed him? Would he think I had changed? Would he still like me and find me attractive? Would he see himself in Timmy?* There was no more time for questions. Our hostess tapped me on the shoulder and said, "Timmy, Mrs. Getty, we're over Paris now."

I looked out. There it was, that glorious city on the Seine. "Look, Tim. There's the Eiffel Tower and that . . . that's Notre Dame. We've arrived. Isn't it thrilling?"

He pulled my arm, leaned very close, and whispered, "Mom, do you think Daddy will remember me? Does he still love me?"

"Of course, darling. How could anyone forget my little redhead? Here, let me brush it. My, you look sharp. But, Tim . . . How do I look?"

"My beautiful mom, you always look beautiful."

"Tim—be serious. How do I really look? Am I okay?"

"Yes, really, Mom. You look beautiful, but be sure to wear the flowers the airline gave you."

We landed easily, and in seconds we were in the airport. From that moment I wasn't aware of anything except looking for Paul. And there he was, scanning the crowd for us. He looked wonderful. Just then, the customs officer said, smiling, "You may go, madame." Timmy and I moved along down the ramp, and at that exact moment Paul saw us, too. He waved, and we both rushed toward him like the UCLA football team.

After giving us a very warm welcome, as though we had never

parted, Paul drove us back to Paris, the three of us sitting in the front seat. He drove right down the Champs Élysées to the Hotel George V, where we found our rooms ready for us—and—we were ready for them.

Paul noted our meeting in his diary entry of June 5, 1955:

Drove my new '55 Cad to Orly, saw Teddy and Timmy 50 yds. away going thru Customs, Teddy looked very glamorous—was wearing an orchid. Timmy looked much larger than I remembered him. Soon I greeted my dear ones. So glad to be with them. 4 years! They came to my room, #801 after an hour in their room, #533. Timmy has some vision and is now wearing glasses. He seems bright and well. He runs and plays. I love him dearly and admire him.

That evening we three had dinner at the Tour D'Argent. As we left the George V we saw Jack Forester. Teddy hadn't seen him since 1940 in Rome.

She had had dinner with Jack and Frank Ryan just as war broke out. Teddy looks about the same as she did 4 years ago and was good enough to say that I did too.

That evening, Paul was invited to go to a huge party given on a barge floating down the River Seine. He wanted me to go with him, but I couldn't leave Timmy. The next morning, Paul called to tell us what the party was like. It sounded fabulous.

When I read Paul's diary, years after this trip, I found passages describing that visit from Paul's point of view:

June 11, 1955

Timmy came to my room alone—he found it alright. We

*had quite a talk. He then asked me to name a few dinosaurs. I
remembered all but one, triceratops. Timmy laughed and said,
"Daddy, just remember, 'Try-Cereal-Tops.' It's CEREAL, like the
kind you eat at breakfast." This made me laugh, and now I'll never
forget it.*

June 14, 1955

*Timmy is 9 years old today. So glad to be with him. Gave him
30,000 francs for his birthday present and a big birthday cake at
dinner that evening with Teddy and me. Surprisingly, Marion
Anderson and her son, Jan, joined us. They're here visiting Paris.
Now Timmy has someone to play with, though Jan is a few years
older.*

Our routine during our stay was simple. Paul would call us every
morning to let us know when he could see us, for he was extremely busy.
I'd ask Marion and Jan to spend that time with us visiting the most
important places one must see when in Paris—Notre Dame, the Eiffel
Tower, and especially Versailles.

Sometimes Timmy seemed tired and would have to rest, but
moments later he'd say, "I'm okay now, Mom." And we'd go on. But we'd
take it very easy.

One afternoon we went to Montmartre, where we browsed through
a few art galleries. At one, we met the artist Michel-Marie Poulain, who,
fortunately for us, was at the gallery showing his work. It was exciting
for Timmy to meet a real artist. Poulain was known for his portraits of
young people, and Timmy saw two that he wished to buy with his birthday money. One, a pretty girl surrounded by several French sailors at a
dance hall, and the other, a young girl smiling.

On meeting the artist, we were not only captivated by his work, but by his charm and the fact that he was known all over the world. We sent these paintings back to Santa Monica, only after *first* showing them to Paul, who approved of his nine-year-old son's charming taste.

When Marion went away for a week, she asked if Jan could stay with us. I ordered another bed to be put in with Timmy and me, much to the amazement of the waiter who brought us breakfast the following morning. Also amazed was the maid who was to clean our room. Later, when she assumed we'd left for the day, she made the mistake of looking through the keyhole of our door to see if we'd left. The boys were waiting for her with a water gun, which sent her dripping down the hall.

Once or twice that week, Timmy went out in the morning with Jan, both of them wearing blue-and-white-striped sweaters and berets. I wouldn't know where they were for hours. I didn't think Timmy could see very well, but he saw well enough to get around, and always knew how to get back to the hotel.

One morning, an extremely upset manager knocked on our door and demanded to see the boys. When they appeared, he looked at them and firmly asked, "Did you two change the shoes at everyone's door on this floor last night?"

I looked at my son and said, "Timmy, did you boys do this?"

"Yes, Mom," he answered. "We did, and I'm sorry."

"Me, too!" Jan added.

"Well, go put those shoes back where they belong, and apologize at once to this gentleman," I said.

I then turned to the hotel manager, threw up my hands, and said, *"Je regrette aussi, monsieur."*

He bowed and said, *"Ça ne fait rien, Madame Getty,"* and followed the boys out.

The next day we headed for Calais to take the ferry to Dover.

We stayed in London for a month. Not only did they see the sights, but Timmy and Jan were taken out to Whipsnade, the famous zoo, by Paul's special friend, Penelope Kitson, to see the Kodiak bear, among the other animals. When they returned, Timmy told me he'd had a great time, but decided Penelope wasn't a very good mother.

"Why?" asked Paul.

"Because she doesn't know how to make a peanut butter sandwich."

"Oh," Paul said, smiling.

That evening when we arrived at Paul's apartment, Ronnie Getty was there. The boys were surprised and happy to see each other. Their last meeting had been four years earlier, in April of 1951, up at the Ranch in Malibu, when Eda Edson and her crew filmed Paul showing his art collection.

While waiting to see their father, the boys and I played cards on the floor of his drawing room. When Paul joined us, both boys jumped up and greeted their father. Then Paul walked over to greet me. I looked up at him. He seemed concerned.

"What's wrong, Paul?" I asked.

"I just realized I'm in need of another name for our company. It seems Pacific Western doesn't register well with the people of Europe. It sounds more like an island in the Pacific than the name of an oil company." And he started to laugh.

I thought for a minute, then I looked up at him. "Why don't you call it Getty Oil? It's your name—use it like your friend, Harry Sinclair, the Sinclair Oil Company."

"That's a good idea, Teddy." Months later Paul wrote Timmy from Saudi Arabia on Pacific Western letterhead. Above it was stamped *Getty Oil Company.*

Before we left London, I had a meeting with Paul and his lawyer, Tom Dockweiler, in Paul's suite. I sat down with both, and when we started talking about Timmy, I burst into tears and ran out on the terrace. When I returned, I saw Paul had tears in his eyes. I thought they were just sentimental tears, brought on by my mentioning Timmy's courage and faith in God. Paul told me then, and never stopped telling me, that I was a wonderful mother—that my love and devotion to Timmy was inspiring to all.

When Paul left the room, I turned to Tom. "I *must* get a divorce," I said.

"Why?" he replied. "You have a wonderful agreement."

"Are you mad, Tom? It may be good for Paul, but not for me, a mother with a son who needs a father. Don't you realize Paul hasn't seen Timmy for the last four years?! He never came home for that first horrifying operation, after he promised me he would. And when Timmy was finally well enough to travel, Paul wouldn't let me bring him over to see him."

"Well, if you divorce Paul, will you marry again?"

"I'd have to fall in love," I replied. "I can't live this way any longer, Tom, to condone a marriage used as a protection for either of us. I loved him and believed he loved me. I thought the trial separation would save our marriage, hoping someday we'd get together again, but it hasn't worked. I'm miserable living like this. Paul always said, 'Put a value on yourself, Teddy'—and I think it's about time I did. I can't be married any longer to a man who's constantly having extramarital affairs. It's not right—I must be free."

"My dear Teddy, I understand, but for the moment, take care of your son. And when he's well enough, then talk of divorce."

After Timmy left with Marion and Jan for supper and a movie, Paul and I were to have dinner alone in the hotel. I was sitting at the dressing table in my suite, getting ready, when I heard the click of a key, heard the door open, and called out, "Who's there?"

"Your husband, dear," Paul answered, walking in.

I was surprised to hear those words; they jolted me back into reality.

"Just give me a minute and I'll slip into a dress," I called out. But coming up from behind, he leaned down, kissed me on the cheek, and smiled at me from the mirror before us. I smiled back.

"You look beautiful, darling," he said, as his hands moved down my body, caressing my breasts.

I pushed his hands away, stood up, reached for my negligee, turned, and kissed him right on the mouth. "Wait here. I'll be ready in a minute."

"Why?" he said, pulling me back, kissing me again and holding me.

I slipped out of his arms and walked into the bedroom. Shutting the door, I leaned against it, my heart pounding. I wanted to make love to this man more than ever. He must have felt this. It brought back our life together at the beach all over again. *Stop it, Teddy!* I thought to myself. *It can never be the same. And just stop dreaming. He'll never be a husband. You live in an empty home.*

Paul knocked. "Need help?" he said, laughing.

"I'm fine, almost ready!" I called out, wiping tears from my eyes. I then hurriedly put on my dress, reached for my handbag, and opened the door. He was standing there.

"You know, you really haven't changed a bit, Teddy Boo. You're still the same adorable girl I've always loved."

"No, Paul, I'm a woman. Now, let's go eat."

The restaurant was very quiet that evening; only the orchestra was playing. After we were seated, Paul ordered dinner and a bottle of wine, then studied me a minute, smiled, and said, "I'm really sorry you're leaving. I wish you and Tim could stay longer."

"Maybe you can arrange to see Timmy more often, for he has asked if you still love him. He's a brilliant little boy, capable of doing something great in life . . . And you, his father, should be the one to guide him."

"I want to."

"Well, if you really do, Paul, don't wait too long."

I suddenly noticed the orchestra had started playing again. Our eyes met, we smiled. It was "Alone Together"—our song. He took my hand and led me onto the dance floor. The passion, chemistry, and love we had had for each other hadn't changed from the night we had met in 1935 . . . *but time had changed us.*

He held me close. We danced in silence. I longed to go back, longed for those days, and in a whisper I said, "Darling, we must dissolve this marriage."

He looked at me. "Teddy!"

"This separation agreement isn't working for me. You seem to be happy, but I'm not. I need to be free . . . free to love . . . you understand, don't you?"

"Teddy. Don't you love me anymore?"

"Of course I do, but I want a whole marriage."

"Teddy."

"Paul, you've been absent from my life these past four years. You want me to be happy, too, don't you?"

"Yes, but . . . what will this do to Timmy?"

"He'll understand. However, I won't start proceedings until he's completely well."

The day we were to leave for America, Paul called Timmy into his office, and they stayed there for almost an hour, talking. When they came out, Paul had his arm around his son and though they were both smiling, Paul looked as though he had tears in his eyes. I could see that Timmy was touched by his father's embrace, especially when Paul leaned down and said, "I hate to see you go, son, but come back after your next school break."

"I will, Daddy, and thanks, I've had a real good time with you."

I joined them, and we all walked out of the hotel where Lee, Paul's chauffeur, was waiting for us with the car.

Timmy kissed Paul, and turning to me asked, "Mom, may I sit in the front seat with Lee?"

"Of course, dear," I replied. Lee took Timmy by the hand, led him to the front of the car, and buckled him into his seat.

I looked at Paul. He pulled me to him, put his arms around me, kissed me tenderly, and said, "I wish I were going with you, Teddy Boo."

I smiled and said, "Me, too, Paul." Then I turned and stepped into the car. Lee closed the door, and I closed my eyes, not wanting to say good-bye.

Lee drove us to Southampton, where we boarded the *Queen Mary* at night. It was exciting because there was a full moon and the sea was calm, and a huge bouquet of flowers from Paul greeted us as we walked into our cabin. It was a great trip, but rather sad. Timmy sometimes felt ill, but we walked the decks every morning, swam in the pool, listened to concerts, and watched movies.

Upon arriving in New York we were met by Ware who drove us out

to the Silvermine Tavern, where he arranged for me to lease a charming little furnished house . . . Timmy returned to Daycroft for the school year.

Each day after homework, Tim would practice his drums (a Christmas gift from his dad), and during the days while Tim was at school, I'd keep myself busy studying concert pieces on a piano I rented, or sometimes meet with other mothers from Timmy's school for brunch to arrange lectures and fundraisers. We had our own maid who came each day to help us.

In the evenings, the sound of the river would put us to sleep, in winter, snowstorms would make us grateful for that huge fireplace. It was a different life than the one we knew in Santa Monica. Across the road and up a ways was the area called the Silvermine Art Colony. It was there young artists studied while others showed their paintings for sale. There were several antiques shops and best of all, a small café, where you could order a cup of coffee and a sandwich. The only market within miles was on Valley Road, where one could walk safely and happily enjoy the river and the lush countryside, undisturbed by city traffic.

Soon after we arrived, I called Bill to let him know that we were home. He was in Maine and asked that I bring Timmy up to his island. "It's great weather now. Tommy's here, and it'll be good for Timmy. Furthermore, it'll be good for you, too, Teddy."

A few days later, after getting settled in our new home, we drove to Rockland, Maine, and took the ferry to Vinalhaven. Bill and Tommy met us, and off we went in his boat to Crotch Island, which seemed from afar nothing more than a forest rising out of the sea. Then, as we drew closer, it was absolutely fascinating, for we landed there just as the sun was setting. The first thing I noticed as I stepped onto the dock was a

beautiful green lawn with a tree in the middle of it, a rowboat beside it with a wooden mermaid standing in it, and flowers planted around the tree and boat.

Beyond stood the huge log house Bill had built himself years ago. There was a long porch the length of the house, with two inviting hammocks. Walking in, we found ourselves in a living area with an amazing fireplace at one end constructed out of enormous granite rocks. On the far side of the room, just two steps up, was a raised dining room that could seat twenty persons. Later, I learned Bill had built it as a stage to present plays.

Bill cooked the dinner that evening. We ate the lobsters Tommy had just pulled from his trap, and fresh beans and corn Bill had grown in his island garden. It was the beginning of a great week for Timmy and me. With no electricity and only a generator used for the television, lasting about an hour and a half, it would be a calamity if it suddenly stopped before the end of a program you were watching. Bill carefully chose programs that started and stopped within the allotted time. I quickly learned how difficult it was to do the chores that have to be done if one lives in a house on a privately owned island without the conveniences of electricity, furnaces, washer-dryers, refrigerators . . . or servants.

Timmy, under Tommy's instruction, was taught all about lobsters—how to tell their age, their sex, and whether they were big enough to keep. If they weren't a certain size, one had to throw them back into the sea immediately. If you were caught by the Marine Police, you'd be fined. Red Phillips, Bill's good friend from Vinalhaven, took Timmy fishing several days, telling him stories of his life at sea.

One night, after the boys had gone to bed, Bill and I were sitting on

the big couch in front of the fireplace. He asked, "Teddy, tell me . . . are you and Paul divorced?"

I looked over at him. "No, I wanted a divorce, but he wanted a separation agreement, and then, when Timmy became ill, I just couldn't. These years have been horrific. Paul wouldn't come home and wouldn't let me bring Timmy to him until this year."

I sighed, got up, walked over to the fireplace, turned, and looked at Bill. Then, feeling I'd cry, I turned away.

"You know, Teddy," Bill said, "Paul never mentioned when we met in Paris that Timmy had gone through such serious operations. He only said you were in California—so why don't you call her?"

I looked at him for a long moment, smiled and said, "Well, you did, and it's been wonderful, not only for Tim, but for me."

"Then stay for a few more days." With that, Bill pulled me to him and kissed me. For the first time in years, I felt safe, with a sense of belonging.

CHAPTER 40

CALIFORNIA OR BUST

In February 1956, I took Timmy into New York to see Dr. Hoen. All seemed well.

On February 21, after we decided to separate, Paul wrote a very loving letter to me.

> *Teddy Boo,*
>
> *It does seem strange doesn't it, after all these years! I'm so glad that there was so little publicity and no quarreling or recrimination. Little Teddy Boo, is, as always, a thoroughbred.*
>
> *I think of the old days, really the young days, very often.*
>
> *Love, Paul*

A day later, he wrote this to Timmy.

Feb. 22, 1956
Darling Timmy,
  You are my treasure.
  I was very glad to get your letter.
  I hope to see you soon.
    Love Daddy

In March, I received another letter from Paul.

March 18, 1956
Dearest Teddy,
  Your letter was most welcome. I hope to see you and Timmy in
the U.S. in May.
  All love to you both,
  Paul

Sadly, Paul was unable to keep that promise, so when summer came, I accepted Bill's offer for us to spend any weekend we could at his home in New Canaan, because he was planning to be at his island with his sons in the summer. While there, I bought a large screened tent, and placed it out on the lawn overlooking the river in front of Bill's house. That way Timmy, his nurse Louella, and I could spend time outside, for it was very hot in Connecticut and there were lots of bugs flying around. Sometimes he'd sleep out there with our beloved puppy, Clover, who would always go along with us in the ambulance up the Merritt Parkway on our way back and forth from University Hospital. Spending the summer at Bill's house with his puppy dog and different friends from school coming

to lunch and play with him was just what Timmy needed. By September, he was back in school.

Paul's letter to Timmy dated December 8, 1956, from Geneva showed how much he seemed to miss us and how he wished we could all be together at Christmas.

Darling Timmy,

I wish we could be together this Christmas. I wonder what Santa Claus will bring you. I remember our Christmas together in Santa Monica and how handsome you looked and how well you sang during the Christmas song and the march to the Christmas tree. Happy Days!

With all love to you and your dear Mother,

Father

Upon receiving this, I felt Paul was for the moment longing for the simple days of Santa Monica and the beach he loved.

In July of 1957, we returned to New York and were seen by Dr. Hoen and Dr. Wright, the very loving woman doctor who had created the serum made from the tumor that they had taken from Timmy.

Later, Dr. Wright asked to see me alone. She came to my room, sat down, and said, "Teddy, I'm leaving soon for Africa and want you to know if for any reason an order for serum is given, the platelet count *must* register over one hundred (one-hundred thousand platelets per liter of blood) or it must not be given. All the doctors know this." I thanked her so much and wished her a happy trip.

In the meantime, Timmy seemed to be doing better, and back we went to Bill's home in Connecticut with his puppy and Louella, his

nurse, for the rest of the summer. Then, sometime in August, Timmy began having nausea and headaches. Dr. Hoen suggested I bring him to the University Hospital.

On the way back to New York in the ambulance that early morning of August 15, 1957, with little Clover curled up beside him, Timmy looked up at me, smiled, and said, "Mom, have you a pencil? If so, please write this down."

And he proceeded very slowly to say these words, as if he were reading them.

God protects me through the night
God will help me win each fight
I know that God is ever near
I know in God, I cannot fear
God will show me day by day
If I follow in His way

"Timmy, where did you get this?"

"I just made it up, Mom. It's my prayer."

"It's so beautiful."

I wrote it down, handed it to him, and he folded it up carefully and put it in his pocket. Months later, Arden Clar, the composer and father of Timmy's friends from Daycroft, came by to pick up his children from Bill's house. Sitting down at the piano with Timmy by his side, he put this little prayer to music. It was published in 1959 under the title "Timmy's Prayer," with the credit line "Words by: Timothy Getty. Music by: Arden Clar."

Arriving at University Hospital, Timmy saw Dr. Hoen, and though

nothing seemed to be wrong, he asked us to stay. He wanted to run tests. I slept in the room next to Timmy's. To keep cool during those hot New York summer days, I'd run down the street and bring back ice cream every afternoon, which we shared with his nurses, Louella and Scarlett.

During this summer, Ware and his family were up at the Vineyard; Bill was in Maine, Mom and my sisters out on the Coast sent messages of love . . . but from Paul, no word.

On Thanksgiving and through Christmas of 1957, Timmy's headaches and nausea returned, so I stayed very close to him and prayed. Though we didn't know it at the time, we were in the hospital when it was announced that "J. PAUL GETTY HAS BECOME AMERICA'S FIRST BILLIONAIRE."

By New Year's 1958, hope filled my heart when Timmy overcame these attacks. In February he started rehabilitation, and in April, he asked Louella to turn the shades in his room down as the light was too bright. I remember Louella and I looking at each other shocked, but so happy.

Dr. Hoen decided Timmy was making such progress that we could start making arrangements to go back to California. We had a calendar on the wall of Timmy's hospital room, and with each passing day we were getting closer to going home. Sometime in July I made our plane reservations, and wrote on the wall, *California or Bust!*

Then Dr. Hoen suggested that, before we leave, Timmy have plastic surgery to smooth out the bump on his forehead caused by all of his operations.

"Absolutely *no*, Doctor," I said. "Wait a year. Please give Timmy a chance to get his strength back, just let us go home."

Paul, who was in Europe when questioned by Hoen, firmly said, "No," but finally agreed, giving the order that "*nothing* but plastic surgery be done." I agreed with Paul, and reluctantly gave my consent. The operation was scheduled for Thursday, August 14, 1958.

About the first week in August we were sent to the Rusk Institute, where Timmy was reevaluated. It looked good. While there, Timmy met the famous baseball player Roy Campanella, who was also a patient at the Rusk Institute, due to an automobile accident that left him paralyzed.

Mr. Campanella recounted the meeting this way in his memoir, *It's Good to Be Alive*:

I was sitting outside on 34th Street one day when a nurse came over and said, "Mr. Campanella, will you be here for a while?" I said I would and she came back with a boy who looked to be about eleven or twelve years old. He was a fine-looking youngster, but he had a cut from the top of his head right down between his eyes. He was wearing dark sunglasses. He was very friendly and spoke very intelligently and I liked him right away. He was a real little gentleman. He was very much interested in baseball, and we talked quite a bit about it. I was so impressed by him I had a baseball up in my room autographed by all the Dodgers that I wanted him to have. He was very happy about that, so I had the nurse wheel me to the elevator and we went to my room.

The baseball was on the dresser and the nurse took the ball and gave it to the boy. He held the ball in his hands and told me he would say a little prayer for me that night before going to bed. I told him I would do the same.

"I'm sorry I can't put my name on it, too," I told him as he was about to leave. "I can't hold a pen in my hand yet."

"That's all right, Mr. Campanella," he said. "I can't see."

It was like someone hit me over the head with a baseball bat. It never had entered my head that he couldn't see. I didn't even know who he was. He told me his name was Timmy, but that didn't ring any bell. He was just a nice kid. It was not until later that I learned his name was Timothy Getty, the son of the oil and railroad tycoon, Jean Paul Getty, who had been called the richest man in the world.

Timmy was released from the Rusk Institute a week before the scheduled surgery, so back we drove by ambulance along the Merritt Parkway with his puppy, nurses, and luggage to Bill's home on the Silvermine River to wait for the day of Timmy's plastic surgery and freedom. We had a fun time that week out at Bill's. Timmy's school friends came to see him, Ware and his family, too. Paul called from Europe, regarding the plastic surgery, and was just as furious with the doctors as I was, for to us there was no urgency.

We should have just left on a plane. However, Dr. Hoen had insisted, "You should do this before you leave for Santa Monica." So Paul and I finally agreed for Timmy to have the operation, but absolutely they were to do nothing more.

On Wednesday, August 13, we left the countryside and drove back into New York. That morning I got up very early, walked over to Timmy's bed, knelt down, and said, "Timmy, dear, Mommy has made many mistakes, and if ever I've made one that's hurt you, please tell me. I only know I'm trying to do what's right for you, and I get afraid my judgment isn't too good and I might hurt you. I'd die if I did."

He leaned up, kissed me, and said, "You're the best mommy in the whole wide world—you couldn't do wrong—and if you did, I'd forgive you even before you did it."

I gave him a kiss and a hug, then said, "Thanks, Tim."

The next few days, he seemed so well. Everyone came in to see him. Bill brought him a pair of moccasins from Maine. Ware brought him a boat carved out of wood that someone had made. Then on Thursday morning, I kissed him, and they took him down to the OR.

CHAPTER 41

GOING HOME

The operation lasted about three hours. Tim came up from the recovery room at about 11 A.M. He was alert, but the tube and needle in his thigh, which was feeding him glucose, was bothering him. He said, "Hello, Uncle Ware," as he passed by my room, and when I said, "Hi, my lamb," he cried out, "Oh, Mommy!" and my heart burst.

As they put him into bed, Dr. Hoen came in and said, "How's my Timoshenko?"

Tim said, "My side hurts."

Dr. Hoen said, "Take this needle out. Tim can have a drink. How about a Coke?"

Tim said, "Thank you, you blessed man!"

When the nurse got the Coke, Tim offered it first to Hoen. (He always wanted to share what he had.) Then he put his hands about the doctor's head, kissed him, and said, "I love you, Dr. Hoen."

Dr. Hoen said, "Well, boy, I love you. The bump's gone, you're okay, and now you're going home to California."

I stood there beside Timmy and thanked God as I never had before, for it seemed at that moment that we had won our battle. He was free, he was fine, and we were going home. Tim was in a kidding mood, full of spirits. His pupils were small and he looked so very healthy—he was. He moved his left hand and leg, and we were all so gloriously happy.

On Friday, he was fine, full of love, kissing everyone (his nurses and me, mostly). He played his radio and listened to stories. We read our lesson from the Bible, and Ware decided he'd fly up to the Vineyard that night, since Tim was well. I was in Tim's room every few hours all night Friday night. I asked the telephone operator to waken me every hour, and I went in to let the night nurse (who slept on duty) go out for coffee. I looked at Tim, who slept quietly. I looked at his chart, noticed that the night nurse hadn't given him more than a sip of water, and that he had voided more than he had taken in. I spoke of this to her at about 6 A.M.

She said, "He just didn't want it."

"You must make him drink!" I replied. "He needs it."

The nurse took his temperature. It was 102. Dr. Vargas, from Mexico City, who was supposed to have checked on Tim during the night, didn't walk in until 7 A.M. He came in before Tim was awake and spoke in broken English to the nurse who said to him, "He is very lethargic."

The doctor didn't understand. He smiled, said, "Dr. Shaccter is coming on at eight o'clock," and left.

Then at 7:30 Tim stirred, and I asked the nurse to give him orange juice. He took a sip, then said, "No more."

I went over to him, kissed him, and he felt warm. I said, "Angel, Mommy's here. Are you okay?"

He said, "I feel awful."

Usually, after a glass of orange juice or Coca-Cola, he perked up and was fine.

At 7:40, I felt something was going on that was wrong. Just then his day nurse, Louella, came in. The night nurse told her he was lethargic, and took out the thermometer which read 102 (rectal). Louella went over to him, said, "Hello, precious, how's my precious? Do I get a kiss?"

He put his arms about her neck, kissed her, and went into a state of shock—just collapsed. They put the thermometer back in; it was 104. I said, "Get some ice!"

We put the ice mattress on and started trying to cool him off. I asked Louella what the temperature was. She said, "Higher!!" She was afraid that I'd get afraid. I demanded to know. She said, "106."

I picked up the phone and called Dr. Hoen. I also asked for the resident, Dr. Shaccter, who apparently wasn't due until nine. Louella went out and came in with an oxygen siphon and tube, which she put up his nose. She was quick, thank God. The night nurse and I cooled Tim off with ice and alcohol, and Louella put an aspirin suppository in. Hoen didn't come until 11 A.M., but Dr. Shaccter came at 9 A.M. and told me to get out. I went to my room and prayed.

I didn't know what was wrong. I found out later that during Tim's surgery, one of the doctors had ordered the serum without knowing his platelet count. When the doctor came to see Tim on Friday, the nurse who had asked him if they hadn't better do a platelet count was told it could wait until Monday. I hadn't even thought about the serum, because

I never dreamed they'd give it to him. But it was the serum, given on Thursday, that immediately began to destroy the platelets in his blood so that he went into shock on Saturday morning.

Dr. Shaccter ordered steroids—Cortex, Cortisone, ACTH, and others, in quantities—so I asked the operator to get Dr. Kupperman, the endocrinologist. Dr. Bloom was off. Shaccter, who knew the case but hadn't been with us since February, I didn't care for. He was a rough young man.

Kupperman was out on an emergency call and didn't call until later that afternoon. In the meantime, Shaccter gave Tim great doses of steroids. Perhaps they did him good. Perhaps they caused the hemorrhaging at 5 A.M. the next morning. ACTH is a dangerous drug and in large amounts can do terrible things to the body. Kupperman, the great endocrinologist, was employed to help Tim. But in Tim's greatest need, he wasn't available.

The doctors seemed to have forgotten that they'd given Tim the serum Dr. Wright had told them not to give him unless his platelets were over one hundred. The following was done to Tim on Saturday. They: 1) tapped his spine, 2) blew out his stomach, 3) gave him oxygen by tube, and 4) put a tube through the other nostril into his stomach. His respirations were 76; his blood pressure and pulse too low to read. So: 5) They gave him steroids by vein, and 6) blood plasma.

I never left my room. I was alone, praying. Dr. Hoen finally came in and said he "couldn't understand what was happening." Then, at about 5 P.M., they did a cardiograph. Apparently he was okay. I was praying for his blood pressure, pulse, and respiration to normalize. At about ten on Saturday night, when Dr. Hoen came in, I asked if I might see Tim.

He said, "What will it do to you?"

I said, "Never mind me. If it's helpful for me to go in and talk to him, let me go."

I called Mr. Pittman in Boston, my Christian Scientist adviser and friend, who I'd been talking to all day; he was out. I called my friend Vera Shepherd. She told me to go in and talk quietly, calmly, and reassure Tim, even if he seemed not to hear or recognize me. I went to see him.

There he was with needles in him, tubes in his nose, breathing heavily. Three nurses were there, also Dr. Shaccter and Dr. Hoen. I went up to Timmy and whispered into his ear, "Darling, it's Mommy here. I'm with you, God's with you, and we are not going to leave you. Don't be afraid anymore, all is well." I put my hand on his diaphragm and patted it; he was breathing hard. Then, as I talked to him about God and His love for Timmy, telling him he must not be afraid, he suddenly relaxed and his respirations came slower.

I looked at Dr. Hoen and he nodded. Tim tried to speak, and I whispered to him, "Don't try to speak, baby, I love you. You're okay, and I know you love me. Take it easy now. God is here. He is your breath, your life. Be not afraid."

The room was cold—the air conditioner on, ice mattress, too. It was horrible to see him lying there. I couldn't collapse for his sake. I simply stayed by his side and held his hand and talked. Then I put his hand in Louella's and went out of the room to speak to Dr. Hoen. He seemed in the dark about why this happened. Shaccter had the room next to mine. He and I were in and out of Tim's room all night. I had had no sleep for days and was so tired, I told the telephone operator to call me

every hour so I could go in to Tim and rest in between. I couldn't think anymore—or pray, either. I was alone and frightened.

Sunday at 5:00 A.M., Louella, who stayed on for seventy-two hours, day and night, came in and said Tim was expelling "coffee grinds"—dead blood from his stomach. I called Dr. Hoen and told him. He said to call Shaccter, and have Shaccter report to him.

I don't know what they did, but I think they pumped his stomach. Hoen said, "If it's 'coffee grinds,' it's old blood. We don't want him to hemorrhage fresh blood . . . watch it."

I called Mr. Pittman at 5:30 A.M. to tell him. Hoen came in sometime in the morning. Then, after seeing Tim, he came back to see me. I spoke about the steroids starting the hemorrhaging, asked him to cut them, especially ACTH and Cortex. Then I asked him where Kupperman was, and if he could reach him. If he couldn't, I wanted him to get Dr. Tuckman back quickly to make sure the doses were correct. I kept saying, "If Kupperman is the medical consultant for steroids, why isn't he here?" I guess I'll never know the answer to this one.

On Sunday, at about 2:30 P.M., they did some sort of test and found the hemoglobin was at 11 instead of 12 or 14. They gave him blood; his breathing was less labored. He was better at 3:30 than at 3, and better at 4:30 than at 4. Sometime Sunday afternoon, Hoen started to put the platelets back in thru the IV. When I heard this, I was grateful, but I didn't connect it with anything except that apparently he was putting platelets and blood plasma and steroids and Dilantin (a drug against convulsions) all in, by tube. The oxygen tube was still in the right nostril, the stomach tube in the left. Hoen left at about 6 P.M. "Tony" Holmes, his day nurse, left at 8 P.M. She stopped by my room

to tell me good night, and said, "It looks good now. His temperature is 100, pulse 140, blood pressure 110/60, and respiration 40. I'll see you in the morning."

I thanked her and went back into my room, combed my hair, and decided to go in and see the night nurse, Louella, who had been on most of the day and night before, as was Ruth, another nurse. Louella was oiling Timmy and I went up to him and kissed him. I saw the platelets going in slowly, noticed his skin color was pink and good, but he was cold because the air conditioner was on. Louella rubbed his body with oil and talked to him. His breathing was better, 40 respirations. (I took it.) I looked at him closely. He acted like a fighter who had won a hard battle and was resting, or trying to rest. I prayed for him to take it easy.

Louella said, "Precious, we are going to have you eating in the morning, you're okay." She said to me, "They gave him something to make him void . . . at seven o'clock." (He had a catheter on him.)

To look at him made me almost faint, but I felt he'd won the battle. I thought, *Oh, so gently we must let him climb back and get his strength.* A man came in to take his hemoglobin. He pricked his finger. Timmy didn't seem to feel it. I thought it was because he was cold, or had had so many of those for the past year he didn't care anymore.

I turned to the nurses and said, "What can I order you both to be sent in from the restaurant?" Louella said lobster salad, and Ruth asked for a chicken sandwich, and then Dr. Shaccter came in. He looked at Tim, picked up the chart, and said, "Give me the phone." He called Dr. Hoen and said, "I'm going now. Things look good here." Then he said, "Dr. Hoen wants to talk with you," and handed me the phone.

———

Hoen said, "Teddy, things look good. Nancy [Hoen's wife] wants to come over with me and visit with you. Would you like that?"

I said, "Fine." But I was tired and wanted to just stand there and be near Timmy.

I gave up the phone to Shaccter, and the man with the hemoglobin report came in and told Shaccter something.

Shaccter said, "It couldn't be. Do it again." Then Shaccter hung up the phone and started out of the room, saying, "Good night. I'm off now, and another doctor will be on call. Everything looks fine." Then he took one last look, and walked back to Tim. He studied him a moment, asked for a stethoscope, and listened to his breathing. His respirations were still fine at 40, with his pulse 140, temperature 100, and blood pressure 110/60. Turning to Louella, Shaccter asked for the aspirator. He took the place where I'd been standing. I walked around the bed to the other side, held Tim's hand very tightly, and told him in his ear, "Tim, boy, you are all right, right now. God is here. Don't be afraid, all is well." And then I put his hand to my lips and kissed it and kissed his cheek, and called Louella to hold his hand, for I hated what Shaccter was going to do and hated to watch, and felt it would hurt Tim.

Shaccter, like some bulldog, took the oxygen tube out of Tim's nose and put the aspirator, a suction pump, in. Then he took Tim's head in his hand and forced open his mouth and put the aspirator down his throat as I looked at Shaccter, horrified at his seeming roughness. All I could do was pray Timmy would hang on—and I wanted to bash this man's head in.

Then Tim seemed to gasp and he stopped breathing. This I saw. This I shall never forget. Tim couldn't fight or breathe and his heart

stopped as mine wanted to. I heard Shaccter say, "Please leave the room, Mrs. Getty."

I left, not daring to believe what I thought was happening *was* happening. I went to my room, called Mr. Pittman, and told him I thought Tim had stopped breathing.

I waited alone there in my room, fighting the fear. I prayed for Tim to gather strength, prayed for him to fight, and it seemed like hours later, but was only a little while, when Nancy came in, looking very alarmed. Hoen had gone straight into Tim's room.

I said, "Please go see how Tim is." She never came back. She fainted in the kitchen. Dr. Hoen came in almost at once.

I said, "What is it?"

"The worst," he said.

"Oh my God, please, go back and try," I begged. He went out, and I don't remember anything except calling Mr. Pittman, who asked me to go into Tim's room and talk to him . . . But Hoen stopped me at the door. "Don't go in, Teddy. There's nothing to be done. I don't know what happened, it was so sudden."

I screamed, "Shaccter took the oxygen tube out, aspirated him, and he gasped. That's what happened! He was too weak to fight. You and your doctors killed him! Where were they—Kupperman, Golomb, and Bloom? None of you were here! Timmy trusted you, and *you* let him down."

Hoen had tears in his eyes. I stared at him, turned, and ran to the open window. It was pouring rain—it seemed like the whole world was crying. I wanted to throw myself out; Louella's hand stopped me. The phone was ringing, it was Paul. I told him, and he burst into tears sobbing, "Oh my poor boy, my poor boy . . ."

I told him I had been so jubilant when I'd gone in to see Tim at

8:15 P.M., and the nurses had told me that his vital signs were better. I knew I had reason to be happy—it just seemed that finally the battle was won. Though Tim was tired, he was breathing easier and then in walked Dr. Shaccter.

Perhaps Tim would have gone that night anyway, but, before God, he *did* look better. I sensed he was just sort of holding his own, and if that damned fool had left him alone and not roughly opened his mouth and forced the aspirator in, I feel we could have weathered that night. Why did he do it? Why didn't I stop him?

The final report on his hemoglobin was 7, which meant that his blood was getting lower . . . and ties in with my observation that, had they not given the serum in the first place (which tore down the platelets in his bloodstream), had they obeyed their own man-made laws and not given it against their own report, which said, *Don't give it when the count is under 100,000*, then all the complications would not have happened—the hemoglobin going down, the platelet count going still farther down.

They started blood plasma on Saturday, which helped, but they should have checked the platelets and given those Saturday, too. They stopped the plasma when they gave the platelets on Sunday. The agony of it all is that it was sheer disobedience on all their parts—Hoen, and Drs. Golomb, Shaccter, Kupperman, and Bloom. Tim and I obeyed God, and obeyed them, too. We clung to the truth like you've never seen, even while they lied to us and let us down.

I told Hoen to do an autopsy. It showed the entire tumor had gone. There was not a particle of it left in Timmy. Also, there was not one tumorous cell in him, either, which meant that they had had no reason to give the tumor serum anymore, and should not have given it at the time

of surgery. There was also no sign of hemorrhaging in the stomach, so whatever was coming up was due to the steroids. Hoen said the autopsy showed it was his heart that gave out. Well, you tell me whose heart can keep going when his platelets are as low as 78,000, they put tumor serum in you that kills more platelets, and lowers your hemoglobin from 12 to 7. How could you survive when, after rallying for two days someone forcibly takes out your oxygen tube, forces your mouth open, and aspirates you so roughly you just gag and stop breathing.

This, before God, is the truth. I never left Tim's side. I saw it all. He was well and happy in the country, and we both wanted to go home. It was not the operation, but what happened afterward. My little Timmy, my child whom I loved so dearly, is gone. The torture is over, and the fight we won is lost. Never has there been such courage, for Tim knew fear, yet bravely faced the battles. Never has there been such love, for he blessed those that hurt him and forgave the doctors when they did make mistakes. (Once one dropped mercurochrome in his eye and he said, "I forgive you, Dr. Bloom. You didn't mean it.")

Always we'd talk of being obedient to the doctors, and trusting God. When they took a long time tapping him, or giving the serum, he'd cry a bit, then say, "How much longer, sir?" He'd grit his teeth, and tell me to call his practitioner for help. He never complained—he was always cheerful. He trusted Dr. Hoen. He turned in agony to God. He was grateful to everyone—the nurses, maids, and aides. He was always so happy when someone thought of him, or called him up, or wrote a note, or sent a flower, or remembered him. He loved his Bible lessons, which we did every day, and he taught me what they meant. He was so pure in heart that he saw the Truth. When things were hard to bear, he'd call Mr. Pittman and grow in hope.

———

He was a child, and loved Donald Duck and Teddy Bear, and slept with Teddy folded in his arms. But he was a man in wisdom. He quoted from the Bible, and he listened to the news. He was aware, alert, far superior to most men in judgment. He spoke sharply to those who were cross, ugly, or wrong. He had compassion for the world, for others who were sick. He had a memory perhaps better than most, because he never remembered but the good. He said, "Don't clutter up your thinking with the bad." His sense of humor was all the more touching because he never lost it in moments of pain. One day, he called his doctors, who were whispering about output and intake, over to him, and said, "Gentlemen . . ." Then he sang, "You belong to the Mutual Tabulation Society, my baby and me!" He felt he would see again, walk again, and he had been seeing light for the previous two months. The day after his last operation he asked Louella to cover the mirror and the pictures because of the glare.

He was proud of being a "teenager." He was five-two and weighed 122 pounds. He had a beautiful little body. His hair was like spun red gold, and he had an elegance about him as a young prince of long ago.

We had spent every weekend of that summer in Connecticut at Bill Gaston's house while he and his sons were in Maine. I'd built a little ramp for him to be wheeled in and out. I'd bought a screen house for him to sit and lunch in, or sleep in, for outside. I'd bought a rubber pool for him to be naked in out on the lawn. Tim loved the sound of the river, loved the warmth of the sun. He adored little Clover, his puppy, who we picked up from the dog kennel each time we drove out to the country in the ambulance—Clover would lick Timmy's face, and they'd cuddle together as we sped along the Merritt Parkway. I put blocks under the piano so he could roll his wheelchair under it. We had picnics out in the tent. The nurses and I would read to him and play his favorite records. I cooked

all the things he loved—"specials"—and he was so dear and loving and grateful.

Sometimes I'd get down on my knees and hold him close, and he'd put his arms around me and tell me not to worry. Then we'd talk of going home. I thanked him for being my dear friend, and giving me so much love and help, and we'd speak of all the memories of good times together. He'd say, "Mom, there will be more to come."

He was full of love for his dad. He never knew he was the richest man in the world. He'd heard it but he'd say, "That's what the world sees. I see him as my own darling daddy, whom I love." How he missed Paul! Sometimes I sat quietly beside him while he seemed to be thinking and he'd suddenly say, "When will he come home? I wish I had a daddy like other boys have. Do you think he really loves me? I wish I could talk to him."

"Well, let's talk to him," I'd say, and we'd call Paul. He'd tell everyone then for days that he'd spoken with his father. He never asked for any material thing, all he wanted was to see his dad. He never begrudged the fact that Paul never came. He was too loving . . . and yet in his heart, he needed a father.

He was proud of being "the last of the Getty boys," proud and loving about all of his brothers, especially Gordon, who had come to see him that last September. Neither Ronnie nor Paul Jr. had time when they passed through, but Clyde Beatty, the animal trainer, came and brought him a lion's claw. Eda Edson came from California. Ware came every day, and Bill, when he was in town, came over with gifts like woolly slippers from South America, or a duck call. Audrey Davis brought books, people sent flowers, and all the telephone operators, maids, and bellboys at the Pierre called or asked for him and prayed for him.

Out in the country, during the last weeks, he had a few children over from Daycroft—the Clar family with three sweet kids—and these weekends gave him a sense of being home. He loved it so out in the country and didn't want to go back to the rehab or the hospital. I wish I hadn't let him. I wish we'd said no. I wish Dr. Hoen had kept his word, and done only what he said he would do.

Tim said, "I don't dare believe," when I told him Hoen promised we'd go home right after he fixed the bump on his head. Well, Tim was right, and Hoen was wrong. He did more than plastic surgery (*all* we signed for him to do). He even photographed the inside of Tim's head in the operating room and put the serum in, without first checking the report . . . And God knows what else he did, for I wasn't there to see. I wish we could drag those doctors before a court of law, for they murdered my son, they didn't follow the laws of medicine. I read the report and it's haunted me my entire life.

I was inspired by Tim's courage, his fighting so long, unwilling to accept defeat—hoping always has made me incapable of comprehending the fact that he's gone! I loved Timmy. I love him now as protectively as a mother lioness her cub, as proudly as an empress her heir, and I miss him just as fiercely. He was a child of our love. He was the answer to my prayers. I just sat there in that cold hospital room with my heart broken. My little lamb dead and I couldn't believe it, for all had been going so well. Exhausted from no sleep for three days, I just sat in that cold room and hoped I'd die, too.

I reached Ware, who flew back from the Vineyard, as did Bill from Maine. The three of us left for Santa Monica, bringing Timmy back home to his beloved California. I held Clover, Timmy's puppy, in my arms the entire flight home. On August 22, 1958, services were held for

Timmy in the Little Church of the Flowers, at Forest Lawn's Memorial Park, where he was interred beside Paul's mother and father.

Paul sent a note expressing his profound sorrow at not being able to attend, but he must have known I didn't expect him.

A mother never gets over the death of a child. All I can do is hold fast to the love I've known, and be proud that Timmy was a true soldier of God, whose Light has not gone out, whose Love is ever present with us, if we will continue in his way, and do good to our fellow man. God is Life, Life is eternal, and His good lives forever.

EPILOGUE

I spent the following week surrounded by my entire family at the beach house. I was crazy with grief and needed them around me. When Ware returned to the Vineyard, Bill took me to his island in Maine and I stayed there with him until the first cold winds of fall drove us down the Old Post Road to his home in New Canaan, Connecticut, the one I had shared with Timmy that past summer. It was there I realized how much Bill meant to me and when he said, "Teddy, I'm in love with you, marry me," I couldn't say no.

Timmy had loved Bill and Bill had helped me through those tragic months. Finally, I was offered a *new* life with a man I now loved. We had a child; a baby girl whom we called Gigi. I never dreamt I would have a child that late in life, but she came and filled a cradle Bill had bought for me with a note attached that read, *Fill it!*

When Gigi was born, Bill was there with me and he picked the baby up, kissed her, then looked at me with tears in his eyes. When a strong man is tender, it heals your heart. Gigi was beautiful and a gift from God.

I thought of Timmy and imagined him raising the flag at the beach house and yelling, "Bravo, Mom! We got a girl!"

I ALWAYS WONDERED why Paul had never come back to see Timmy. It had killed me inside, it was what made me divorce him. After Timmy's death, Paul had said, "Don't leave me, stay married to me, and you can be richer than the Queen of England." I said no. I was too hurt. It was not until 2010 that I found an unopened letter from Paul saying,

Oct. 12, '54

Dearest Teddy,

I wish I knew my plans. I want to return home to the U.S. I am very eager to see Timmy. I think of him every day and long to be with him. 3 years is a long time in a child's life. I've developed an allergy to ships. I dread being on them and don't care for the North Atlantic in winter. I may have to go Saudi Arabia again soon. If so, I don't like the thought of crossing to N.Y. and Cal. then returning across the ocean in a few weeks.

I'm very weary of Europe. I doubt that I'll want to revisit it again once I'm home. The U.S. looks good to me!

The Neutral Zone is different now since this is the first year of production and sales. There is much to do both here and in the Zone, but I dread the long 8 day rail trip there. Why don't I fly? Why am I so childishly timid about flying?? Anyhow, I plan to be back in the U.S. within six months—and stay there. My dread of the ocean will keep me there. And, as you know, I used to like ocean travel. And, even went sailing with you at Martha's Vineyard!

What had I better do? Let me know. And tell me all about Timmy—and what school does he go to? Ronny said that you and Timmy both looked fine. I've written to LA regarding the

trade-in of Timmy's car—but what good will it do until you return to Cal?

Love to you both.

Paul

He had reached out to me in this letter, wanting to come home to us, his family, and I had never opened it until 2010! I had never known. Would I have stayed with him if I had? I don't know.

Years later, I did see Paul. It was 1975, and Gigi, my sister Nancy, her daughter Lisa, and I were in Europe. When Paul heard we were there, he asked us to visit him at Sutton Place, Guilford, England. Hearing his voice over the telephone, after all those years, I couldn't say no. I felt I needed to see him again—he must have felt it, too.

Upon arriving at Sutton Place, Paul's butler, Bulimore, opened the door, and there stood Paul. I walked right into his arms and he kissed me, then embraced Nancy and, smiling, took the hands of each girl as they curtsied, and said, "I'm so happy you are all here. Barbara will show you to your rooms. And now, if you'll excuse us, Teddy, come with me." And taking my hand, we walked up the staircase to the second floor, down the long hall to his suite, through his bedroom, into his bathroom and stopping before a marble washstand, where Paul surprised me by getting down on his knees.

"Paul, what are you doing?" I asked.

"I have a surprise for you." And with that, he opened the drawer and pulled out a rather faded little Donald Duck. Yes, *the* Donald Duck—the one I'd given him in 1935, the year we met.

Handing him to me, he smiled and said, "Look, Teddy Boo, I've kept him all these years, but he now desperately needs your help." It was then

that I saw the red crayoned heart I'd drawn on Donald's rear end had faded, he needed mending, and his shoelaces had come undone. It brought tears to my eyes. I looked at Paul deeply, and said, "I still have mine!"

"Well then, if you will, I'll ask Mrs. Bannerman, our housekeeper, to lend you her sewing kit and you can sew up my Donald before you leave." And that's exactly what I did.

We sat out in the garden one afternoon. I repaired Donald, and Paul sat beside me, reminiscing about our life at the beach house. He spoke of the walks we'd take with Timmy and the dogs, Hildy and Jocko, up the beach to the pier and back—stopping to watch those mad little sandpipers as they raced one another in and out of the waves barely missing being swept out to sea; and just as the sun disappeared beyond the horizon leaving a red golden sky, flocks of seagulls could be seen heading for the hills to roost each night.

When Paul passed away the following year, on June 6, 1976, I received a small box from England with Donald Duck carefully wrapped up inside—and outside, there hung a name tag marked *For Teddy*.

ACKNOWLEDGMENTS

Special thanks go to my brother Ware, who inspired me as a kid to sing; my two sisters, Nancy and Bobby; my dear sweet mother; J. Paul Getty, who taught me to keep going no matter how difficult the going was; Dan Halpern, who had the courage to sign a woman of ninety-eight to a book deal!; Digby Diehl, for working with me; Hilary Redmon, a great editor who knows how to cut and not lose me; Richard Currier, for had he not been by my side holding my hand these past four years, I might not have finished the book; Robert Hill; Tom Hopke; Carol Carter; my friend Carola Stoner, a great spirit who helped me find Dan; Anne Getty; Kay Diehl; Sophie B. Hawkins; my dear nurses Mary, Maggie, and Nan; my teachers Blanche Marchesi, Sara Cahier, and Julio Moreski; the spirited Colleen Camp; and my lifelong friends Jean Donnley, Jean Pochna, Ethi Junger, Betzi Beaton, Jean Appleton, Kostya, Norene Nash, Beverly Petal, Leslie Sank, Valorie Gross, Dorothy Roeder, and Deborah Haase; and my ex-husband William Gaston, who introduced me to blue jeans, sailboats, and Maine.